Government by Agency

Lessons from the Social Program
Grants-in-Aid Experience

This is a volume of

Quantitative Studies in Social Relations

Consulting Editor: Peter H. Rossi, University of Massachusetts, Amherst, Massachusetts

A complete list of titles in this series appears at the end of this volume.

Government by Agency

Lessons from the Social Program Grants-in-Aid Experience

WALTER WILLIAMS

Institute of Governmental Research and
Graduate School of Public Affairs
University of Washington
Seattle, Washington

with the assistance of

BETTY JANE NARVER

Institute of Governmental Research
University of Washington
Seattle, Washington

ACADEMIC PRESS
A Subsidiary of Harcourt Brace Jovanovich, Publishers
New York   London   Toronto   Sydney   San Francisco

ACADEMIC PRESS, INC.
111 Fifth Avenue, New York, New York 10003

United Kingdom Edition published by
ACADEMIC PRESS, INC. (LONDON) LTD.
24/28 Oval Road, London NW1   7DX

Library of Congress Cataloging in Publication Data

Williams, Walter.
    Government by agency.

    (Quantitative studies in social relations series)
    Includes index.
    1. Administrative agencies––United States––Manage–
ment. 2. Grants–in–aid––United States. 3. United
States––Social policy. 4. United States––Politics
and government––1969–1974. 5. United States––Pol–
itics and government––1974–1977. I. Narver, Betty
Jane, joint author. II. Title.
JK421.W474   353.0084   80–527
ISBN 0–12–755950–7

PRINTED IN THE UNITED STATES OF AMERICA

80 81 82 83   9 8 7 6 5 4 3 2 1

To David Block Williams

Contents

Preface

Social agency leaders must reorient and redirect organizational efforts toward the field where social services are being delivered. This is the main theme of *Government by Agency*, which urges agency political executives to devise a management strategy that redistributes agency resources in order to increase local commitment to federal performance objectives and local capacity to deliver services. When local entities, rather than the federal government, deliver services, they ultimately determine policy. A new agency strategy should no longer view fund recipients as the enemy, who must be forced to comply, but rather as the delivery arm of policy that must be aided through federal activity.

The book focuses on the field efforts of the social agency to manage service delivery programs funded by federal grants-in-aid. Once Congress and the president have made the major political decisions about the allocation and distribution of social program funds, the action passes to the social agencies. These organizations are the chosen federal vehicles for implementing and administering grants-in-aid in the social service delivery areas. The federal government has allocated almost all of its resources to the agencies so that they can manage a vast array of federal social programs.

The role the social agency plays as manager of these federally funded, but state or locally operated, programs has become important only in the past quarter century. Federal grants to state and local governments for all activities except transfer payments came to a little over $800 million in 1950. In the next decade and a half, grants-in-aid were mainly used for physical investments, particularly highways. Only in the mid-1960s did the federal government begin funding social programs either in areas that had traditionally been the domain of state and local governments, such as education, or in areas such as community development where little government activity at any level had taken place.

The Great Society programs thrust the social agencies into a most uneasy partnership with state and local governments in the shared governance of social service delivery programs. As the social agencies have grown in size and importance, the difficulties of management have increased to a point where we must question the extent to which the social agencies are governable. This study tries to formulate a partial answer to this question.

A major segment of this book reports on a field study of the efforts of the Department of Labor (DOL) and the Department of Housing and Urban Development (HUD) to implement the Comprehensive Employment and Training Act (CETA) and the Community Development Block Grant (CDBG) programs. The study centered on the federal regional offices that were intended as the key linkage between agency headquarters and grant recipients. The regional office appeared to be an important element in the emerging New Federalism effort to decentralize authority over social service delivery programs. Power was to be shifted mainly to local governments in reaction to the perceived overcentralization of the federal government during the Great Society period.

When this study began, little had been written about these regional offices. Hard questions about the regional offices and their relationships to headquarters and grantees needed to be asked. Did the headquarters office send information to the regional offices on time? Did the regional offices pass this information on to the local governments and send back information to headquarters without distortion? Did the technical services at the regional offices assist local grantees in carrying out programs? Were the regional offices paper tigers in their ability to levy sanctions against balky local governments? Had regional offices become a dumping ground or a haven for petty, inept federal bureaucrats? In sum, were regional offices anything more than troublesome barriers that hinder local governments in their efforts to administer federal programs funded through grants-in-aid?

These questions were asked in 1974, just as DOL and HUD were starting to put CETA and CDBG into the field. Massive implementation problems immediately arose, partly because traditional relationships were disrupted by the New Federalism programs. Even with the change to the Carter administration, the study found that many of the regional office problems still existed, especially in regard to their relationships with central offices in Washington and local grantees.

The depth of some of the problems was startling. I was surprised by how little substantive programmatic help grantees received from the social agencies and their regional offices. Moreover, there was marked intensity of feeling by recipients of social agency funds against the "feds." No one would expect to hear paeans of praise for federal staffs from local CETA and CDBG administrators. But there was an unexpected level of unconcealed anger and frustration (especially among CETA people) directed toward the regional office staff, the headquarters' staff who had responsibility in the field, and toward the agency and Congress generally. The people who were most upset were those who appeared to understand the way the whole system worked and those who seemed to have a high level of competence. A typical view was that the regional office, whatever its stated function, spent much of its time fouling up local people. At best, it was considered a necessary hindrance around which one had to work.

The field study reported on in this book and similar studies by other researchers indicate continuing problems in social agency management of grants-in-aid. A look at the local fund recipients shows a host of problems, too. The assumption under the New Federalism that the locals could dramatically improve social programs if the federal government gave them more power did not hold up. Shared governance has been a rocky road for both partners.

Where does this leave us? Should the partnership be dissolved and one of the partners—either the federal government or the local government—have sole responsibility for federally funded social service delivery programs? Should we go even further and provide funds directly to consumers to purchase social services as in a voucher system, thereby relying on the free market rather than on government? In the cases of funds going only to local governments or to consumers, the social agencies would, at most, be check writers in the social service delivery programs. Are we ready to accept that the social agencies are unable to govern the social program grants-in-aid and that they should be removed from their management role?

In seeking an answer, the first thing to note is that Congress, in the near future, will almost certainly continue the shared governance through grants-in-aid that charges the social agencies with management responsibility and subnational governments with operational responsibility. So it could be said that any realistic answer should recognize this stark fact, even if we think that local government autonomy or consumer sovereignty is a superior solution. However, I will argue that even if Congress were willing to make this basic change, such change would be premature. Shared governance is the alternative most compatible with the varied demands of democratic federalism. The federal government will continue to need the social agency in a pivotal role to resolve the conflict between federal and local interests in the field.

At this point it is simply too early to eliminate the agency management role. Sufficient evidence is not available to tell us whether the social agencies should have done a much better job during the past fifteen years that were marked by such great turbulence, or to assess whether alternatives to shared governance would have produced superior results. It is unrealistic to expect that our social institutions, including the social agencies, could have adjusted so rapidly to the demands of the grants-in-aid era.

But how long should the nation wait to see whether social agency political executives can manage these vast institutions that are responsible for grants-in-aid programs? The question is complicated by the recognition that social agencies are not oriented or organized to meet the demands of shared governance. Agency redirection requires a management strategy that recognizes the centrality of the local service delivery organization. The critical objective of the federal field effort must be to increase both the commitment on the part of local organizations to perform and their capacity to deliver services.

A management strategy that redirects the agency toward the field will work only with a thorough reorganization and reallocation of agency resources. It will require real leadership from political executives who come and go rapidly in federal government. Even with such leadership, critical organizational changes in agencies with vast bureaucracies will be most difficult. But a start must be made. This book explores how the social agencies can devise a strategy that will allow them to focus management attention and resources on the field where the federal government's multibillion-dollar social service programs are being delivered.

Acknowledgments

For several years, I have been thinking about the issues considered in this book and have benefited both from grants and from discussions with numerous people. As to the grants, I have been aided by the National Science Foundation, the Ford Foundation, and the Law Enforcement Assistance Administration of the U.S. Department of Justice. However, the author, not these organizations nor any of the individuals cited below, is solely responsible for the final product.

I first wish to recognize the many anonymous individuals interviewed in the field study that makes up a major segment of this book. The Department of Labor and the Department of Housing and Urban Development staff members in both the regional offices and headquarters allowed my staff to conduct lengthy interviews. The same was true for those fund recipients of DOL and HUD grants to whom we talked. The field study also benefited from discussions with federal executive office staff; congressional staff; personnel in the Department of Health, Education and Welfare, where interviews were conducted to provide more understanding of federal field operations; and a few people not in the government, particularly staffs of public interest groups. I cannot overstate my gratitude to this large number of busy, knowledgeable people who were willing to provide factual information and to discuss issues.

Richard Elmore, my colleague at the Graduate School of Public Affairs and Institute of Governmental Research, read various drafts of the manuscript and offered invaluable comments. Robert McPherson, now

at the University of Texas and previously the head of the King-Snoho-
mish Manpower Consortium (a major CETA fund recipient), and
Charles Bean, staff member of the Department of Housing and Urban
Development, commented extensively on draft chapters about CETA
and CDBG.

Betty Jane Narver, who assisted me throughout the preparation of
the entire manuscript, headed the field interviewing during a critical
juncture, provided many insights both through numerous discussions
and through her comments on multiple chapter drafts, and was
primarily responsible for writing the two chapters on the implementation of CETA and CDBG. Finally, I am indebted to Thelma Brown who
typed and retyped the manuscript and frequently pointed out where it
did not make sense.

Government by Agency

Lessons from the Social Program
Grants-in-Aid Experience

1 INTRODUCTION

The early years of the 1960s marked the start of America's second social program revolution. Tremendous confidence in the power of the federal government created a host of new social programs in the areas of manpower training, education, community action and development, and the delivery of social and health services. State and local governments were seen as contributors to the complex social and economic problems facing the country. The civil rights movement focused attention on minorities and the poor—groups that had often been victimized by local governments. The only hope seemed to lie in a strong federal hand from Washington carrying the message of the nation's goals of equal opportunity.

The federal categorical programs that emerged often were highly specific, telling local organizations not only what they should do but how they should do it and to whom. As very detailed cures failed to solve the problems, new programs directed at new categories of recipients were developed. Complexity in programmatic and administrative terms characterized these services. Program techniques that would bring satisfactory improvements, such as long-run increases in earnings capacity or educational achievement, were difficult to develop. Political and organizational problems beset these federally funded and administered, but locally operated programs. Over the years, few things proved more frustrating or complicated than the relationships between the federal government and local organizations, particularly local governments.

1

Discontent with this highly centralized federal role began during the last years of the Johnson administration. By its end, the federal government's shotgun approach to economic and social programs was seen as part of the problem. The call was for more local control—a New Federalism.

The achievements of social goals envisioned in the period before the Vietnam buildup and the urban riots simply did not materialize. In the first few years after the end of the Johnson administration, it was fashionable to claim that the Great Society programs had been total failures. Indeed, some saw them as a contributing factor to the tensions that marked the turbulent years of the late 1960s and early 1970s. This was a period of seeking scapegoats.

A revisionist view recently has recognized the major contributions of the social service delivery programs.[1] Enough has been seen of the approach of the New Federalism to provide a basis of comparison with the Great Society. We are not, as earlier, forced to the always unfair comparison of *performance* against *promise*.

The flavor of the newer, perhaps more balanced perspective, is captured in Levitan and Taggart's statement that their "interpretation emphasizes the half-full rather than the half-empty cup, and the positive rather than the negative."[2] If we are realistic about the great difficulties of treating the socioeconomic problems toward which these programs are aimed, even moderate gains are an accomplishment. But the social conditions remain. The Great Society issues still call for action.

In examining these social conditions, the first critical questions are those of basic allocation and distribution: What should be the nation's major social goals, how much should be spent on each goal, and who should benefit? Although the answers to these questions are mainly political, they may also depend upon available means to carry them out. However, the political system may opt for a larger or smaller effort in education or manpower despite a most limited knowledge of programmatic and organizational approaches.

Once the broad political determinations about social goals and

[1] Several recent books present attempts by a number of authors to assess the programs of the Great Society years from the perspective of the 1970s. See David C. Warner (editor), *Toward New Human Rights: The Social Policies of the Kennedy and Johnson Administrations*, Lyndon B. Johnson School of Public Affairs, The University of Texas at Austin, 1977; Sar A. Levitan and Robert Taggart, *The Promise of Greatness: The Social Programs of the Last Decade and Their Major Achievements*, Harvard University Press, Cambridge, Massachusetts, 1976; and Robert H. Haveman (editor), *A Decade of Federal Antipoverty Programs: Achievements, Failures, and Lessons*, Academic Press, New York, 1977.

[2] Levitan and Taggart, *The Promise of Greatness*, p. viii.

levels of expenditures have been made, the next set of questions concerns means available to the federal government to pursue these goals and within the feasible alternatives, how it should pursue them. Here the balance shifts from philosophical toward more pragmatic concerns. What are effective means of delivering social services? How do we get more benefits per dollar of social service delivery program expenditure? One's philosophical position should be played out against the realities of operating delivery programs in the complex milieu in which both federal and local governments as well as nongovernmental organizations have significant roles.

This book treats certain aspects of this second set of questions in asking generally how the federal government should manage its programs.[3] *The primary focus is the governance efforts by the social agencies which are the chosen federal vehicle for implementing and administering grants-in-aid in the social service delivery areas once the decisions about broad social goals and basic allocations and distributions have been made.*

Generally, the terms *governance* and *management* will be used interchangeably in what follows. The former, however, will be more appropriate at times especially when we treat the crucial issue of social programs under the joint jurisdiction of two governments—what we label as *shared governance.*

Social agency governance or management will be used as a broad concept in contrast to some cases in the public sector where the terms *public management* and *public manager* have been employed in a restricted sense to refer to the way in which public administrators (mainly career civil servants) behave in carrying out relatively routine tasks. Management, however, will be employed as it now is in the private sector. As Andrews observed in *The Concept of Corporate Strategy:* "Management itself may be regarded as leadership in the informed, planned, purposeful conduct of complex organized activity."[4] Social agency governance or management applies to the bundle of

---

[3] One area not considered in any detail is the kind of research effort that might be devised to aid policymaking. The senior author has treated these research questions earlier. See Walter Williams, *Social Policy Research and Analysis,* American Elsevier, New York, 1971, especially pp. 150–168; and Walter Williams, "The Capacity of Social Science Organizations to Perform Large-Scale Evaluative Research," in Peter H. Rossi and Walter Williams (editors), *Evaluating Social Programs,* Seminar Press, New York, 1972, pp. 287–314.

[4] Kenneth R. Andrews, *The Concept of a Corporate Strategy,* Dow-Jones-Irwin, Homewood, Illinois, 1971, p. 2. For an interesting notion of private and public managers which views public management almost as broadly as we do, see Joseph L. Bower and Charles L. Christenson, *Public Management: Text and Cases,* Richard D. Irwin, Homewood, Illinois, 1978, pp. vii–ix, 1–4.

issues faced by agency leaders concerning both what the social agency *can* do within the context of broadly established social goals; and within these limits, what it should do and how it should do it.

Let us now consider the perspective from which the major issues of federal management will be investigated. It is helpful to divide this long federal governance process from Congress to local service project operators into three parts, labeled the "decision," "administrative and support," and "operations" domains. The decision domain includes Congress and the top decision makers in the executive branch who make the "big decisions" that others down the line are expected to execute. At the other end, the operations domain comprises the social service delivery organizations dealing directly with project participants. Here is where the big decisions become operating policies and are tested in terms of organizational performance and program outcomes. The administrative and support domain is the area in between. The decision and operations domains are fairly clearly delineated. In contrast, the in-between space is a loosely drawn configuration of various levels of the federal and subnational governments peopled by both bureaucrats and politicians. The administrative and support domain stretches from the middle levels of a social agency through the administrative structures of local governments. It is held together by a flow of federal program funds and a set of traditional program and personal allegiances. However loosely connected by the common bond of money, it is this domain that must link decisions to operations. It not only links but forms a kind of gelatinous filter through which the big decisions must pass in order to be implemented.

The administrative and support domain has been neglected. Interest has focused mainly on the high intensity and visibility of big decisions in Congress and at the top of the agency or on the immediacy and personal involvement in direct service delivery. In between, the grayish hue of bureaucracy and the tediousness of regulations and fiscal procedures get ignored. But this is where the message of the top decision makers must be translated into operational terms. It is at this point that various administrative and support services should be carried out to improve the capacity of local operators to deliver services.

Our efforts to investigate issues of federal management will concentrate on the administrative and support domain. The main focus will be on field activities, exploring in particular federal field staffs and their relationships with their own headquarters staff and with local organizations including governments.

The ground for the administration of federal social service delivery programs is laid by Congress and the social agencies as they come to terms on specific programmatic objectives and agency responsibilities. The most critical element of federal governance, however, is the social agencies' efforts to work with local organizations to increase their commitment to federal objectives and to improve their capacity to implement and administer social service delivery programs.

Those at the top—elected officials, appointed political executives, high-level civil servants—must look down when they seek to improve the management of social programs that deliver services. The case materials that focus generally on the administrative and support domain and particularly on federal field staffs (regional offices) provide a look at how field governance gets carried out. It should be kept in mind that the messages from the field experiences are relevant not only to those in the administrative and support domain but also to those in the decision domain charged by law with the basic responsibility of governance. *Better agency field governance is the key change needed in federal efforts to improve social service delivery programs.*

THE CASE STUDY[5]

This analysis of social agency governance draws its detailed field information primarily from a study of the effort during the Nixon and Ford administrations to implement two key pieces of New Federalism legislation: The Comprehensive Employment and Training Act of 1973 (Public Law 93–203, 28 December 1973) and the Community Development Block Grant portion of the Housing and Community Development Act of 1974 (Public Law 93–383, 22 August 1974).[6] The stated intent of

---

[5] This case study joins a rapidly growing body of research concerned with issues arising out of efforts to put in place new social program legislation or program modifications. References are now far too numerous to cite except to note works containing extensive bibliographical references. See Walter Williams and Richard F. Elmore (editors), *Social Program Implementation*, Academic Press, New York, 1976, which considers briefly earlier implementation studies and presents several papers with extended bibliographies on implementation efforts in education, community development, and income maintenance. For references to works on general implementation questions plus additional case materials, see Erwin C. Hargrove, *The Missing Link: The Study of the Implementation of Social Policy*, Urban Institute, Washington, D.C., 1975; and Eugene Bardach, *The Implementation Game: What Happens after a Bill Becomes a Law*, MIT Press, Cambridge, Massachusetts, 1977.

[6] General accounts of the origins of the New Federalism are found in Michael D. Reagan, *The New Federalism*, Oxford University Press, New York, 1972 (this is a good extended discussion with a useful bibliography); and Richard P. Nathan, *The Plot that Failed: Nixon and the Administrative Presidency*, Wiley, New York, 1975. Reagan traces the fiscal relief element of the New Federalism back to a 1958 revenue sharing proposal

both these programs was to give local governments more program flexibility and to shift power over federally funded programs toward the local level.

The New Federalism's two main thrusts have been labeled "decategorization" and "decentralization." The former indicates an effort to consolidate a number of specific programs under a single heading so as to simplify procedures, reduce complexities, and permit greater flexibility in the mix of programs chosen by a local government. Decentralization describes the attempt to shift responsibility and authority broadly from the federal government and specifically from the headquarters units of federal agencies to organizations in the field.

The initial legislative phase of the New Federalism ended with passage of the State and Local Fiscal Assistance Act of 1972, popularly entitled "general revenue sharing," which provided federal funds to subnational government to help them support general purpose activities.[7] The second phase was intended to decategorize large numbers of programs and package the funds in broad "block grants" to localities in specific areas such as employment and training. As Stenberg and Walker observe: "[A] block grant may be defined as a program in which funds are provided chiefly to general purpose governmental units in accordance with a statutory formula for use in a broad functional area largely at the recipient's discretion."[8]

When the study began in the summer of 1974, the Comprehensive Employment and Training Act (CETA) had been passed and the early im-

---

by then Republican Representative Melvin Laird and 1960 writings by Democrat Walter Heller of the University of Minnesota. Neither the Laird bill nor the professor's efforts received much attention at the time. See Reagan, pp. 89–92. The Nathan book is a good behind-the-scenes account by a key member of the Nixon New Federalism team. It includes the background for the Nixon television address of 8 August 1969 in which he announced his New Federalism initiatives (see pp. 16–18).

[7] For a detailed discussion of general revenue sharing written just after it was enacted, including an interesting account of its politics, see Richard E. Thompson, *Revenue Sharing: A New Era in Federalism?*, Revenue Sharing Advisory Service, Washington, D.C., 1973. For a recent critique, see Richard P. Nathan, Charles F. Adams, Jr., and Associates, *Revenue Sharing: The Second Round*, Brookings Institution, Washington, D.C., 1977.

[8] Carl W. Stenberg and David B. Walker, "The Block Grant: Lessons from Two Early Experiments," PUBLIUS, *Journal of Federalism*, Spring 1977, p. 34. This article provides a good overview of block grant efforts in the past and a critique of the first two block grants—the Partnership for Health Act of 1966 and the Omnibus Crime Control and Safe Streets Act of 1968. While Stenberg and Walker view these two acts as the first true pieces of block grant legislation, they observe on p. 31: "[P]rograms embodying block grant features are of relatively recent origin, [but] a somewhat similar approach was taken by the federal government during the 19th century in making direct cash grants to states and localities for banking, education, agriculture, defense, and internal im-

plementation effort was under way (the law became effective July 1974). The Community Development Block Grant program (CDBG) was approaching enactment (August 1974). Our primary field investigation included the 2½ years ending at the change of the presidential administrations in January 1977. This period permitted us to see both the initial implementation phase and the following period in which efforts were made to stabilize the field administration and operations.

Although the administrative and support domain was our primary target, our starting point of analysis was the decision domain. We looked first at the events that led to the passage of CETA and CDBG and the specific provisions of the legislation. The two pieces of legislation were shaky, unclear compromises between the Nixon administration, which expressed the intent to turn programs over completely to state and local governments, and the Democratic Congress, which was reluctant to give up so much federal power. That initial congressional intent was unclear and made agency interpretations of national intent difficult, thereby placing a heavy burden on headquarters and regional offices.

Regional offices are the passage point in the administrative and support domain from headquarters to the field. Here is where the word of federal intention is provided to the "locals" and the point at which the federal government is supposed to see that its intent is being followed. We centered our detailed field investigation on federal regional offices, looking both to their relationships with local governments and to the ways in which these agency field offices related to headquarters units in Washington.

Regional offices at the beginning of the New Federalism appeared to be institutions of growing importance in the social agencies. "Regionalization" was designed to shift federal decision making to these offices, giving more independence from headquarters in their dealings with local government. On 27 March 1969, President Nixon instructed a number of agencies, including all the major social agencies, to adopt common regional boundaries and a common regional office location (10 regions was the final result). In making these changes, Nixon stressed the importance of the role of the staff who implement the law in the field. Regional offices were to be the focal point in what we have termed the administrative and support domain.

---

provements." For a full discussion see Daniel J. Elazar, *The American Partnership: Intergovernmental Cooperation in the Nineteenth Century United States,* University of Chicago Press, Chicago, 1962. Further, some Great Society legislation such as Title I of the Elementary and Secondary Act of 1965 operated much like block grants with few federal strings. At the same time, it is not until the New Federalism period that block grants become an important funding device.

For our study, we conducted interviews with regional office staff, local elected and appointed (e.g., CETA and CDBG administrators) officials, local project operators, agency headquarters staff, staffs in the executive office and the Congress, and others who have had a direct involvement in the formation and monitoring of the programs, particularly what have come to be labeled public interest groups, such as the National League of Cities and the National Association of Counties.

Description has been an important part of the study. Little had been written on regional offices. They had been a kind of intellectual backwater of almost no interest either to academics or to government officials who write about federal policy. Even the agencies had given little time or thought on the role of the regional offices in the stage prior to and during the implementation of the two block grant programs. Regional offices simply had expanded as a largely unplanned result of the massive growth of social service delivery programs in the 1960s.

Description is therefore necessary in order to analyze who has what actual responsibilities and to determine how these responsibilities are carried out by agency headquarters offices, federal regional offices, subnational governments, and program and project sponsors and operators. Far more important than the formal relationships are the perceptions of the key actors concerning themselves and each other. What did headquarters really expect from the regional offices? What did the regional offices see as their mission in the field? How powerful did the local organizations receiving federal funds perceive the regional office to be vis-à-vis headquarters? What did the regional staff perceive as their real roles with local organizations that administered programs or delivered services? Another critical set of questions concerns capabilities. Did the agency organizational structure allow good communications between headquarters and the field? How well were various administrative and support activities such as technical assistance and monitoring carried out? The inquiry focuses on how power and capacity manifest themselves in the administrative and support domain.

The greatest number of interviews were conducted in the Department of Labor (DOL) and Department of Housing and Urban Development (HUD) regional offices, restricting most of our effort to the west coast (Regions IX and X), where several follow-up interviews were conducted.[9] The Boston regional office (Region I) was visited once, in part

---

[9] Neither interview sites nor interviewees were chosen at random. Rather, we were guided by such factors as proximity of the interview site to Seattle, importance of the position of the person interviewed, issues to be pursued, need to verify information, and indications that a person should be talked to ("You really ought to see John Smith on this

to consider the question of how much effect location (e.g., proximity to Washington) had on various sets of relationships.[10]

The local level was the second main concern. In a limited number of cases, we have looked at the relationships first between regional offices and the local governments that administer the CETA and CDBG funds and to a lesser extent between those governments and the organizations with which they may contract to operate specific projects.[11] Also interviewed were a number of individuals, such as the CETA or CDBG specialists in public interest groups, who have had broad contacts with regional offices, local governments, and project operators throughout the nation.

Looking up from the regional office toward Washington, a complex chain of relationships stretches through the agencies into the executive office (e.g., the Office of Management and Budget) and congressional committees and subcommittees. To understand fully the headquarters–regional office relationship undoubtedly would require a series of interviews exploring many intricate byways (for example, the continuing relationships between major agency bureaus and their House and Senate subcommittees). Time and money considerations prevented us from tracing these more distant relationships in any depth through interviews, so we relied on secondary sources.

In the field we were able to interview most of the high-level officials in local governments and the officials actually responsible for administering the CETA and CDBG programs that we sought to see. Our contacts in Washington, D.C., were more limited. Also our time and money restrictions and the busy schedules of federal officials prevented some desired interviews. But the federal government at this level is watched more closely than the regions and written about more frequently, so alternative information sources were available.[12]

As suggested earlier, when we began our study there was little published on regional offices. Fortunately, during the same general

---

issue."). An appendix discusses our interview efforts in detail, including a presentation of an interview schedule for a region showing the job positions of the persons interviewed and some illustrative questions.

[10] DOL had a major technical assistance and training effort under way that led us to Boston rather than another office near Washington.

[11] In CETA, funds go to governments that contract with other organizations to run some of the local manpower projects. Under CDBG, the local government that receives the community development funds is likely to operate projects directly.

[12] For example, a knowledgeable "outsider" from a public interest group, a congressional staff, or a person from another part of an agency may know about as much, tell a lot more, and offer a more balanced perspective than the assistant secretary we did not see.

period as our work, several studies, including some quite large ones, were undertaken that looked at various aspects of the CETA and CDBG implementation efforts and/or the reorganization of the agencies.[13] Although the emphases in these studies were somewhat different from ours, there is considerable overlap and complementarity. These other studies provide details we do not have (e.g., one study considered HUD organizational issues, including an extended investigation of the top of the agency).

Our interview efforts have focused mainly on what happened during the period starting with the block grant legislation and ending with the close of the Ford administration—a time we label loosely the "New Federalism period." Using the same interview techniques with a lesser number of people located in the field and in Washington, we have looked at the efforts in the first years of the Carter administration to move away from the New Federalism both by recentralizing power in Washington and by going back to categorical programs. These attempted changes, and perhaps more importantly the rationale for the attempts, broaden and deepen our understanding of the New Federalism period. That is, the changes of the new administration are partly a response to perceived problems of the last administration and furnish another validation point for our own observations. But at the same time, it is important to record that the New Federalism period also shaped and constrained what was done in the early Carter years. We get a far better understanding of social agency governance from seeing the relationship of the New Federalism period not only to its past but also to the period that followed.

AN OVERVIEW OF THE
CONCEPTUAL FRAMEWORK

The next several chapters offer an extended picture of the DOL and HUD efforts to implement and administer the new block grant programs. We have chosen to get down to cases in these descriptive chapters without a detailed treatment of the framework of analysis. Many of the concepts to be developed can be handled more efficiently by drawing on the field details. However, it is necessary to have the main elements of the analysis before us.

[13] These studies will be cited and discussed in the chapters that treat the CETA and CDBG implementation efforts.

Basic Assumptions

The discussion of social agency governance has two basic assumptions as anchor points. The most basic assumption is that Congress, or Congress in conjunction with the president, wants legislation to improve the socioeconomic conditions of participants in social service delivery programs. That is, the basic national intent of federal legislation is bettering the lot of those who receive social services. Legislators may disagree about the specifics concerning outcomes, but we assume they desire that employment and training programs help people acquire skills that lead to better (higher paying, more secure) jobs than they now can get and that they want community development activities to produce better living conditions for people. We do not take reelection and institutional maintenance as the only drives in Congress.[14] At the same time, we are not postulating that Congress will be precise in what it wants, only that in general it desires better outcomes for those who participate in social service delivery programs.

The second major assumption is that Congress will charge the social agencies with management responsibilities for grants-in-aid but will give the grants to subnational organizations to administer and/or operate these programs in the field. Congress will opt neither for full federal responsibility for social program operations nor for the federal government to do no more than sign checks. In the latter case full responsibility will not be given to local authorities (citizen sovereignty) nor to recipients through schemes such as vouchers (consumer sovereignty). Rather social service delivery programs will be funded under a shared power or responsibility model—"shared governance." The federal government will be involved in varying degrees in the specification of priorities and objectives, the determination of the nature of the process through which decisions are made at the local and state levels, and the assessment of how locally operated programs perform.

Over time, the pendulum is likely to swing back and forth between attempts at more federal control as in the Great Society period and less federal control as was the case under the New Federalism. The oscillation is a key factor in our analysis, since it complicates the issue of responsibility and authority. In all these swings, however, significant amounts of responsibility will continue to be shared by the federal and local levels in the federally funded programs we are examining.

[14] For a brilliant account of basic congressional drives, see David R. Mayhew, *Congress: The Electoral Connection,* Yale University Press, New Haven, 1974. This book also has an excellent bibliography.

The Framework of Analysis

The examination of social agency governance starts with the federal laws establishing social service delivery programs. Legislation such as CETA and CDBG tells the social agencies, subnational governments, and other funded organizations what Congress wants to happen. The legislation as elaborated on by agency regulations and guidelines may specify a number of inputs, including procedural requirements having to do with administrative aspects (e.g., accounting or information systems, or application or reporting forms to be used) and specific project elements. The legislation may indicate the desired organizational behavior by staff members in serving clients and administering the funded organization as an institution. Finally, desired objectives or outcomes will be set out to indicate the kinds of benefits that recipients of the service are expected to receive.

These expectations, cast in terms of relationships among inputs, organizational behavior, and outcomes, in essence lay out a theory or hypothesis about performance. When a law is passed, the ostensible assumption is that program inputs and actions (organizational behavior) will produce the desired level of organizational performance that in turn will yield the expected outcomes and thus the desired level of program performance. For example, the explicit (or at least implicit) theory behind legislation providing funds for training is that if training is done in certain prescribed ways, the earnings power of trainees will be increased. This is a hypothesis about cause and effect postulating that the use of certain human and other resources (inputs and behavior) will bring the desired outcomes of social legislation.

The legislation also fixes federal responsibility for field governance in the agencies. These organizations as the chosen vehicle of federal field activities are provided resources available to no other federal entity. Such resources are expected to be employed to induce funded organizations to move toward the legislation's desired results—the national intent.

The social agencies are large-scale public organizations (bureaucracies) characterized by a long, hierarchical chain of command. Such a chain presents several power problems for the decision domain political executives—the persons charged by law with responsibility for agency governance. First, they must manage through permanent civil servants, almost all of whom are strangers and most of whom are in the administrative and support domain.[15] The exercise of power is

[15] This critical notion of governance by strangers is treated superbly in Hugh Heclo, *A Government of Strangers: Executive Politics in Washington*, Brookings Institution, Washington, D.C., 1977.

further complicated "because of the high degree of permeability of the federal agency to outside influence," which means that internal control issues may involve "significant actors in the power setting outside."[16] The involvement of local governments brings problems for the social agency of "management control across jurisdictional boundaries."[17] Here the agency must operate within the broad confines of democratic federalism, where each level of government has powers deriving from the constitution itself and from a long history of past relationships.

Power is the basic issue of agency governance. What power do social agencies have to affect directly or indirectly what happens in the field when they are two or three layers removed from operations and dealing through subnational governments? What power do the political executives explicitly charged with managing agency resources have to induce nonfederal field elements to move toward desired organizational behavior and social goals?

Throughout the book, we will be using three similar terms that need to be distinguished—*power, control, and influence.* Power will be our broadest concept. It indicates what ability government has to bring about desired commitments, decisions, actions, or outcomes or to block unwanted behavior or results. It is our all-purpose term for the capacity to get what is wanted or stop what is not desired. Control is used more restrictively, speaking to the extent to which management—that is, the upper echelons in various organizational hierarchies—has the capacity to direct decisions, actions, and outcomes. It is a concept more of command and to some extent coercion. A basic issue will be the degree of management or hierarchical control political executives in social agencies have over their own bureaucracies and the organizations that operate social projects. Influence as used here is a softer, less coercive notion than control.[18] Influence comes about from inducing or guiding

[16] Donald P. Warwick, A Theory of Public Bureaucracy: Politics, Personality, and Organization in the State Department, Harvard University Press, Cambridge, Massachusetts, 1975, p. 199.

[17] Richard F. Elmore, "Organizational Models of Social Program Implementation," Public Policy, Spring 1978, p. 198.

[18] Influence could have been used as our broadest concept instead of power. For such usage, see Edward C. Banfield, Political Influence, Free Press, New York, 1961. Banfield on pp. 4–5 specifies these types of influence: "(a) influence which rests upon a sense of obligation ('authority,' 'respect'); (b) influence which depends upon the wish of the influencee to gratify the influencer ('friendship,' 'benevolence'); (c) influence which works by improving the logic or the information of the influencee ('rational persuasion'); (d) influence which works by changing the influencee's perception of the behavior alternatives open to him or his evaluation of them, and which does so otherwise than by rational persuasion (e.g., 'selling,' 'suggestion,' 'fraud,' 'deception'); and (e) influence which works by changing the behavior alternatives objectively open to the influencee, thus either absolutely precluding him from adopting an alternative unacceptable to the in-

organizational commitments, decisions, and actions and participant outcomes through various direct or indirect means. Social agency power in social service delivery programs can come from management control or from influence, with the two flowing from different strategies of exercising power.

THE LIMITS OF POWER

Our inquiry into social agency governance begins with the limits to power. Of critical concern in our analysis are certain limiting factors that over time may block the desired results of social legislation. The first are exogenous factors, defined as those variables over which governments or particular elements of government have no short-run and only possible long-run impacts. These exogenous factors may be dominant. For example, innate intelligence, socioeconomic status, and prior job experience may determine increased earnings far more than government policies.

Political and bureaucratic forces further reduce social agency capacity to govern the programs it is charged with administering. Actions on the part of Congress or of state and local governments can create barriers to program implementation. Bureaucratic blockages both within an agency and in sources external to the agency can have the same effect.

The resources of governance available to the agencies are limited. Constraints may come because of deficiencies in explicit or implicit agency authority, a basic lack of program or organizational knowledge, weaknesses in the techniques available to provide programmatic and organizational assistance or to develop and use information, and deficiencies in staff expertise or organizational structure within the agency.

These limits are crucial to social agency governance—to the basic decision about responsibilities and hence what the agencies are to be accountable for in terms of governance. Even though the determination of a social agency's mission is ultimately a normative one, this choice should be constrained by what the social agency really can do. If the agency is given an unrealistic mission, it may end up having less power than it might otherwise have over results it is able to influence.

If more power is desired, why not take it directly? Here we confront one of the many paradoxes of power in the shared responsibilities arrangement. If the search for more power overreaches on respon-

---

fluencer ('*coercion*') or inducing him to select as his preferred (or least objectionable) alternative the one chosen for him by the influencer ('positive or negative inducement').'' We restrict the term to the less coercive aspects of Banfield's broad listing.

sibilities, it can create confusion in the field and loss of credibility, both of which cut into agency power. Harassment of local governments may result as federal field staff chase the unreachable responsibilities.

AGENCY RESOURCES AND FUNCTIONS

Resources are the base for the exercise of aid or coercion in agency governance. At basic issue is how the agency uses available resources or develops additional resources to pursue objectives. Agency resources can include funding authority, political and organizational clout, organizational and programmatic techniques, the store of information and the means of developing and analyzing it, and managerial and staff skills.

We can think of resources much like the hand dealt in cards or the assets on a balance sheet. Or resources may be conceived of as capacities or potential capacities. That is, the agency resources, such as money, matériel, knowledge and staff, can be translated into various capacities required for governance.

Resources need to be considered in terms of the functions in which the agency should engage to execute its mission. In particular, what functions are needed for field governance, and what resources or capacities are required to carry out these functions? Our analysis of the agency field governance of social service delivery programs will concentrate on three main functions: approval, information development and analysis, and technical assistance.

The *approval function* is a continuing activity performed by an administrative unit (a) to specify how the provisions of legislation and executive agency directives are to be carried out by other administrative units and operating elements; and (b) to determine the level and allocation of a grantee's funds and the administrative, organizational, and programmatic requirements and restrictions attaching to a grant.[19]

The *information development and analysis function* involves efforts to provide quantitative and qualitative data and analysis in support of agency decisions and actions generally and the other functions specifically. In what follows, we will distinguish among various techniques that might be used in developing and analyzing information. The same techniques, it should be noted, can serve different activities. Thus, the information derived from evaluation or monitoring, both of which are discussed below, can support either compliance or advisory

---

[19] As will be clear from the discussions that follow, the related checking efforts to determine if grantees are doing what was approved and technical assistance efforts to enforce compliance are treated as separate functions.

technical assistance. The information development and analysis function is a cross-cutting activity, and the purpose of information use will be an important issue in later chapters. But now we will make distinctions only as to techniques.

The two field techniques that will concern us most are *monitoring* and *evaluation*. Williams has observed that "agency monitoring [is an assessment technique that] generally involves site visits [to] consider such factors as administrative management practices, adherence to stated guidelines, and staff capability."[20] Evaluations are assessment efforts to measure the extent to which program participants benefit from services delivered. Monitoring is focused on procedures used and services delivered while evaluations address whether participants receiving services actually experience positive outcomes.[21]

The other major information activity is *policy analysis and research,* which describes the application of a variety of techniques to develop, search for, and synthesize information so as to provide a basis for making policy decisions and developing implementation strategies. These activities, especially research, have traditionally been specialized headquarters efforts. But the question of the extent to which research and policy analysis capability are being used in the administrative and support domain is an important one.

The technical assistance function involves the provision by one administrative unit to another administrative or operating unit of supportive services aimed at improving that second unit's administrative, organizational, or programmatic techniques and procedures. Distinctions need to be made as to the degree of the coercion in technical assistance and its scope. *Compliance technical assistance* speaks to actions or changes by the recipient of the technical assistance that the provider of such assistance deems as required in order to be in compliance with legislation or administrative regulations and guidelines. *Advisory technical assistance* involves efforts to provide alternative actions or changes to be considered by the recipient of the technical assistance. Compliance technical assistance is a directive; advisory technical assistance is a suggestion.

It also is useful to distinguish between *procedural* and *substantive* technical assistance. As to the former, one important aspect is helping establish the administrative mechanisms and accounting and informa-

---

[20] Walter Williams, "Implementation Analysis and Assessment," in Walter Williams and Richard F. Elmore (editors), *Social Program Implementation,* Academic Press, New York, 1976, p. 285.

[21] As discussed in a subsequent chapter, the basic distinctions between monitoring and evaluation made here do not always hold in the field.

tion procedures required by the agency for fiscal accountability. Procedural technical assistance also is part of the daily business of agency staff, whether the question it provides quick answers to is what a particular regulation means, how a form is to be filled out, or whether some action of a grantee is permissible. Such questions usually are directed at compliance issues associated with the approval function, and answering them is an integral part of the program line operation. Substantive technical assistance involves consultation, training, or other means of trying to improve a specific effort or to raise general capacity over time. It may be aimed at compliance issues and viewed as a basic part of the line operation. However, it is more likely to be performance oriented and may well be intended as advice rather than specific direction.

An analysis of functions forces a concern with programmatic and administrative techniques and skills—the capacities—that need to be available to support adequate field performance. Whatever organizations are charged with doing and however great are their perceived powers, what actually can be done will be bounded both by the available information base and by the underlying technical capability of the organization in question. In considering how these three main functions are performed in the administrative and support domain, we will be looking at the basic building blocks of social agency governance in the field.

THE SEARCH FOR A STRATEGY OF
SOCIAL AGENCY GOVERNANCE

In the less than two decades since the start of the Great Society programs, the social agencies have become vast institutions having a material influence on the lives of American citizens. *Time* magazine observed in an article entitled "The Beneficent Monster": "If one institution were to be singled out as having the most impact on American life today, it would not be church or school, private corporation or political party. It would be the United States Department of Health, Education and Welfare."[22]

As the social agencies have grown in size and importance, the difficulties of social agency management—particularly that of social service delivery program grants-in-aid—have increased to a point where one must ask the extent to which the social agencies are governable. Where are we to find the leadership to move these vast public institutions that have become a permanent part of the American social struc-

[22] *Time*, 12 June 1978, pp. 24–32, the quote is found at p. 24.

ture toward the accomplishment of basic social goals? How is agency management going to keep the various organizations in the grants-in-aid process, from the decision domain down, focused on perform-ance—on the substantive problems of how to offer better services?

The Dilemma of Field Performance. Social legislation such as CETA and CDBG fixes federal management responsibility directly on the agency secretary and more broadly on the "high ranking political executives" at the top of the agency.[23] The charge to the political ex-ecutives will be most specific, stating "the secretary shall" carry out a host of tasks that add up to federal responsibility for *all* performance in the field.

At the same time, the present political system creates an almost im-possible situation for the agency executives. Hugh Heclo has made the point most vividly:

> [To] the inherent electoral changes, the American executive political system adds a considerably greater range of nonelectoral uncertainty to political leadership. This system produces top executives who are both expendable over time and in a relatively weak, uncertain position at any one time. . . .
>
> [W]ithout a very steep learning curve, political appointees are likely to find that their capacities for effective action have matured at just about the time they are leaving office. . . . The entire process does not produce long-suffering policymakers who realize their major changes will come gradually through persistence. Most political appointees are more impatient. Any civil servant who offers the standard and often sensible bureaucratic advice to watch, wait, and be careful can expect to arouse more than a little suspicion.[24]

How well would corporations perform if their chief executive officer and a number of senior vice presidents came in and went out roughly every 18 months to 2 years, which is the average life expectancy for federal agency political executives, and worked with a staff of cor-porate career personnel who were strangers to the new executives? Even if political executives concentrate on program substance, it is hard for them to take a long view, embracing goals that can be ac-complished only long after they have left the scene.

The problem of moving the agency toward field performance has another related, complicating dimension. The rhetoric of legislation is explicit that the governance of social programs should have a primary objective of improving the delivery of social service benefits to pro-gram participants. But a host of factors set political executives off

---

[23] The phrase is from Heclo, *A Government of Strangers*, p. 2.

[24] Ibid., p. 110.

in a different direction. Political, organizational, and bureaucratic pressures push the political executives and other managers to maximize "organization health, defined usually in terms of bodies assigned and dollars appropriated."[25] Organizational health speaks to concerns about organizational status, comfort, and safety, not capacity to perform.

A basic dilemma of agency governance is the hard resource tradeoffs forced by the competing requirements of organizational health and organizational performance capacity. Agency management, which must answer for play in both games, is being asked to do battle on two widely separate fronts with different demands and time frames.

Organizational health threats are highly visible, with the potential for immediate disaster in the decision domain. Therefore, good health becomes the first order of business for the agency, with the obvious justification that the agency cannot carry out its basic mission if it is in political trouble. But staying out of trouble so often demands constant attention. Avoiding problems with Congress or with a local government can distract attention and resources from the performance game. Moreover, organizational health well may determine the saliency of issues even when the agency looks toward the field. Issues of compliance such as fraud and distributional outcomes, not organizational capability or final outcomes, predominate because these are areas of political volatility.

The performance game in contrast requires attention to a long, slow buildup of field resources where achievements are difficult to measure and long in coming. The ultimate irony may be that the inherent complexity of social service delivery programs that makes detection of poor performance so difficult and progress so slow provides less pressure to do well and less danger of explosive events that shatter the agency. The result is that commitment to a continuing, extended effort to improve performance capability is hard to sustain and often loses out at the margin to issues of organizational health. The agencies make a poor trade off between organizational health and capacity that so often leaves them unfocused on performance.

The Management Challenge. Gruber and Niles argue: "Today, the successful management of our institutions . . . has become the central intellectual question of our times." [26] Frederic Malek after stints in business and government claims: "There can be no question that public

[25] Graham T. Allison, *Essence of Decision,* Little, Brown, Boston, 1971, p. 82.

[26] William H. Gruber and John S. Niles, *The New Management: Line Executive and Staff Professional in the Future Firm,* McGraw-Hill, New York, 1976, p. 39.

management is the toughest job in the country."[27] And surely there is no harder management task than that facing the political executives who must operate in the milieu of the shared governance of social service delivery program grants-in-aid.

Few would deny the difficulty for management of turning the social agencies toward a sustained commitment to performance and of raising the capacity for performance in social service delivery programs. Far more realism is required in establishing expectations of what social agency political executives and other agency managers can do. Improvements in management are likely to be neither rapid nor dramatic. But without adequate management performance by the political executives and key career civil servants, what can we expect from the social programs that now are so prominent? As Malek observes after his previous statement of the difficulty of public management:

> The stakes are so high, the demands so constant, that public purposes can be achieved only if our governments are managed by the most able, the best prepared, and the most totally committed people. Yet few elected chief executives have harnessed the power of their career bureaucracies, and this is an important reason government doesn't work as it should . . . .
>
> It has been my experience that career government employees are as intelligent, talented, and dedicated as any group of people in any private organization in the country. There is no acceptable reason why they should convey an image of un-motivated people interested only in their own job security and spending more than their share of the taxpayers' dollars. To repeat: *the core of the problem is the typical failure of substandard political appointees to rise to the demanding challenge of providing genuine leadership to the careerist.*[28]

The challenge of social agency governance is great. Yet can we continue to justify the major management role of social agencies in social

---

[27] Frederic V. Malek, *Washington's Hidden Tragedy: The Failure to Make Government Work*, Free Press, New York, 1978, p. 94. Recently there have been a number of books and articles by people such as Malek who have occupied high executive positions in government and business and now argue both how different public management is from private management and how much more difficult public management is. In addition to Malek, see Michael Blumenthal, "Candid Reflections of a Businessman in Washington," *Fortune*, January 29, 1979, pp. 36–49 and Donald Rumsfeld, "A Politician Turned Executive," *Fortune*, September 10, 1979, pp. 88–94. For a good review of how public and private management differ and how hard public management is compared to private management, see Graham T. Allison, Jr., "Public and Private Management: Are They Fundamentally Alike in All Unimportant Respects?," a paper presented at the Public Management Research Conference, Brookings Institution, Washington, D.C., 19–20 November, 1979.

[28] Malek, *Washington's Hidden Tragedy*, pp. 94–95, italics added.

service delivery program grants-in-aid if improved agency governance is not forthcoming?

The Agency Management Strategy. We will argue that better agency governance is going to require a fundamental recasting of how social agencies approach policy development and execution. A basic need is a strategy indicating where the agency should be going (its long-run objectives) and how it should get there (how it will allocate its resources). Devising such a strategy is the most fundamental task of agency leadership. The agency management strategy must shape the direction of agency efforts including its organizational structure if the agency is to move toward better organizational and program performance. Required is an agency strategy that takes account of both limits and resources, especially realistic future capacities—a matching of opportunities and constraints.

A critical objective of the agency management strategy should be increased local commitment to performance objectives and capacity to perform in the field.[29] If the social agency is to be reoriented toward the field, agency leaders must develop a management strategy that induces those in the field who ultimately determine policy to move toward performance objectives compatible with national intent, strengthens the institutional setting that supports the exercise of discretion, and makes available resources likely to help in making better choices over time.

---

[29] As will be discussed in Chapters 5 and 10, we are drawing on the work in the business sector on strategy and structure. See Alfred D. Chandler, Jr., *Strategy and Structure: Chapters in the History of the American Industrial Enterprise*, MIT Press, Cambridge, Massachusetts, 1962.

2 | THE GRANTS-IN-AID ERA

This chapter will discuss the major events leading up to the passage of CETA and CDBG including the categorical programs that were decategorized, the main provisions of the new legislation, and the general situation in the agencies at the time of implementation. We will be sweeping quickly from the New Deal social legislation through the enactment of CETA and CDBG so as to bring us to the start of field implementation.

Before turning to the historical section, a comment on historical relevance is needed. We will be looking at both the principles that underlay the New Federalism and the action taken to implement that notion. Much of the early Carter administration was a clear flight from principles and activities of the Nixon–Ford days. In part, these changes can be attributed to "pure politics." The Democrats undid what the Republicans had done, just as the Republicans felt compelled politically to reverse the trends of the Great Society programs. But the change also reflects substantive concerns. Both of these swings indicate what the incoming administration viewed as wrong directions.

If past programs tend to bring a particular reaction, they also carry predictable restraints. We will emphasize in both Chapters 3 and 4 how much the Great Society categorical programs of the Johnson administration shaped what could be done in the New Federalism period. In turn, what happened during the New Federalism established very clear boundaries of what could be done by a new administration.

Moreover, these notions of restraint hold for the operation of the social agencies as well as for funding philosophies. For example, HUD "began" the New Federalism period in organizational confusion, and these organizational problems bedeviled the implementation effort. When the Carter administration turned immediately to a reorganization of HUD, the past problems not only defined what needed to be done but bounded most severely what actually could be carried out in the reorganization. In addition, many of the same people, particularly at the middle level of management, stayed in place performing the same functions despite reorganization and changes in administration or program emphases.

One final point: Although we attach general titles such as the Great Society or the New Federalism, the federal experience is really seamless. We should not fall into our own trap by believing that these labels define clear boundary points.

A RAPID RUN THROUGH FOUR DECADES
OF FEDERAL PROGRAMS

In this section we begin our look at two interrelated but separable aspects of the federal grants-in-aid era. The first may be labeled "fiscal federalism." At issue is the extent to which the federal government undertakes total or partial funding of programs operated by subnational organizations. The second aspect of federalism to be concerned with is "shared governance." At issue is the nature of the programmatic responsibilities shared by federal and subnational governments in these grants-in-aid programs.

This section covers more than 4 decades of federal programs starting with the mid-1930s. The focus is on aggregate expenditure data, considering first the major change in the direction of federal spending from defense to social outlays and then the change from direct federal service delivery to grants-in-aid.

Twice in this century—in the middle years of the 1930s and the 1960s—a president and a Congress produced in relatively short order a host of new social programs that dominated the years that followed. From that earlier period came the basic superstructure of United States income maintenance policy. The Social Security Act of 1935 established both the Old Age Survivors Insurance program (the disability and health portions were to come later, the latter in the second burst of social programs) and the federal–state public welfare system. More important at the time were a number of temporary programs, such as the Works Progress Administration (WPA), the Public Works Administration (PWA), and the Civilian Conservation Corps (CCC). These were the ancestors of the Great Society social service delivery programs, particularly those in the areas of employment and business aid. Like the programs of the 1960s, many projects were scattered throughout the United States, presenting crucial problems of management. The federal government was not organized to meet these problems and had to search out new mechanisms.[1]

In the main, the social service delivery programs of the 1930s disappeared as World War II wiped out unemployment and established the base for the prosperity of the postwar period. Social concerns again became prominent in the 1960s, but in the intervening 3 decades little social legislation had passed. Then, in a period of a few months, Congress enacted the Economic Opportunity Act of 1964, the Elementary and Secondary Education Act of 1965 (ESEA), the Public Works and Economic Development Act of 1965 (EDA), the Housing and Urban Development Act of 1965 (which established HUD), Medicare and Medicaid in 1965, the Civil Rights Act of 1964, and the Voting Rights Act of 1965. The Great Society had arrived.

Aggregate data on federal expenditures demonstrate the extent of the second social program revolution.[2] From 1955 to 1977,[3] the foreign affairs and defense portion of the federal budget fell from 62 to 27%, even though actual outlays more than doubled. Total federal domestic expenditures, which have been dominated by social transfer payments and services, rose from $65.7 billion in 1965 to $115.4 billion in 1970 to an estimated $292.2 billion in 1977. Transfer payments to individuals for retirement and disability (mainly social security payments), unemployment, and low-income assistance are approaching 60% of all domestic expenditures. Here is where the major dollar growth has occurred with an increase of over $136 billion between 1965 and 1977.

But it is the category that Schultze in his analysis of federal spending labeled "social investment and services" that has shown the

---

[1] For an account of the management issues written during that period, see James W. Fesler, "Executive Management and the Federal Field Service," in *President's Committee on Administrative Management*, U.S. Government Printing Office, Washington, D.C., 1937.

[2] The most useful recent review of federal expenditures over time is found in Charles L. Schultze, "Federal Spending: Past, Present, and Future," in Henry Owen and Charles L. Schultze (editors), *Setting National Priorities: The Next Ten Years*, Brookings Institution, Washington, D.C., 1976, pp. 323–369. The data in this paragraph are from Tables 8–2 and 8–6, pp. 328, 334.

[3] All data in this section are taken from tables reporting fiscal year information, but the fiscal year designation has been deleted.

greatest percentage increases since 1965.[4] These expenditures more than tripled in the years between 1965 and 1970 from $4.9 to $16.3 billion and then increased about two and a half times over the next 7 years to $40.9 billion in 1977.

Social service delivery programs starting from a low base at the outset of the Great Society exhibited an even more phenomenal growth rate than other domestic programs. Several Brookings Institution analysts, discussing the period 1963–1973, which extended from just before the Economic Opportunity Act to just before the passage of CETA, observed

> [F]ederal expenditures on grants for social programs amounted to only about $1.3 billion in 1963 and grew almost twelvefold in the following decade. A small part of this growth came through the expansion of programs that were already on the books in 1963. Most of the growth, however, was attributable to new programs enacted in the 1960s. By 1973 spending for these new programs amounted to $11.1 billion, 70% of which was in four major areas: grants for elementary and second-ary education, principally under ESEA; manpower training and public employ-ment programs; urban development grants, about half of which are for the model cities program; and grants to the states for social services designed to reduce welfare dependency.[5]

It was these social service delivery programs growing so rapidly in percentage terms from the early 1960s that stirred the New Federalism debate.

Henry Aaron, using the same data as Schultze, provides another perspective on federal spending by concentrating on what he labels as expenditures on human resources and cash transfers and looking at the degree to which these expenditures are either focused exclusively on the poor or not focused exclusively on the poor. Aaron observes

> During the Kennedy–Johnson years, expenditures focused on the poor as a fraction of full-employment gross national product rose from .8% (1961) to 1.4% (1967). . . . Growth in human resource and transfer programs focused on the poor continued during the first Nixon administration, but was reversed after 1973. Despite the con-cern about the "welfare mess" of growing rolls and rising budgets, cash and in-kind transfers focused on the poor actually declined between 1973 and 1976, from 1.8% to 1.5% full-employment GNP and were about what they were in 1971.[6]

---

[4] Schultze's social investment and services category is broader than social service delivery programs, including, for example, $9.6 billion in FY 1977 for veteran's health and education benefits, but the figure does provide a bail park estimate of social service delivery program growth.

[5] Edward R. Fried, Alice M. Rivlin, Charles L. Schultze, and Nancy H. Teeters, *Set-ting National Priorities: The 1974 Budget*, Brookings Institution, Washington, D.C., 1973, p. 180.

[6] Henry J. Aaron, *Politics and the Professors: The Great Society in Perspective*, Brookings Institution, Washington, D.C., 1978, p. 6. Aaron's data presentation is con-

It should be stressed that the two block grant programs to which we turn shortly are key elements of this shift in direction in the second part of the Nixon–Ford administration from the focus of funds exclusively on the poor.

American federalism has experienced important changes with the rapid growth of federal grants-in-aid.[7] In the social service delivery areas, grants-in-aid required that federal agencies and subnational governments share program responsibilities in two kinds of areas: (a) those such as elementary and secondary education that had been the sole responsibility of subnational governments; and (b) those such as community development for which neither government had taken responsibility. Moveover, these grants forced an uneasy partnership in efforts aimed at aiding the disadvantaged, often in programmatic areas where there was little or no experience. And particularly in the key social service delivery areas, the forced relationship was a direct one between federal and local governments.

The remainder of this section concentrates on the broad dimensions of fiscal federalism indicating both the magnitude of federal grants-in-aid other than transfer payments and their direction. The rest of this chapter and the subsequent case material chapters in particular provide an in-depth look at this sharing of program responsibilities during a critical phase of the emerging federalism.

While federal grants-in-aid can be traced back to the eighteenth century, the amounts generally were small, especially before the Depression, and were dominated from that time until the 1950s by welfare payments established under the Social Security Act.[8] Up until the post-World War II (post-Korean War) period, almost all federal

---

tained on pp. 4–15. Aaron's category of human resources and transfers parallels roughly Schultze's categories of payments to individuals and social investment and services.

[7] For useful discussions of the changes in federalism, see Michael D. Reagan, *The New Federalism*, Oxford University Press, New York, 1972; Deil S. Wright, *Understanding Intergovernmental Relations*, Duxbury, North Scituate, Massachusetts, 1978; and Ellis Katz and Benjamin R. Schuster (editors), *The Practice of American Federalism*, A Roundtable Discussion on Recent Developments in American Federalism and Intergovernmental Relations, held at the Center for the Study of Federalism, Temple University, Philadelphia, 28 February 1979. Professor Wright argues for using the term *intergovernmental relations* rather than *federalism* to describe the complex set of federal–state–local relationships, because the historic term federalism carries so much baggage from its diverse usage over time. For our purposes, however, we will stick with federalism as a general rule and employ it interchangeably with intergovernmental relations.

[8] For an extended, useful discussion of federal grants-in-aid, see Special Analysis H entitled "Federal Aid to State and Local Governments" in *Special Analyses: Budget of the United States Government, Fiscal Year 1980*, Office of Management and Budget, Washington, D.C., 1979, pp. 212–246.

domestic expenditures fell into the categories of (a) transfer payments and subsidies going directly to individuals or businesses; and (b) services to special groups such as veterans, provided directly by federal employees without a subnational government or nongovernment intermediary.

Table 2.1 shows the dramatic growth of federal grants-in-aid over the last quarter of a century. In 1950, federal grants-in-aid, the bulk coming from transfer payments to individuals, made up a little over 10% of state and local outlays. In the early and mid-1950s, less than $1 in every $20 of state and local government outlays came from all other federal grants (column 5). By 1978 (the last year for actual, as opposed to projected, data), total federal grants-in-aid represented nearly 27% of state and local outlays. Of total state and local outlays, $1 in $5 was financed by federal grants-in-aid exclusive of the transfers. The shift in fiscal federalism is seen most vividly in the rise in other (nontransfer payment) grants to governments for various services and investments from less than $1 billion in 1950 to over $53 billion in 1978 (column 3).

The period to 1965 brought grants-in-aid increases mainly in physical investment programs. Then came the shift to social program grants-in-aid. The change is best illustrated by transportation, the dominant physical investment area. In 1963, transportation accounted for 36% of total grants-in-aid. Fifteen years later, after major absolute dollar increases for transportation, it represented only 11% of grants-in-aid.[9]

Another facet of the changing fiscal federalism discussed in Special Analysis H merits brief discussion. The analysis reports the percentage of federal grants-in-aid going for grants described as "general purpose" (mainly general revenue sharing) or "broad based" (CETA, CDBG, social services, and local public works being the main ones). These kinds of grants are intended to give grantees much greater discretion than categorical funds. From 1972, before general revenue sharing, through 1978, the general-purpose and broad-based grants rose from less than 10% to 27% of federal grants. Two brief comments are needed. First, categorical grants still predominate. Second, even though these figures can be misleading as subsequent discussion will show, the broad effort in the New Federalism period to shift funds to more discretionary grants does come through clearly in the macro data on outlays.[10]

One final aspect of grants-in-aid is important—the receipt of

---

[9] Ibid., Table H-4, p. 223.
[10] Ibid., Table H-9, p. 230.

TABLE 2.1

Historical Trend of Federal Grants-in-Aid, 1950–1978 (Fiscal Years, in Millions of Dollars)

	(1) Total grants ($)	(2) Grants for payments to indivi- duals[a] ($)	(3) Other grants to govern- ment[b] ($)	(4) Federal grants as a percentage of state and local outlays (%)	(5) Other grants as a percentage of state and local outlays (%)
1950	2253	1421	832	10.4	3.8
1955	3207	1770	1437	10.1	4.5
1960	7020	2735	4285	14.7	9.0
1965	10,904	3954	6950	15.3	9.8
1970	24,018	8867	15,151	19.4	12.2
1975	49,832	16,217	33,615	22.9	15.4
1978	77,889	24,765	53,124	26.7	18.2

Source: Table H-7, p. 225 in Special Analysis H, "Federal Aid to State and Local Governments" from *Special Analyses: Budget of the United States Government, Fiscal Year 1980*, Office of Management and Budget, U.S. Government Printing Office, Washington, D.C., 1979.

[a] The main categories of transfer payments are public assistance, medicaid, housing assistance, and child nutrition programs.

[b] Other grants to government is a catchall category for all grants going to subnational entities except for transfer payments.

federal support by localities without major state involvement. As a team of Brookings researchers observed

> The share of federal aid given directly to local governments has risen to about one-third of all federal grants, and the dollar amounts have increased sharply. If welfare grants (AFDC and Medicaid), which go to the states, are eliminated from consideration—as we would argue they should be for these purposes—*half* of all remaining federal grants to states and localities in 1978 go to local governments. This trend toward increased *direct* federal–local grants represents a fundamental change in American federalism.[11]

This section, in presenting the broadest fiscal dimensions of the grants-in-aid era, has carried us beyond the time period that is the main focus of our study. So we now step back, in this chapter, to look at the origins of the two key pieces of New Federalism legislation and then, in

[11] Paul R. Dommel and others, *Decentralizing Community Development*, Second Report on the Brookings Institution Monitoring Study of the Community Development Block Grant Program, U.S. Department of Housing and Urban Development, Washington, D.C., 2 June 1978, p. 56, italics in the original.

the next several chapters, to follow their implementation and administration. Here we see the social agency's efforts to govern in relatively new and extremely complex programmatic areas with local governments.

FACTORS LEADING UP TO THE
NEW FEDERALISM LEGISLATION[12]

Five overlapping and interrelated factors shaped the first two pieces of block grant legislation: concern with rapid growth and increased categorization of programs; changing economic conditions; shifting social concerns; failures in efforts to coordinate projects at the local level; and changing views about who should make decisions concerning federal programs at the local level. The experience with manpower programs in the 1960s and early 1970s illustrates well how these emerged as the central factors that produced a basic questioning of the federal social service delivery programs. The five factors are so intertwined that they will be considered together, with the discussion divided only between the direct employment and training experience and a more general disscusion concerning President Nixon and the direction of the New Federalism. Then we will look in more detail at the complex events leading to CDBG that extend and elaborate on earlier points in the section.

Manpower Programs Prior to CETA

Unemployment was well above average in the last years of the Eisenhower administration as compared to the period following World War II. It jumped from 4.3% in 1957 to 6.8% in 1958 and, after a drop, returned to 6.7% in 1961. The Area Redevelopment Act of 1961 and the Manpower Development and Training Act (MDTA) of 1962 reflected the economic concerns of this period. MDTA, as Marshall has observed, "was initiated to provide retraining for workers displaced by

---

[12] A number of studies have investigated (a) the decision domain development of earlier manpower (e.g., the Manpower Training and Development Act) and community development (e.g., model cities) policies and how these influenced the development of CETA and CDBG; and (b) the operation of manpower and community development projects in local communities. We have chosen to summarize briefly only the most pertinent evidence, because the available information on legislative and operational level problems is so large that an extensive treatment of it would expand this book greatly.

technological change."[13] MDTA had two main components—institutional training (mainly classroom vocational education) and on-the-job training (OJT). Its efforts were concentrated on people with extensive employment experience who were out of work because of the employment downturn. Particularly in OJT, the typical participant was likely to be a white male high school graduate with several years of full-time work experience.

In the mid-1960s, with declining unemployment, the focus of social policy turned toward the elimination of poverty and the provision of equal opportunity for disadvantaged persons.[14] The Economic Opportunity Act (EOA) of 1964, which created the Office of Economic Opportunity (OEO), established a number of categorical manpower programs, such as the Job Corps, the Neighborhood Youth Corps, and Work Experience. Subsequent amendments to the EOA created additional categorical manpower programs to serve the disadvantaged. The EOA also established the Community Action Program (CAP) and its local operating elements, the community action agencies (CAAs), which were to play a prominent role in manpower program development during the Johnson administration. In larger cities, the CAAs (the majority of which were nonprofit organizations rather than elements of local government) served concentrated geographic areas with high incidence of poverty. CAAs challenged the existing local decision-making arrangements. As Hallman has observed: "[Many OEO staff members] possessed deep suspicion of municipal government and other parts of local 'establishments.' They were talking about power for the poor."[15]

The United States Employment Service (USES), established in the Wagner–Peyser Act of 1933, was the Department of Labor's main operating element in the field. With strong ties to subnational governments, USES was an established part of the state and local manpower

---

[13] Ray Marshall, "Microemployment Programs of the 1960s," in David C. Warner (editor), *Toward New Human Rights,* Lyndon B. Johnson School of Public Affairs, University of Texas, Austin, 1977, p. 82.

[14] For a good discussion of the differences between the antipoverty and equal opportunity objectives, see Robert A. Levine, *The Poor Ye Not Have with You: Lessons from the War on Poverty,* MIT Press, Cambridge, Mass., 1970, especially Chapter 3. This book and James L. Sundquist, *Politics and Policy,* Brookings Institution, Washington, D.C., 1968, provide excellent accounts of the origins of the War on Poverty. Two chapters by Levine entitled "A Biased History of the War on Poverty" and "An Equally Biased Evaluation of the War on Poverty" are illuminating accounts of the War on Poverty by an insider who was the senior policy analyst at the Office of Economic Opportunity.

[15] Howard W. Hallman, "Historical Highlights of the Poverty Program," a paper prepared for the Airlie House Conference sponsored by the Urban Coalition, Warrentown, Virginia, January 1969, p. 8.

effort but had limited experience in serving the disadvantaged.[16] The Department of Labor (DOL) became an important part of the antipoverty effort when the EOA legislation delegated responsiblity to it for the Neighborhood Youth Corps. In 1967, OEO delegated its adult manpower programs to DOL. DOL was required to use the OEO poverty standards for determining eligible participants in the delegated programs, and it began to concentrate more on helping disadvantaged people in its own programs.

As manpower policy shifted toward serving the hard-core disadvantaged in concentrated poverty areas, coordination became a critical problem. In response, the President's Committee on Manpower (PCOM), a cabinet-level committee established by a 1964 executive order, sent three-person teams from DOL, OEO, and the Department of Health, Education and Welfare (HEW) to 30 areas (mainly large cities). As Williams observed

> What the PCOM teams found were: (1) a large number of federally funded manpower programs operating alongside private and local government programs, and administered under a bewildering set of funding and operational requirements that often made the intermeshing of the programs difficult if not impossible . . . ; (2) a lack of coordination or cooperation among programs of different agencies at all levels of government; and (3) a general inadequacy of most individual programs to serve adequately or even to reach many disadvantaged persons, particularly hard-core unemployed ghetto residents.[17]

The most important effort to coordinate local manpower programs was the Concentrated Employment Program (CEP), which attempted to concentrate manpower resources in a geographic area even smaller than that served by the CAA.[18] In CEP there was a presumption that the local CAA would be the "prime sponsor" of CEP projects and that USES would be the primary deliverer of all manpower services in CEP.

---

[16] For an account of problems faced by USES in shifting over to serving the disadvantaged, see Miriam Johnson, Counter Point: The Changing Employment Service, Olympus, Salt Lake City, Utah, 1973; and Stanley H. Ruttenberg and Jocelyn Gutchess, The Federal–State Employment Service: A Critique, Johns Hopkins University Press, Baltimore, 1970.

[17] Walter Williams, Social Policy Research and Analysis, American Elsevier, New York, 1971, p. 39.

[18] Differing views of the CEP experience are presented by the senior author, who was in the policy analysis office at OEO and involved in the development of CEP, and Stanley Ruttenberg, who was the DOL assistant secretary heading the Manpower Administration. See ibid., pp. 36–49; and Stanley H. Ruttenberg, Manpower Challenge of the 1970s: Institutions and Social Change, Johns Hopkins University Press, Baltimore, 1970, pp. 30–39, 64–71.

CEP forced together the two main federal actors, and often antagonists, in the local manpower arena.

Coordination, however, did not work. As Marshall observed: "[CEP] attempted unsuccessfully to solve the coordination problem by providing *block grants* to local groups to plan, operate, and coordinate local programs in selected low-income areas."[19] It seems a fair appraisal. This coordination effort, as others in the Great Society years, was based on the premise that federal agencies working together could reconcile many overlapping field concerns so that *all* agencies would gain. The coordinators would not face basic power issues. Coordination efforts among equals are almost always certain to yield minor, superficial changes that do not alter the power balance. DOL, OEO, and to some extent HEW simply would never give up any power in the field and were not willing to have a superior authority decide among equals.[20]

During the 1960s and early 1970s, categorical manpower programs continued to grow in dollar size and number. Marshall reports manpower program outlays of $450 million in FY 1964; $2596 million in FY 1970 at the end of the Great Society years; and $4952 million in FY 1973 just before the block grant legislation.[21] In FY 1964, about 60% of the funds went to USES and the long-established vocational rehabilitation program in HEW. Of the new programs, only MDTA was on the books. Then in the remainder of the 1960s, the nation tried a host of new approaches, such as heavy business involvement (Jobs in the Business Sector [JOBS]), concentrated employment in poverty areas (CEP), and public employment in several categories including the young (Neighborhood Youth Corps), older people, particularly those in depressed rural areas (Operation Mainstream), and people seeking new paraprofessional jobs (New Careers). Cities hired consultants or established new staff positions to find out how to qualify for the ever growing and changing categoricals. Mirengoff and Rindler summed up the manpower program situation as follows

> By the end of the 1960s, there were more than 17 programs, each with its own legislative and organizational base, funding source, and regulations. Out of these so-called categorical programs flowed 10,000 or more specific manpower projects,

[19] Marshall, "Microemployment Programs of the 1960s," in Warner (editor), *Toward New Human Rights*, p. 83, italics added.

[20] The best treatment available of local-level coordination is found in James L. Sundquist, *Making Federalism Work: A Study of Program Coordination at the Community Level*, Brookings Institution, Washington, D.C., 1969.

[21] Marshall, "Microemployment Programs of the 1960s," in Warner (editor), *Toward New Human Rights*, Table 1, p. 87.

often several in the same community competing for the same clientele and resources. These programs generally were conducted through public and nonpublic agencies but not through the local governments themselves.[22]

The prevailing view of the incoming Nixon administration was that there were too many categorical manpower programs, too much federal regulation and supervision, too little control by local government, and too few manpower programs yielding positive benefits for participants.[23]

Economic conditions and social concerns were changing in the early 1970s. The unemployment picture began to resemble that of the late Eisenhower years. The disadvantaged were joined in the unemployment lines by people unaccustomed to being out of a job. As Mirengoff and Rindler point out: "[The Emergency Employment Act of 1971], which subsidized state and local public service jobs for a two-year period, was designed to put unemployed people—*not necessarily the most disadvantaged*—into employment quickly while providing badly needed public services in local communities."[24] The focus of social concern in manpower programs had started to shift.

Nixon, Congress, and the New Federalism

We need to consider briefly some broader ideas, including two strongly held notions of President Nixon, that shaped the New Federalism in broad dimension and also had an important impact upon CETA and CDBG. First was Nixon's distaste for community action in general and for the CAAs in particular. The thing that seemed to bother him most was that CAAs had some independence from local governments and that citizens had a goodly amount of influence over the CAAs. He was against citizen participation as it had developed in the

[22] William Mirengoff and Lester Rindler, *The Comprehensive Employment and Training Act: Impact on People, Places, Programs—Interim Report*, National Academy of Sciences, Washington, D.C., 1976, p. 2. This book contains a brief but useful summary of the categorical program experience. For a more detailed discussion of manpower programs see the references in footnote 23 (the Levin paper has an extensive bibliography).

[23] Three appraisals from the perspective of the 1970s are Marshall, "Microemployment Programs of the 1960s," in Warner (editor), *Toward New Human Rights*, pp. 75–94; Henry M. Levin, "A Decade of Policy Developments in Improving Education and Training for Low-Income Populations," in Robert H. Haveman (editor), *A Decade of Federal Antipoverty Programs*, Academic Press, New York, 1977, pp. 123–188; and Sar A. Levitan and Robert Taggart, *The Promise of Greatness*, Harvard University Press, Cambridge, Mass., 1976, pp. 134–149.

[24] Mirengoff and Rindler, *Comprehensive Employment and Training Act*, pp. 1–2, italics added.

OEO programs and others. The model cities program is a good example. In the Johnson administration, model cities had been ambivalent about letting the City Demonstration Agencies (CDA), which were new entities outside of the jurisdiction of city hall and which tended to be citizen dominated, run programs rather than just plan them. But as Brown and Frieden have observed "HUD's vacillation on this issue ended with the advent of the Nixon administration. HUD officials soon began denying CDA requests for authority to operate programs."[25] President Nixon wanted power in city hall.[26]

Second, Nixon was strongly "antibureaucracy." In his 8 August 1969 television address, in which he discussed the notion of the New Federalism, President Nixon observed "[The New Federalism] would decentralize administration, gradually moving it away from the Washington bureaucracy and turning it over to States and localities." Richard Nathan, who was a principal Nixon advisor on the New Federalism, argued "that many governmental decisions should not be relegated to experts [federal bureaucrats] but should, instead, reflect the popular will through democratic decision processes."[27] Such a statement may seem to conflict with President Nixon's anticommunity action views. However, the reconciliation appears to be that President Nixon wanted to take power from *both* federal bureaucrats and poverty area citizens and give it to elected officials who represented *all* the people. It is not clear whether or not he foresaw that those same officials would delegate that power to their local bureaucrats.

Future historians will decide whether President Nixon's New Federalism was a federal cop-out intended to scuttle the social pro-

---

[25] Lawrence D. Brown and Bernard J. Frieden, "Rulemaking by Improvision: Guidelines and Goals in the Model Cities Program," *Policy Sciences*, 7, 1976, p. 472.

[26] There is now a vast literature on community action. For an extended discussion and a large bibliography of materials written before and during the Johnson administration, see Sar A. Levitan, *The Great Society's Poor Law*, Johns Hopkins University Press, Baltimore, 1969. For a more recent discussion with an excellent bibliography of more recent work, see Paul E. Peterson and J. David Greenstone, "Racial Change and Citizen Participation: The Mobilization of Low-Income Communities through Community Action," in Haveman (editor), *A Decade of Federal Antipoverty Programs*, pp. 241–278. Finally, mention should be made of Daniel P. Moynihan, *Maximum Feasible Misunderstanding*, Free Press, New York, 1969. This quite negative view of the CAAs by a close Nixon advisor surely must have influenced the president's thinking on community action.

[27] Richard P. Nathan, *The Plot that Failed*, Wiley, New York, 1975, p. 85. The term *antibureaucracy* is taken from the Nathan book, which presents a good discussion of Nixon's views on the bureaucracy and his efforts to gain control of the federal bureaucrats. The Nixon television address on 8 August 1969, can be found on pp. 101–112. The quote in this paragraph is on p. 107. This and other references to the same article are under copyright © 1975 by John Wiley & Sons, Inc. Reprinted by permission of John Wiley & Sons, Inc.

grams of the 1960s.[28] We do know that President Nixon did propose specific social programs such as the Family Assistance Plan and that a heavily Democratic Congress enacted both general revenue sharing in 1972 and CETA and CDBG, all of which contained important elements of the Nixon philosophy.

Whatever the underlying philosophical motives, it does seem clear that the New Federalism evidenced a federal tiredness and frustration, particularly in the Congress. The nation had lost the optimism of the beginning of the Great Society years. It was worn out from the vast number of categorical programs that came first in optimism and then in frustration and fright over the social animosities of the mid-1960s. Finally, there was a quite justifiable questioning of federal management. But when the reaction came, it was unrealistic. Local weaknesses were ignored. Somehow locals could solve the problems federal officials could not handle. *Wrapped in the rhetoric of the wonders of the democratic process, giving money to local elected officials offered an ingenious way of passing on to somebody else the problems of programs, of coordination, and of the growing number of minority groups who wanted part of the action.* These delusions were part of the legislation that emerged.

Background of CDBG

The community development efforts under CDBG are both more poorly defined and more complex than the CETA manpower programs. As an Advisory Commission on Intergovernmental Relations (ACIR) study has observed "Community development has, from time to time, included programs related to physical development, human services, environmental protection, and political organization. More than many other programs, its meaning has varied depending upon the particular program, its objectives, and the participants involved."[29] The CDBG legislation for the first time explicitly linked community development

---

[28] For a more extended discussion of such allegations, including a critique of the views of various critics of the New Federalism when general revenue sharing was before the Congress, see Reagan, *The New Federalism*, pp. 130–131.

[29] *Community Development: The Workings of a Federal–Local Block Grant*, Advisory Commission on Intergovernmental Relations, A-57, Washington, D.C., March 1977, p. 1. This ACIR study is an excellent summary of prior legislation, the development of the CDBG legislation, and provisions of the act. This section relies heavily upon the ACIR study. Another good summary covering much the same materials is Richard P. Nathan and others, *Block Grants for Community Development*, First Report on the Brookings Institution Monitoring Study of the Community Development Block Grant Program, U.S. Department of Housing and Urban Development, Washington, D.C., January 1977. Both works have extensive bibliographies.

and housing programs. This forced concern with housing added a dimension that made implementation more difficult.[30]

COMMUNITY DEVELOPMENT PROGRAM
PRIOR TO CDBG

In 1892 Congress appropriated $20,000 to finance a study of urban slum conditions. Sixteen years later, another study group created by Theodore Roosevelt examined slum conditions.[31] But there was no federal action. Only with the impetus of the wholesale social and economic ravages brought by the Great Depression of the 1930s did the federal government step directly into the battle to save cities. Emergency housing and slum clearance legislation were seen as job-creating devices to stimulate economic recovery.[32]

The Housing Act of 1949, where the term *community development* was first used explicitly in federal legislation, was a landmark piece of legislation that provided the foundation for widespread federal support of housing and community development activities. However, despite a broad interpretation of housing in this legislation, Congress interpreted community development primarily as land acquisition, slum clearance, preparation of the blighted land, and resale of the prepared site to private developers. This approach to community development was generally designated "urban redevelopment."

The Housing Act of 1954 expanded the 1949 redevelopment concept, labeling it officially "urban renewal." The act contained a requirement for a "Workable Program for Community Improvement," which included provisions for planning and for citizen participation components. The citizen participation requirements were largely perfunctory and provided little opportunity for community members, particularly poor and minority representatives, to make any impact on planning. Section 701 of the act provided planning funds to towns with populations below 25,000 and to area-wide planning bodies for larger cities. Communities were to come up with an urban renewal plan

[30] For brief discussions of all housing and community development legislation through 1974, see *Evolution of Role of the Federal Government in Housing and Community Development: A Chronology of Legislative and Selected Executive Actions, 1892–1974*, Subcommittee on Housing and Community Development of the Committee on Banking, Currency and Housing, U.S. House of Representatives, 94th Congress, First Session, October 1975, U.S. Government Printing Office, Washington, D.C. This publication, which runs to well over 200 pages, is an exhaustive list of programs and their provisions. A quick look at it should convince the reader who is unfamiliar with basic housing legislation of the vastness and complexity of this area.

[31] Ibid., p. 1.

[32] Nathan and others, *Block Grants for Community Development*, p. 20.

rather than to perform piecemeal slum clearance operations. The concept of "urban planning" was changed to "comprehensive planning" in the Housing Act of 1968 and implied that all grants must be made to official planning bodies that had official planning powers.

Programs enacted through 1965 continued the physical approach in federally assisted community development. Title VIII of the Housing Act of 1961 provided for the preservation of open spaces, urban beautification, and historic sites. In the Housing Act of 1965, Title VII made provision for grants for water and sewer systems, neighborhood facilities, and advance acquisition of land. The emphasis of the urban renewal programs was primarily on physical rehabilitation, in part because the results were visible and measurable. At that time, the concept prevailed that changing slum dwellers' physical environments would substantially solve their problems.

The Demonstration Cities and Metropolitan Development Act of 1966 sharply changed the focus of community development efforts by addressing social and economic problems as well as those of physical improvement. Its Title I (model cities) provided funds for job training, employment, and a variety of social services, as well as for neighborhood improvement efforts. Also, the planning emphasis shifted from physical planning on a project-by-project basis to a comprehensive plan reflecting physical, social, and economic aspects.

Comparisons and contrasts of model cities agencies with the community action agencies (CAAs) established in the 1964 Economic Opportunity Act are important to note. In large urban areas, model cities agencies, just as the CAAs, were concentrated in slum and blighted areas that were smaller than the city itself and referred to as model neighborhoods. However, model cities watered down or modified two major thrusts in the Economic Opportunity Act. First, funds went to a city demonstration agency that had to be housed in an existing department within the local government or a public agency established or designated by the local government to administer the model cities grant. Second, model cities' "extensive participation" requirement for model neighborhood residents was stronger than earlier HUD community development legislation but not as strong as the "maximum feasible participation" requirements for CAA neighborhood residents. As early as 1966, President Johnson and the Congress wanted programs more under the control of city hall with less direct citizen involvement.

It is also worth noting that model cities was originally considered to be very much like a block grant. However, as Kaplan has observed

"[E]ven in such an ostensibly home-rule oriented program as model cities, the requirement that the Secretary approve local plans was converted initially into weighty, often obtuse, guidelines; irrelevant administrative prescriptives concerning local planning processes (understandable only to Ph.D. students and clearly out of sorts with the planning state of the arts); and, often, extended torturous handbooks.[33]

Model cities stood as a forewarning to those who would develop block grants in the Nixon administration.[34]

The problems with model cities and other community development efforts led to a number of changes that foreshadowed CDBG. Three need brief discussion. Neighborhood Development Programs (NDPs) provisions in the Housing Act of 1968 near the end of the Johnson administration allowed a community to receive assistance for planning and carrying out urban renewal projects. This approach facilitated implementation of renewal projects with immediate starts on rehabilitation, public improvements, redevelopment activities, and less complicated procedures. By 1972, all new renewal projects were executed under NDPs.

The 1971 Annual Arrangement (AA) provisions stipulated yearly negotiations between representatives of participating jurisdictions and HUD officials. At this time, the two groups would develop a "package" of community development activities for that particular jurisdiction that would be funded by HUD. This approach was supposed to allow for earmarking of HUD funds for a full-year program based upon a comprehensive assessment of local needs and priorities. Besides providing better coordination, the ACIR study argues that the AA process was viewed by the Nixon administration as a stopgap block grant arrangement until its community development special revenue sharing package passed Congress: "HUD believed the AA process would enable mayors to select desired projects for funding much the same way as with a no-strings-attached community development block grant."[35]

Planned Variations (PV), started in 1971, was a broader program than Annual Arrangements, permitting a city-wide model cities pro-

[33] Marshall Kaplan, "Model Cities and the New Inventory," in Joseph D. Sneed and Steven A. Waldhorn (editors), *Restructuring the Federal System*, Crane, Russak, New York, 1975, p. 81.

[34] For excellent accounts of model cities based on the Johnson administration experience, see James L. Sundquist, *Making a Federalism Work*, Brookings Institution, Washington, D.C., 1969, pp. 79–129; and Edward C. Banfield, "Making a New Federal Program: Model Cities, 1964–68" in Walter Williams and Richard F. Elmore (editors), *Social Program Implementation*, Academic Press, New York, 1976, pp. 183–218. For a good account of community development efforts from a later perspective and with more recent references, see Bernard Frieden and Marshall Kaplan, "Community Development and the Model Cities Legacy," in David C. Warner (editor), *Toward New Human Rights*, Lyndon B. Johnson School of Public Affairs, University of Texas, Austin, 1977, pp. 277–314.

[35] *Community Development: The Workings of a Federal–Local Block Grant*, p. 5.

gram for a jurisdiction. In addition, it made provision for "chief executive review and comment" that gave local chief executives substantial coordinating responsibility, review power over related applications for federal assistance to their community, and funding for the review. There also was a "minimization of review" section through which HUD committed itself to curtail involvement in the review process and to delegate the major portion of its review powers to local chief executives.

None of these efforts provided enough of the no-strings environment envisioned by the Nixon administration. As the ACIR study concluded:

> The categorical limitations which were placed on HUD funds proved to be an obstacle to program coordination and flexibility. First, the existence of a finite funding source within each program category placed an automatic limitation upon the cities. . . .
> Additionally, cities found it difficult to change priorities in community development projects where the funds had already been allocated. Previous commitment to ongoing programs curtailed the flexibility of the funds involved.[36]

THE FIGHT OVER COMMUNITY DEVELOPMENT AND HOUSING

The fight was long and acrimonious between President Nixon and the Congress and within the Congress itself over the shape of what finally emerged as the Housing and Community Development Act (HCDA) of 1974.[37] It was exactly 40 months to the day from the introduction by the Nixon administration of the Urban Community Development Revenue Sharing Act on 22 April 1971, to the final enactment of HCDA on 22 August 1974. During the interim the perhaps most bitter clash between President Nixon's no-strings-attached approach, usually labeled "special revenue sharing," and a more restrictive concept with significant federal control, usually called "block grants," occurred. There were other key issues, including whether funds would go to urban counties, the extent to which funds would continue to go to social services as in the model cities program, and the linkage between community development and housing.

The last go-around on the legislation pitted the Senate, which

---

[36] Ibid., pp. 5–6.

[37] For a good account of the development of the block grant legislation from President Nixon's original efforts through final enactment of CDBG, see Nathan and others, *Block Grants for Community Development*, pp. 31–51.

fought for strong federal control and a basic link between community development and housing, against the House and the administration, which worked together on the drafting of the House version of the bill. The outcome of the various compromises will be discussed in the section on specific provisions. At this point, it is important to emphasize, however, that the extended controversy yielded a complex and often contradictory piece of legislation that was to make implementation exceedingly difficult.

One other aspect of the Nixon–Congress battle needs to be discussed—the so-called Nixon moratorium on housing and community development activities that occurred in 1973. The moratorium was Nixon's means of applying pressure on Congress to push through his 1973 Better Communities Act (a revised version of the 1971 proposal). The tactic placed a temporary freeze on new commitments for water and sewer grants, open space grants, and public facilities loans (all of which were ultimately decategorized in CDBG) until these activities were folded into the special revenue sharing program. A similar "holding action" was to be used with urban renewal and model cities funds at the end of FY 1973. It was a power play by the administration to force Congress' hand by cutting off the flow of HUD funds to cities and counties. However, as the ACIR study observed

> The strategy backfired—despite its purported consequences. . . . It fortified congressional resolve to use its agreement on community development legislation as leverage to obtain acceptable housing proposals. Its ultimate goal was clear: an omnibus housing bill which would ensure the continued use of Federal dollars by local governments to maintain and further national goals and objectives set by Congress during the past 30 years of housing and community development legislative involvement.[38]

The other critical outcome of the moratorium was the demoralization of HUD. As we shall see in subsequent sections, HUD began the CDBG implementation with major problems in organizational structure. The moratorium added greatly to HUD's overall burden in terms of poor morale.

PROVISIONS OF THE BLOCK GRANT LEGISLATION

In this section, the most important provisions of CETA and CDBG will be discussed. Our concern is with the legislation as enacted—the new laws to be implemented at the times they emerged from Congress.

[38] *Community Development: The Workings of a Federal–Local Block Grant,* p. 9.

"Original" CETA Provisions

The Comprehensive Employment and Training Act of 1973 combined programs from the Manpower Development and Training Act, the Emergency Employment Act, and portions of the Economic Opportunity Act. CETA, as amended by the Emergency Jobs and Unemployment Assistance Act of 1974 (Title VI, as discussed in the following summary), became the basic piece of federal manpower legislation. Its stated purpose was "to provide job training and employment opportunities for economically disadvantaged, unemployed, and underemployed persons, and to assure that training and other services lead to maximum employment opportunities and enhance self-sufficiency by establishing a flexible and decentralized system of Federal, State, and local programs."[39] The "original" CETA provisions—the 1973 legislation and the 1974 addition of Title VI—may be summarized as follows

Title I provided funds to state and local governments labeled "prime sponsors" to offer comprehensive manpower services including training, employment, counseling, testing, and placement. Prime sponsors include units of general local government in areas with populations of 100,000 or more; a combination of units of general government that includes at least one unit in an area where the population is 100,000 or more (called a "consortium"); a state; and special areas designated by the secretary of labor. Local governments and consortia predominate.

Eighty percent of the funds provided under this title were to be determined under a formula based on prior levels of funding, the relative number of unemployed persons within a state compared to such numbers in other states, and the relative number of low-income persons. The 20% of the funds not allocated under the formula covered special grants for vocational education, state manpower services, efforts to encourage consortia, and discretionary spending by the secretary.

Title II authorized a program of transitional public service employment in geographic areas of substantial unemployment (a rate of unemployment of 6.5% or more for 3 consecutive months). These programs were to be administered by the prime sponsors established in Title I.

Title III provided funds for special groups including youth, offenders, persons of limited English-speaking ability, and so on. This title also provided funds for research, demonstration, and evaluation efforts administered by the secretary.

Title IV continued Job Corps, which was originally created under the Economic Opportunity Act.

Title V established a National Commission for Manpower Policy, the main function of which was to advise the secretary of labor on manpower issues.

Title VI, which was added in December 1974 through passage of the Emergency Jobs and Unemployment Assistance Act, provided for public service employment jobs much as did Title II but did not restrict funds to areas of substantial unemployment. Title VI funds also went to prime sponsors.

[39] Public Law 93–203, 93rd Congress, S. 1559, 28 December 1973 (87 STAT. 839), p. 1.

Title VII contained administrative and procedural provisions applicable to all titles, covering such areas as discrimination and political activity.

The overall CETA legislation combined a block grant (Title I), which decategorized MDTA and portions of the Economic Opportunity Act, with several categorical programs. There also was a kind of crosscutting decentralization feature in CETA. As Mirengoff and Rindler have observed

> Congressional intent to shift control of programs and funds from federal to state and local authorities was originally reflected only in Titles I and II. The addition of Title VI and a summer youth program as decentralized (although categorized) activities brought the proportion of CETA resources managed by local authorities to 89% in fiscal 1975.[40]

Our concern focuses on the decentralized portion of CETA, particularly the administration of Title I.

CDBG Provisions

The CDBG program—Title I of the Housing and Community Development Act of 1974—like CETA decategorized a number of programs and provided grant funds to local governments through a formula based on total population, the extent of poverty (given double weight), and the extent of overcrowded housing. CDBG decategorized the following programs:

> Urban renewal under Title I of the Housing Act of 1949 and the Neighborhood Development Programs which were made part of the urban renewal provisions in the Housing Act of 1968;
>
> Public facilities loans under Title II of the Housing amendments of 1955;
>
> Open space land grants under Title VI of the Housing Act of 1961;
>
> Rehabilitation loans under Section 312 of the Housing Act of 1964;
>
> Water and sewer facilities grants under Section 702 of the Housing and Urban Development Act of 1965;
>
> Neighborhood and facilities grants under Section 703 of the Housing and Urban Development Act of 1965;
>
> Model cities under Title I of the Demonstration Cities and Metropolitan Development Act of 1966.[41]

---

[40] Mirengoff and Rindler, The Comprehensive Employment and Training Act, p. 5.

[41] For a summary of the decategorized programs as originally passed, see Evolution of Role of the Federal·Government in Housing and Community Development: A Chronology of Legislative and Selected Executive Actions, 1892–1974, pp. 25–27, 51–52, 90, 79–80, 98–99, 114–119.

A major initial result of the decategorization was simplified requirements, as this HUD statement indicates "CDBG regulations
printed in the Federal Register total 25 pages as compared to about
2600 pages of regulations in HUD handbooks for categorical grant programs."[42]

The legislation states that the primary objective of CDBG is "the
development of viable urban communities, by providing decent housing and a suitable living environment and expanding economic opportunities, principally for persons of low and moderate income."[43] Title I
then goes on to set out that federal assistance under that title is to support community development efforts aimed at seven specific national
objectives:

(1) the elimination of slums and blight and the prevention of blighting influences
and the deterioration of property and neighborhood and community facilities of
importance to the welfare of the community, principally persons of low and
moderate income;
(2) the elimination of conditions which are detrimental to health, safety, and
public welfare, through code enforcement, demolition, interim rehabilitation
assistance, and related activities;
(3) the conservation and expansion of the Nation's housing stock in order to provide a decent home and a suitable living environment for all persons, but principally those of low and moderate income;
(4) the expansion and improvement of the quantity and quality of community services, principally for persons of low and moderate income, which are essential for
sound community development and for the development of viable urban communities;
(5) a more rational utilization of land and other natural resources and the better arrangement of residential, commercial, industrial, recreational, and other needed
activity centers;
(6) the reduction of the isolation of income groups within communities and
geographical areas and the promotion of an increase in the diversity and vitality of
neighborhoods through the spatial deconcentration of housing opportunities for
persons of lower income and the revitalization of deteriorating or deteriorated
neighborhoods to attract persons of higher income; and
(7) the restoration and preservation of properties of special value for historic, ar-
chitectural, or esthetic reasons.[44]

Specific Provisions

Let us consider in somewhat more detail several important aspects
of the two pieces of legislation. We will be picking and choosing from

---

[42] *Community Development Block Grant Program: First Annual Report,* U.S. Department of Housing and Urban Development, Washington, D.C., December 1975, p. 3.

[43] Public Law 93–383, 93rd Congress, S. 3066, 22 August 1974, p. 1.

[44] Ibid., pp. 1–2.

CETA and CDBG to illustrate important changes from the categorical programs embodied in the block grants.

THE POWER SHIFT TO LOCAL GOVERNMENTS

Both CETA and CDBG at their inception were seen as means of shifting power from the national to the local level. The most basic change under CETA was the provision of block grants to local units of government. Prime sponsors were empowered to determine both the mix of manpower services offered in their communities and the organizations that would deliver these services. The prime sponsor had the option either of providing manpower services directly or of contracting with outside organizations for such delivery.

CETA shifted power *to* the prime sponsors and their electorate *from* DOL; local nongovernmental organizations, including those representing poverty areas; residents of poverty areas; and certain national organizations that had local units that administered manpower programs. The power shift derived in part from a basic change in relationships. First, rather than dealing directly with well over 10,000 grantees for specific manpower projects, DOL was to administer something over 400 grants to prime sponsors. These prime sponsors in turn were to administer and (if they chose) to operate manpower projects. DOL was now one more layer removed from actual project operations.

Second, manpower project operators had to negotiate directly with local governments rather than with regional and area offices or DOL headquarters. In the latter case, national organizations such as the National Urban League formerly had been able to negotiate directly with Washington for the funding of their local projects. CETA meant the local organizations had to work out their own arrangements at the local level. Finally, manpower funds no longer would go directly to local nongovernmental organizations such as CAAs representing geographic areas. The major thrust of the 1960s, to get funds to poor neighborhoods, was weakened.

In CDBG the key decentralization issue was which local jurisdiction was to get funds. One of the most fundamental and complicated struggles in the community development legislation concerned the formula distribution of funds to geographical categories. The result of the basic formula distribution decision is simple to state. Urban counties, rapidly growing cities in the South and the Southwest, and nonmetropolitan areas (those outside of Standard Metropolitan Statistical Areas) gained, while larger cities, particularly those in the Northeast and Midwest, lost in the formula distribution of CDBG funds.

CDBG did contain hold-harmless provisions that guaranteed that a community during a specific time period would receive no less funds than it did under the several decategorized programs even though the CDBG formula yields a smaller amount. However, the temporary nature of the hold-harmless arragements indicated that the big cities would lose funds unless Congress changed its mind and extended these provisions.[45]

Within the major cities, where the bulk of the community development funds had gone under the categoricals, the big gainer was general local government (the cities' chief elected officials) and the losers were city demonstration agencies, residents of model neighborhoods, and other relatively independent housing and community development organizations, including those that were part of the local government. In this respect, the change was much like that in CETA with city hall gaining power at the expense of all the other major actors in the area including federal field officials.

PROGRAM AND ELIGIBILITY CHANGES

One of the most important aspects of CETA Title I was that projects funded under this title could do anything programmatically that had been done under earlier legislation and could provide these services under less restrictive requirements for eligible participants. All types of projects funded under MDTA and EOA remained eligible activities under CETA. The basic change in participant eligibility requirements was to include unemployed and underemployed persons—much less restrictive categories than had been the case either under EOA-funded programs, where poverty standards were applied, or under MDTA programs, where changes had reoriented services toward those who were suffering continuing economic disadvantages derived from such factors as race or age.

In sharp contrast to CETA, CDBG demanded difficult changes. Further, these changes reflected the unclear nature of the compromises in the final legislation. Changes included a requirement to stress service to low- and moderate-income persons in all programs, a shift away from social services toward physical development, and a linkage between community development and housing.

The original Senate bill had specified that at least 80% of a locality's community development funds be spent on low- or moderate-

---

[45] The ACIR study devotes the bulk of its discussion of the major issues of CDBG to a consideration of funding decisions. See *Community Development: The Workings of a Federal–Local Block Grant*, pp. 17–29.

income people or blighted areas. The final compromise in the law stated that "any grant under this title shall be made only on condition that the applicant certify to the satisfaction of the Secretary that the Community Development Program has been developed so as to give *maximum feasible priority* to activities which benefit low- or moderate-income families or aid in the prevention or elimination of slums or blight."[46] The term *maximum feasible priority* had emerged in the conference committee report, but no definition was given. As the ACIR study indicated, maximum feasible priority appeared to be the rough equivalent of *maximum feasible participation*, the term that had caused endless confusion in the poverty program.[47] It was anybody's guess as to what constituted giving maximum feasible priority to expenditures that benefited low-income people or attacked blight and slums. To complicate matters, various activities clearly eligible under the categorical legislation became questionable under CDBG.

A second compromise moved away from a Senate requirement that no more than 20% of the community development funds could be spent on social services (referred to in the legislation as "public services" and sometimes called "software" as opposed to physical development, labeled "hardware"). What came out of the conference committee was almost as restrictive and much more confusing. Section 105 (a)(8) set out a number of restrictions, including one that the public service must be in areas where CDBG activities are concentrated, that "such services are determined to be necessary or appropriate to support such other activities" (physical services), and that "such services under other applicable Federal laws or programs have been applied for and denied or not made available within a reasonable period of time."[48] CDBG did not allow cities much discretion in developing a mix between physical development and social service programs. The real dilemma developed in cities deeply involved in model cities projects where a return to hardware cut into established social services previously provided by HUD funds in the model neighborhood.[49]

By far the most troublesome of the several planning documents that the applicant for CDBG funds had to submit to the secretary under Section 104 (a) was the Housing Assistance Plan (HAP). The HAP is the only document that cannot be waived for smaller cities. The HAP was

[46] Public Law 93–383, Section 104 (b) (2), p. 6, italics added.
[47] See *Community Development: The Workings of a Federal–Local Block Grant*, pp. 12–13, 31.
[48] Public Law 93–383, pp. 8–9.
[49] For a discussion of social (public) service expenditures in the first year of CDBG, see *Community Development Block Grant Program: First Annual Report*, pp. 31–33.

seen as the way to ensure that local governments attended to housing needs in their communities when planning their community development program. As a House subcommittee observed

> [T]he experience gained from twenty-five years of federally-assisted community development activities. . . demonstrate[s] that, almost universally, housing activities were not coordinated with local community development activities in any systematic way to the detriment of both types of activity. For this reason the housing assistance provisions in Title II of the Act were to be melded with the community development assistance provided in Title I through the HAP.[50]

However much the housing–community development link was needed, the HAP put a severe new burden on community development applicants. The law required that the HAP "accurately surveys the condition of the housing stock in the community and assesses the housing assistance needs of lower-income persons . . . specifies a realistic annual goal for the number of dwelling units or persons to be assisted [and] indicates the general locations of proposed housing for lower-income persons."[51] It was a demanding requirement in terms both of data and of analytic competence.

THE SHIFT IN EMPHASIS FROM
PROGRAM TO PROCESS

Both CETA and CDBG shifted focus from program specifics to the decision-making process used in determining those specifics. CETA Title I illustrates this point vividly. That title embodied a crucial shift of attention from types of programs where there was roughly 10 years of experience to a complex intergovernmental and citizen decision-making process for determining particular projects where there was little or no experience in the employment and training areas.

The contrast between CETA Titles I and IV (Job Corps) shows the differences between the block grant and categorical approaches. The differences occur despite the fact that both titles (a) have similar goals of helping people to become more employable, productive citizens; and (b) involved long-established programs so that those developing the legislation had ample basis for elaborating on program package specifics.

Title IV in several places elaborated in great detail on the program

---

[50] *Community Development Block Grant Program,* Subcommittee on Housing and Community Development of the Committee on Banking, Finance and Urban Affairs, House of Representatives, 95th Congress, 1st Session, February 1977, U.S. Government Printing Office, Washington, D.C., p. 27.

[51] Public Law 93–383, p. 5.

package that "shall" exist in each Job Corps center. In contrast, Title I offered a laundry list of eligible comprehensive manpower services that previously had been provided under MDTA and EOA, but without presenting programmatic details. For example, despite roughly 12 years of experience with on-the-job-training programs (OJT was in the original 1962 MDTA legislation), Title I only listed "training on the job" as a possible candidate for funding.

CITIZEN INVOLVEMENT

Both pieces of legislation were long on the rhetoric of citizen involvement but at key points lacked specifics that supported such involvement. CDBG offers the best example. Section 104 (a) (6) provides that a grant will not be made by the secretary until

> [the applicant] provides satisfactory assurances that, prior to submission of its application, it has (A) provided citizens with adequate information concerning the amount of funds available for proposed community development and housing activities, the range of activities that may be undertaken, and other program requirements, (B) held public hearings to obtain the views of citizens on community development and housing needs, and (C) provided citizens an adequate opportunity to participate in development of the application; but no part of this paragraph shall be construed to restrict the responsibility and authority of the applicant for the development of the application and the execution of its Community Development Program.[52]

After the quote, Section 104 (b) (4) goes on to state that "the Secretary may accept a certification from the applicant that it has complied with the requirements" of the provisions for citizen involvement.[53] How the term *adequate* was to be defined as it applied to information and the opportunity to participate in the development of the application was not specified in the legislation.

THE ROLE OF THE SECRETARY AND
THE REGIONAL OFFICES

The most confusing aspect of CETA was the intent of Congress concerning DOL's expected role both in headquarters and in the field in administering prime sponsors. On the one hand, the legislation in its statement of purpose established a "flexible and decentralized" system and the mood of the times certainly pointed toward a hands-off policy by the Department of Labor. Moreover, as we have already discussed,

[52] Ibid., pp. 5–6.
[53] Ibid., p. 6.

the prime sponsors were to replace DOL as the administrators of specific manpower projects.

At the same time, CETA spelled out in lengthy detail administrative tasks for the secretary of labor to perform before a prime sponsor could receive funds. Section 105 differs little from the most strict categorical legislation in specifying that the secretary "shall" determine that prime sponsors meet a host of stringent provisions before they can be funded. As a final step, Section 110 (a) provides for a takeover by the secretary of a failed program or of employment and training activities in a geographic area where no prime sponsor qualified such that DOL can "make grants to and enter into contracts with public and private nonprofit agencies and organizations in the same manner and to the same extent as if the Secretary were the prime sponsor for that area."[54]

The final CETA legislation ended up more restrictive in tone and in intent than the Nixon version of special revenue sharing, which would have been more like general revenue sharing—a check sent to local governments to be spent on manpower with few strings attached. Robert McPherson, then director of the King–Snohomish Manpower Consortium in the state of Washington (one of the largest prime sponsors in the country), was correct when he observed that "long before the national bureaucrats wrote the federal regulations and ensuing field memoranda, the basic CETA assumptions were compromised by the legislative process."[55]

The CETA legislation left vague how power and responsibility were to be shared by various levels of government. Nowhere is this made more vivid than in the exchange between Congressmen Carl Perkins of Kentucky and Lloyd Meeds of Washington (both Democrats) just before final House passage of the CETA legislation that had emerged from the conference committee. Perkins argued

> Finally, I have heard this bill described as "special revenue sharing" by some people downtown. Let me say flatly that it is not.
>
> This bill is a compromise between those who favored the so-called revenue sharing approach and those who believe in a strong Federal role and responsibility. . . . [The bill places] squarely with the Secretary of Labor the responsibility for seeing that the conditions and the special requirements of the law, as

[54] Public Law 93–203, p. 11.

[55] Robert McPherson, "CETA—The Basic Assumptions and Future Prospects," a paper prepared for a Conference on Manpower Policy sponsored by the Employment Studies Program, San Francisco State University, San Francisco, October 1976, pp. 21–22.

well as its general purposes, are in fact being carried out. *The ultimate responsibility for success or failure rests with the Secretary and we will hold him strictly accountable.*[56]

Meeds did not agree

There are those who will contend this is not a revenue sharing bill. But it reads like a revenue sharing bill, it works like a revenue sharing bill, it comes from the same people who brought you general revenue sharing—the Nixon administration.[57]

At least some of the Congress, including Mr. Perkins, who chaired DOL's oversight committee in the House, believed the secretary had "ultimate responsibility for success or failure"—that is, accountability for final outcomes. At the other extreme, some saw the bill as doing little more than giving the funds to subnational governments with almost no strings. The legislative language and debate yielded ample supporting evidence for whichever position at the extremes or in between that one chose to take. The new balance of power between the federal government and local governments and organizations was something that had to evolve during the implementation period.

The ambivalence about the degree of federal involvement is even more striking in CDBG. The first thing to observe is that Congress did intend to place limits on fund recipients that would move them toward national priorities. Beyond the demands already discussed in the subsection on program and eligibility changes (see pp. 46–48), the legislation required a maintenance of effort by communities receiving CDBG funds and specified in Section 105 (a) a list of 13 community development program activities deemed eligible. The list is sufficiently inclusive that it did not place excessive restrictions on localities, but it did set out what the Congress preferred.

What was so ambiguous was the role that Congress intended for HUD. On the one hand, the act in the usual overblown legislative language sets out that the secretary "shall" require a host of documents and assurances from potential grantees. On the other hand, the legislation in Section 104 (c) states

The Secretary shall approve an application. . . . unless—

(1) on the basis of significant facts and data, generally available and pertaining to community and housing needs and objectives, the Secretary determines that the applicant's description of such needs and objectives is *plainly inconsistent* with such facts or data; or

---

[56] *Congressional Record—House,* 20 December 1973, H11801, italics added.
[57] Ibid., H11802.

(2) on the basis of the application, the Secretary determines that the activities to be undertaken are *plainly inappropriate* to meeting the needs and objectives identified by the applicant . . . or

(3) the Secretary determines that the application does not comply with the requirements of this title or other applicable law or proposes activities which are ineligible under this title.[58]

Section 104 (f) goes on to set out a "veto only" approach in which an application "shall be deemed approved within 75 days after receipt unless the Secretary informs the applicant of specific reasons for disapproval."[59]

The quoted parts of Section 104 appear to tell the HUD secretary to back off and let the applicants do what they want unless something is proposed that stands out as blatantly wrong or is obviously in direct violation of the law. Surely, such terms as *plainly inconsistent* and *plainly inapplicable* go about as far toward suggesting a hands-off policy for field staff as legislation can go without saying no front-end review at all. However, Section 104 (d) provides for audits and reviews by the secretary "to determine whether the grantee has carried out a program substantially as described in its application, whether that program conformed to the requirements of this title and other applicable laws, and whether the applicant has a continuing capacity to carry out in a timely manner the approved Community Development Program."[60] How carefully was HUD expected to scrutinize in the postreview? Is it to be "easy" as suggested for the front-end review or "tough" with tight interpretation of provisions including the 13 eligible activities in Section 105? A tough audit seems almost certain to intimidate applicants in terms of future choices by telling them that what got by in an application can be questioned and punished in a postreview. As the ACIR report observed in commenting upon the contradictions that emerged in the final legislative compromise:

A heavy emphasis on the preconditions can pull the program away from the block grant format, while a heavy stress on the minimal review provision, if exercised both *prior and subsequent* to the grant, can push the program nearer to the special revenue sharing approach. What emerges, then, as the real test is how these "conditions" are applied in actual administrative practice.[61]

[58] Public Law 93–383, p. 6, italics added.

[59] Ibid., p. 7.

[60] Ibid., pp. 6–7.

[61] *Community Development: The Workings of a Federal–Local Block Grant*, p. 17, italics added.

IMPLEMENTATION RESOURCES AND PROBLEMS

In this section we present in brief form a rough balance sheet first of DOL's and then HUD's resources and problems as implementation began.

CETA

The first factor to note is that CETA did not carry with it new programmatic or participant eligibility problems. In the 1960s, each new categorical program was likely to have a complex, untried program package or to demand services for a hard-core disadvantaged category even more difficult to treat than previous categories. Monitoring during that earlier period was made more difficult in part because of the proliferation of the categories of participants and in part because particular categories technically were harder to verify. In contrast, CETA did not establish any new program approaches. It allowed prime sponsors and project operators to support or use all the types of projects previously eligible under the manpower categoricals, and made eligible groups that were less difficult to treat.

In organizational terms, DOL looked good. First, the Manpower Administration (renamed Employment and Training Administration under CETA) had responsibility for all DOL manpower service programs at the local level. There was no real conflict or overlap with separate DOL programs that were concerned with regulation and labor relations. Second, DOL at the start of the CETA implementation appeared to have a well-established chain of command and procedures for headquarters–field staff relationships. Moreover, there was a veteran staff both at headquarters and in the regional and area offices that had worked together for a number of years in the kinds of manpower programs and projects that were used during the CETA implementation.[62] Finally, compared to other federal departments, DOL has enjoyed a certain singleness of purpose in its basic mission of helping unemployed or underemployed people find work. There were not the contradictory outside interest groups such as HUD had to contend with that drained resources away from direct program concerns.

[62] These impressions are based on one of the author's extended direct experience with DOL in the 1960s and discussions about DOL with others after that time. For an account of that experience, see Williams, *Social Policy Research and Analysis*, p. 41 (footnote 3). No detailed study of DOL's administrative and support domain capability just prior to CETA implementation is available.

There were some difficult problems too. First, as already discussed, the CETA legislation was unclear as to what Congress wanted
in terms of DOL and local government relationships. With all of the
rhetoric about decentralization and the need to let the locals "do their
own thing," DOL field staff were concerned and to some extent
demoralized over what was left for them to do. Second, many of the
new prime sponsors had little or no experience with manpower programs or with the more sophisticated management information systems
that guided manpower program administration. This inexperience
among prime sponsors quickly provided work for the field staff, but it
was often a trying experience, with DOL having to deal with people
who knew nothing about the programs they were to administer. Finally, jumping ahead a bit, the passage of Title VI in December 1974
authorized a 1-year appropriation of $2.5 billion—an extremely large
sum of money to put into a new system whose implementation in the
field had begun roughly one-half a year before.

CDBG

We can portray quickly the HUD balance sheet just prior to the implementation of CDBG by a comparison with DOL. First, CDBG was a
much less clearly defined and far more complex piece of legislation
than CETA. In particular, the link to housing was a new requirement
where HUD had little experience. Second, like DOL, HUD had had
some valuable experience, such as that gained in model cities, the
NDPs, and the AA and PV provisions, that seemed directly relevant to
the new program. Further, HUD had had far more experience than DOL
in working with the local governments that were to receive CDBG
funds. The HUD fund recipients were more likely to be familiar with
community development and housing programs than prime sponsors
were with manpower projects.

In contrast to DOL, HUD was a relatively new department
established in 1965 under the Department of Housing and Urban
Development Act.[63] It was not until 1966 that a separate community
development division was established as one of several divisions under
an assistant secretary for renewal and housing assistance and not until
1971 that the community development office reached assistant
secretary status. Further, HUD, unlike DOL, suffered from internal and
external conflicts that represented basic disagreements in society. The

---

[63] For a discussion of the provisions of that act, see Evolution of Role of Federal
Government in Housing and Community Development, pp. 106–107.

obvious conflicts between the banking and mortgage industries and low-income home owners or potential home buyers exemplifies these problems. Internally, powerful assistant secretaries clashed with each other, and community development simply did not have the field to itself in service delivery as did the Employment and Training Administration.

As we will see in Chapter 4, HUD was beset by organizational problems. Moreover, caught in the power battle between President Nixon and the Congress, HUD staff morale suffered in the Nixon moratorium that occurred not long before the passage of CDBG. Finally, CDBG appeared even more vague than CETA about what field staff were to do.

One final comment before turning to the detailed account of the block grant implementation: The balance sheet is not intended to be a hard assessment of the probability of implementation success, in part because such an analysis after the fact of implementation reflects too much hindsight and in part because detailed data were not available about the two agencies' organizational capabilities prior to implementation. Rather this brief section is meant to orient the reader to issues that will arise in subsequent discussion.

3 | THE IMPLEMENTATION OF CETA

This and the next chapter follow the same basic format. Several sections focus on what happened in the field in the implementation efforts during the New Federalism period. This long segment stresses the details of putting the programs in the field, being concerned with both organizational issues and how federal regional staff interacted with headquarters personnel and fund recipients. The final section will discuss how the various functions defined in Chapter 1 were carried out in the administrative and support domain during the New Federalism period.

In this chapter, all discussion, unless stated explicitly, will concern DOL efforts to implement and administer CETA during the New Federalism period extending to the end of the Ford administration. Exposition is made easier by casting events in the present tense to tell the implementation story as it unfolded. We have not tried to record changes occurring in CETA during the Carter administration except where such changes aid us in elaborating on a specific issue. Hence the reader should not infer that the present tense descriptions are meant to describe CETA today.

THE ETA STRUCTURE FROM THE FEDERAL PERSPECTIVE

This section looks at the structure and workings of the field operations portion of the national office of the Employment and Training Administration (ETA) and then at the regional offices. Much of this material consists of the perceptions of federal regional officials and certain key staff members. We take the approach of first viewing the regional office's mission from an inside position to provide the "on-paper" description. Because such a description deals at least in part with intent rather than reality, this view, without a doubt, will be the most generous picture painted of the regional offices. It is necessary to point out when using these perceptions, however, that there are many regional people who have felt confused about the regional role in the brave new world of the New Federalism. Lack of clarification from the national level combined with the results of new dispersions of power at the local level left some regional office staff uncertain as they carved out a job for themselves and for the office.

Before we turn to the detailed discussion, it may be helpful to the reader to specify the main actors in CETA. Figure 3.1 depicts the organization of a regional office in some detail and shows in most abbreviated form the major elements above and below with which it deals. The primary actors in CETA in addition to the secretary of labor are

The *Employment and Training Administration* (ETA), headed by an assistant secretary, is the largest agency within the Department of Labor and is responsible for DOL's major employment and training programs including CETA and USES.

The *Office of Field Operations* and within that the *field desk officers* are the main contact points in the national ETA office for regional office staff.

The *Office of the Regional Employment and Training Administrator* is the unit in the regional office responsible for CETA. It is headed by a *regional employment and training administrator* (RETA).

Within the Office of the Regional Employment and Training Administrator are the *Office of Program and Technical Services* and the *Office of Administration and Management Services*, which provide staff services including technical assistance.

Also under the RETA is the *area operations office*, which is the line unit responsible for CETA activities. Here are located the *field representatives*, who are the individuals having direct contact with prime sponsors.

Prime sponsors are the subnational governments that receive CETA monies by formula allocation and are responsible for administering or operating employment and training projects.

Project operators are local organizations with which the prime sponsors contract to operate individual employment and training projects. They are the service delivery point.

Until November 1975, the Employment and Training Administration in DOL was called the Manpower Administration. The head of ETA is now called the assistant secretary for employment and training. The administrator for the region is currently called the regional

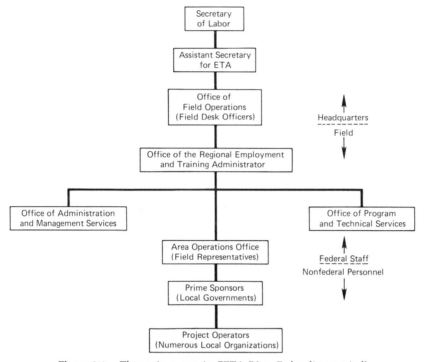

Figure 3.1. The main actors in CETA (New Federalism period).

employment and training administrator (RETA); under the old arrangements, the title was assistant regional administrator for manpower (ARDM). Although much of our research was carried out during the time of the old nomenclature, we will use the current designations of ETA and RETA to avoid confusion.

National-Regional Relationships

Discussion in this section is restricted to ETA, which accounts for the great bulk of DOL's expenditures and administers all of DOL's social service delivery programs. Besides CETA, the main ones are the United States Employment Service (USES) and the Work Incentive Program (WIN), administered jointly with HEW. The key federal figure in the field for CETA is the regional employment and training administrator, who reports directly to the assistant secretary for employment and training. The main point of contact between the regional office and the Washington ETA structure is through the Office of Field Operations, whose director is responsible to the assistant secretary.

At the national level, the secretary of labor and the assistant secretary for employment and training are responsible for setting broad policy directions. The Office of Field Operations provides interpretation and clarification of policy and of regulations through "field memoranda" that are sent out to all regional offices. The content of these memos may be initiated by any of the various offices within ETA, depending on subject matter, but they must all be cleared through the Office of Field Operations before distribution. These field memos, written at the national level, are the mechanism for indicating the broad directions of ETA policy as well as providing more precise information about how these policies should be implemented through the regulations.

Many of the memos are quite detailed and explicit, limiting the flexibility of regional interpretation. Field memoranda come from the national office in great numbers and include information on such diverse areas as new appropriations, policy changes, new regulations and grant modifications, meetings, training sessions, new proposals, and new reporting systems. These memos in specifying national policy on implementation and operations are a crucial communications link between headquarters and the field. They will be discussed in greater detail later in this chapter.

A second major source of communication between the regions and headquarters is the regional field desk officer. These desk officers (one for each region) form the official liaison between field and national offices and are usually the first contact point for regional staff when they deal with headquarters. On any issue of day-to-day operations, the regional office calls its regional desk officer for information and assistance. The desk officer comes to a region generally once a month and while there listens to regional concerns, sits in on quarterly review sessions, and gives help on technical assistance questions. Also, the desk officer generally serves as an advocate for the region in the national office.

In terms of specific headquarters–field staff relations, Administration and Management Services Office staff members have frequent contact with the Office of Field Operations through the desk officer. Staff members in the Office of Program and Technical Services are more likely to work on a regular basis with their counterparts at ETA headquarters. Field representatives, however, are not likely to have frequent contact with Washington. When they do, it is generally with the field desk. According to regional staff, when the field desk officer visits the region, he allots time for discussions with field representatives.

In general, the field desk officers in the Office of Field Operations see their main responsibility as transmitting national directives and then insuring that the regions are carrying them out effectively. They have responsibility for facilitating communications between head-quarters and the regions and for certain housekeeping functions, serving as a clearance point for budget and travel funds. Some field operation liaison staff claim a monitoring responsibility toward their regions, while others identify this oversight task as a kind of "friendly visit" or as "technical assistance" to the regions. Some desk officers indicated that their role includes an identification of regional "weak spots" that can be used as a guide in the content and direction of staff training plans. They can take the initiative in assisting regions to structure their own implementation efforts. Assistance to the regions, according to staff, also includes the circulation of innovative ideas and enough information to communicate "thinking at headquarters" to the regions.

A final element of the communication between headquaraters and the regions is provided by monthly meetings in Washington of all 10 regional employment and training administrators. The RETAs meet with the ETA assistant secretary who chairs the session and various executive staff members of the major offices in ETA. Questions of policy are discussed and information is given on changes in regulations and in legislation. This is one of the main opportunities for the regional administrators to contribute to the development of policy and the refinement of implementation strategies.

Structure of the ETA Field Activities

The regional employment and training administrator is the senior person in the field responsible for CETA, with the direct line of authority running from the ETA assistant secretary.[1] Under the RETA are a deputy regional administrator and five assistant regional administrators (ARA), who head the following offices within the regional office: Unemployment Insurance, Job Corps, Office of Program and Technical Services, Office of Administration and Management Services, and Area Operations Office (hereafter area office). The first two administer established categorical programs and have strong ties with their national counterpart offices. They have no impact on the CETA activities and will not be considered further.

The other three offices have responsibilities for CETA and the United States Employment Service. The Office of Program and Tech-

[1] During the New Federalism period, DOL had a regional director with no responsibility over the RETA. In a minor reorganization during the Carter administration, the regional director position was abolished, so we will ignore it here.

nical Services (PTS) has two elements: program development, and evaluation and technical services units. The Office of Administration and Management Services (AMS) has financial and grant management and ETA data and management systems components. These are staff offices whose responsibilities include advising the RETA and the area office.

The area office performs line functions with direct responsibilities for prime sponsors. Although it is viewed as a separate operation, no field representatives are stationed outside of the regional office no matter how distant the area office is from the prime sponsor. In Region X, for instance, the field representative for Alaska travels from Seattle to that state on a regular basis.

The area office, although included in the regional office, is best viewed as a separate entity. In essence, we have carved out the ETA operation from the entire DOL regional office headed by the regional director and divided the entire ETA structure into two segments: one constitutes the RETA and his staff offices, labeled as the regional office; and the other constitutes line functions, labeled the area office.

The PTS and AMS staff offices have no direct control over the area office. Their job is to service the area office upon request, and this function includes providing help for prime sponsors if a field representative specifically asks for this assistance. In theory the staff offices and the line office have equal status. However, the two staff offices also advise the RETA, and clearly this advice may impinge on the area office. In many cases, staff can exert a strong influence on the RETA interacting with him on an almost daily basis. This kind of "influence" is clear in the activity of the staff offices, which we will consider next.

The staff offices prepare by subject area the regional bulletins that are used by area and prime sponsor staffs in implementing CETA and operating USES. These bulletins are based on the national field memos that give direction on policy and implementation. The bulletin as translated from the memos must be approved by the RETA before it enters official channels within the region. Although the memos are detailed, there may be room for discretionary judgment by the RETA and practices vary from region to region. In some regional offices, these memos are merely retyped under the regional letterhead, while in others, careful attention is paid to the information and the RETA may assume the prerogative to provide regional emphases to the central office directives circulated to regional and area staffs and to local governmental units.

Most regional administrators see their role as middlemen between the national office and local levels of government—a kind of conduit function. Messages are transmitted, with the regional office processing information up and down the system.

The Central Role of the Field Representative

Area offices through their field representatives provide the pivotal point of contact with the prime sponsor. The field representatives are considered generalists in contrast to the specialists in the Offices of Program and Technical Services and Administration and Management Services who provide advice to the regional administrator and specialized technical assistance to the area office. Field representatives (field reps) travel at regular intervals to their designated geographic areas to work on a one-to-one basis with prime sponsors. In Region X, for instance, the region is divided into three areas with seven field reps visiting specific sponsors in Alaska and Idaho, eight working in Oregon, and eight more operating in Washington.

The actual responsibility for putting the CETA program in the field rests with the area office staff. Field reps provide their prime sponsors with information, review plans, and help with applications and plan revisions. These reps are the only "feds" who have extended contact with local governments. Usually more than half their time is spent out in the field, although it must be clearly pointed out that "in the field" almost always means in the office of the prime sponsor rather than on the site of any local operations.

Both the area and the regional office see their responsibilities primarily in relation to the prime sponsor, expecting little or no contact with actual project operators. Sometimes prime sponsors will bypass the area office and contact the regional office and occasionally the national office for information or to apply pressure, but, on the whole, the field representative is the main DOL–ETA contact for the sponsors.

Prior to CETA, the field representative specialized in a particular type of project. Thus, a field rep might have been an "OJT (on-the-job training) man" primarily experienced in the intricacies of writing contracts for that particular categorical program with numerous contractors. They were then responsible for checking on these contractors for compliance with the myriad of detailed regulations attached to the various categorical programs. Field reps worked primarily with local operators, who themselves were considered "specialists" in a particular kind of project.

CETA field reps became generalists in two senses. First and foremost, they deal with local government officials who are "generalists" responsible for administering but not running projects. Second, their concern is with overall CETA activities of prime sponsors, including comprehensive planning, prime sponsor administration of various operators, development of management and information systems, and so on. In essence, they are to deal with the "big picture" of total prime sponsor efforts, not with the details of project operations. They must decide where prime sponsors are falling down over the whole range of CETA activities, where they need help, and what kind of help they need.

After the introduction of CETA, three problems developed around the field representative's shift from the specialist of categorical days to the present overall generalist. First, how was the same field rep who had been the narrow project specialist to become the broad generalist? There was a need for a marked psychological change in attitude toward prime sponsors as compared to contractors. The contractor who ran an individual project had engaged in direct contract negotiation with the field rep who was clearly viewed as a compliance officer in relation to the project. In theory, the CETA field rep was to work with the prime sponsor as a "helper" or a diplomat of sorts involving an indirect, more subtle kind of negotiation. The status of the prime sponsor is quite different from that of the local operator, and the approaches used in dealing with one are not at all the same as those required for the other. The protocol that assured smooth relations with a separate and independent governmental entity was not necessarily included in the field rep's preparation for transition from MDTA to CETA.

Second, the field rep required considerable general knowledge gathered over time about the prime sponsors. Yet, in many regions, field reps have been rotated from one area within a region to another, which made it very difficult to gain knowledge about local conditions, establish continuity with local officials and staff, and identify and work toward solving problems. The rationale given for moving field reps lay primarily in the desire to avoid political entanglements and provide fresh perspectives on local problems. Yet, as one prime sponsor staff person commented upon the arrival of the sixteenth field rep in CETA's short lifetime: "We don't even have time to train the rep properly before he's reassigned."

Third has been the problem of specialized knowledge, since the introduction of CETA has changed regional and area office functions dramatically on paper. Technical assistance and training were seen as major responsibilities of the regions. Yet technical assistance often was in areas such as planning where the field representatives had little or no expertise. This might not have been a big problem if the intended use of regional office staff as specialists had been more successful. But as will be discussed in more detail later, the regional office staffs were not able to fill in this deficiency. In particular, the staff specialists could not provide prime sponsors with substantive, programmatic technical assistance and capacity building.

PRIME SPONSOR'S PERCEPTIONS OF THE ETA REGIONAL OFFICE AND CETA[2]

Both our study and the larger National Academy of Sciences (NAS) study found instances of good regional office–prime sponsor relationships and of strong field representatives in individual cases providing much help, particularly to weaker prime sponsors.[3]However, the prime sponsors' image of DOL activities in the administrative and support domain often has been a negative one. Yet, it is well to keep in mind in this section that the prime sponsors' perceptions have been affected by their own administrative problems and by the real weaknesses and difficulties faced by all administrative units in the field, as well as by actual DOL inadequacies. The prime sponsor interviewees tend to underplay their own weaknesses (some of which come through in the next section) and their self-interest in keeping DOL at arm's length. Prime sponsors often give the impression that they would be far more innovative if only the feds would let them. But as a highly placed DOL headquarters staff person observed in commenting on an earlier draft of this chapter: "*Most* CETA sponsors want to be told what to do ('give us specific guidance') and then be allowed to do it with minimum policing or reporting; they are not seeking discretion but limited supervision."

The Problems of Shifting Roles

Before CETA, the regional office played a prominent role in allocating DOL funds and dealt directly with program operators through contracting and monitoring. Money under CETA comes by formula to the sponsors, excluding ETA regional offices far more than in

---

[2] This and subsequent sections draw heavily upon a study of CETA carried out by the National Academy of Sciences' Committee on Evaluation of Employment and Training Programs. Philip J. Rutledge chaired the committee; William Mirengoff was its study director. Several volumes have now appeared. For our purposes, the two most important ones are William Mirengoff and Lester Rindler, *The Comprehensive Employment and Training Act: Impact on People, Places and Programs—Interim Report,* National Academy of Sciences, Washington, D.C., 1976 (referenced as Mirengoff and Rindler, 1976); and Mirengoff and Rindler, *CETA: Manpower Programs under Local Control,* National Academy of Sciences, Washington, D.C., 1978 (Mirengoff and Rindler, 1978). The NAS study used local observers to investigate 28 of the more than 400 prime sponsors. These prime sponsors included 6 cities, 9 counties, 9 consortia, and 4 states. They ranged in size from a county that served 129 enrollees during FY 1975 to New York City, which served over 25,000 enrollees in CETA during that fiscal year.

[3] For a discussion of the NAS findings, see Mirengoff and Rindler, 1978, pp. 89–90, 271.

the past from both the specific substantive program decisions and the political activities surrounding these decisions.

In CETA prime sponsors either operate projects directly or contract directly with project operators. In the latter case, the prime sponsors are the administrative or management unit dealing with project operators. Thus, contact between DOL and prime sponsors is contact between administrative units.

This shift of focus to the prime sponsors illustrates the most dramatic change brought about by the CETA legislation. During the first year of CETA implementation, prime sponsors had to build their own administrative machinery. Cities that had long experience with manpower programs had the resources to do this, but smaller cities and new consortia faced major problems in developing adequate administrative and technical capabilities to handle the extensive requirements of administering manpower programs. Less sophisticated prime sponsors often were at the mercy of the regional office demands when they did not have the capacity to meet those demands, let alone administer a CETA program effectively.

Many people assumed that both the degree of federal presence and the nature of that presence would change with the new decentralized, decategorized block grant program. There was a supposition by some that the number of staff at the regional level would decrease. Actually, regional office presence was very evident during the early days of CETA, in part because many local officials were inexperienced in developing manpower objectives, programs, and procedural details. Instead of reducing federal staff in the regions, CETA required the same staffing level in the early days and added a nonfederal administrative layer—the prime sponsor—between DOL and the program operators. This newly added layer was made up in part by administrators and staff who had just started learning about the administration of manpower programs.

The work load of the regional office probably increased during the first round of CETA, with heavy demands for processing applications, interpreting complicated guidelines and regulations, disseminating information, and collecting data for the national office. One of the reasons little thought was given to changing the substance of manpower programs lay in the fact that during the first round prime sponsors barely had time to deal with management requirments, let alone programs, in submitting their applications.

There has been a tendency on the part of inexperienced sponsors to respond to every request for information or grant modification. Some of these demands were unexpected and unrealistic in terms of information available and time for compliance. For example, one medium-sized city with limited program experience was told by DOL, which in turn was under pressure from Congress, that the city must spend all its Title II (public employment) funds more quickly than originally planned. The city complied, with serious program repercussions resulting from the early dispensing of funds. Some of the more experienced sponsors we interviewed, when faced with the same demand from DOL, ignored the request and spent the money according to their own needs and plans.

Inexperienced prime sponsors were the most vulnerable to the inevitable conflict between CETA requirements and local governmental procedures. For example, some sponsors, because of city or county requirements, had to take every modification in a program before a governing council and have an ordinance passed for acceptance. One case involved a medium-sized city where the ETA regional office made a $205 error in processing that city's CETA application, putting the entire CETA program for the prime sponsor in jeopardy for over 2 months. The mistake was actually in the city's favor, and it would happily have written the whole amount off. But DOL wanted the matter straightened out before it would approve the grant. In that particular state, deficit spending is illegal, so technically the progam could not operate until the grant was approved. To add another complication, city law required that the city council pass a new ordinance every time even the most minor change was made in a grant package. The problem dragged on exacerbated by DOL's concern with detail and the city's charter rigidities. During the impasse, the local CETA administrator decided to operate the program illegally (violating the state's no deficit spending provision) rather than stop the entire program. Eventually the $205 error was tracked down, the application was modified by the sponsor, and accepted by DOL.

In cities or consortia where manpower programs had been operating for several years, experienced people often moved into the key CETA administration positions for the new prime sponsor. In a city we studied where there had been a strong manpower program, the former manpower staff provided the "new" administrator and top personnel for CETA. The transition to the new program appeared smooth and relatively problem free.

Among the prime sponsors with long manpower experience, different strategies have been used in dealing with the regional office. Some worked out a process of cooperation and accommodation that cut down on DOL interference. This approach allowed substantial freedom and used the system to further sponsor goals and objectives.

Other experienced operators viewed DOL harassment as inconsequential and often ignored requests from the regional office. They have used political pressure to free themselves of federal interference. In either case, the regional office is often circumvented in the belief that it creates bureaucratic barriers to smooth operations.

In the early stages of CETA, the primary function performed by the regional offices, as sponsors were rushing to get their applications submitted, was that of handholding or providing assistance of the most elementary type. However, there was an assumption that a growing responsibility of the regional office during the shift to a more decentralized and decategorized system would be that of substantive technical assistance, including capacity building. Most prime sponsors interviewed felt that the response of the regional offices to these two needs has been most limited. Rather assistance has either (a) answered questions on appropriate forms or on participant eligibility requirements; or (b) aided the sponsor in setting up compatible accounting systems or in other procedural matters.

Little real help was given to the prime sponsors in terms of substantive technical assistance or capacity building. In our interviews, inexperienced sponsors seemed to feel that they were receiving a reasonable level of assistance from the regional office. But when pressed, they indicated that the help was of the processing, eligibility determination variety. The National Academy of Sciences Committee on Evaluation of Employment and Training Programs succinctly captured the DOL approach as a *"preoccupation with procedure instead of program substance."*[4]

A very different picture emerged when we talked to CETA administrators who were sophisticated in terms of manpower programs and perhaps more importantly in terms of intergovernmental relationships. They, more often than not, saw the federal field staff as a negative factor. A CETA administrator with a wide variety of experiences, including some at the national level, characterized DOL as a "pain in the rear." He felt strongly that the regional office not only does not provide assistance to prime sponsors in improving programs, but through low-level harassment and nit-picking hampered sponsors' efforts to put together innovative programs. He described an attempt he had made when first organizing his CETA program to integrate program planning by using CETA youth funds in conjunction with other federal monies and his own county youth services resources to develop

---

[4] Ibid., p. 261, italics added.

a comprehensive youth assistance program. Rather than viewing this as an approach in harmony with the leverage intent of the block grant approach, the ETA regional office refused to allow him to use CETA money in this fashion and wanted it kept in a separate pot. He believed that a later request for a special technical assistance and training grant was turned down because of his resistance to the regional office's scheme for prime sponsor organization.

This administrator felt that there were numerous examples of outright misuse of CETA funds by local organizations but that DOL was impotent to do anything about this. They "negotiated" and made threats but applied few actual sanctions to force compliance. DOL tends to use small, heckling techniques to punish sponsors who show tendencies toward independence. One prime sponsor commented, "DOL sees me as a thorn in its side. They ask me what I think, I tell them, they don't like it and my grant proposals start coming back for very picky reasons."

A number of sponsors indicated that ETA technical assistance training sessions were useless and only served as "exercises in making the process more complicated." In one major city where the CETA operations appeared to us to be running smoothly and effectively, the disdain for technical assistance from the federal government was expressed graphically. The honor of attending the monthly regional technical assistance meeting was extended to the staff person given the "A—of the Month" award.

It appears that ETA has not moved far on the spectrum from providing processing and interpretation information to the more meaty function of substantive technical assistance. Even in Boston, where the Manpower Training Institute began the development of a more sophisticated mechanism in the ETA system to deal with technical assistance, prime sponsors indicated that the help still did not come to grips with substantive issues of programmatic development.

Information and Regulations

Some of the biggest complaints by prime sponsors concern the general lack of useful information, the specific failure of DOL to provide feedback on information developed at the local level, and the growing number of regulations and related reporting requirements. The result has been too much paper work, too little real help, and a great deal of frustration with the DOL bureaucracy.

The role played by the public interest groups (PIGs)[5] in providing services illustrates the information problems prime sponsors experience in working with the DOL. These organizations often provide, through informal channels, valuable information that is not available because of poor communications or bureaucratic blockages. Two examples will be useful. First, the field memoranda sent from headquarters to the regional office can get "hung up" in the multiple clearance and sign-off procedures of the regional office hierarchy even though few changes are made at the regional office level. The public interest groups, on the other hand, mail the Washington memo directly (and immediately) to the sponsors so the locals often get a useful headstart from this simple procedure. Second, the interest groups are usually more knowledgeable about the word from headquarters than are federal field people. Being on-the-spot in Washington gives the PIGs a decided advantage. Often sponsors learn of changes in regulations or grant modifications from the public interest groups long before regional office staff have heard through the normal channels of the field memorandum. In fact, we found regional administrators who regularly called local government's CETA administrators to find out what was going on in Washington.

In response to a real need, the PIGs have attempted to improve the substance of programs by putting local governmental units in touch with each other so that they could share innovative program ideas and improvements in administrative techniques. Often the main contact prime sponsors have had with each other came at area and national conferences organized by various public interest groups. These contacts have filled a vacuum for sponsors, who see something resembling complicity on the part of the feds to keep sponsors isolated from one another.

In addition to the assistance provided by the public interest groups, a new source of nonfederal help from prime sponsors is being developed in some parts of the country. Prime sponsor associations are providing much needed points of contact among sponsors and are moving toward building a system of peer technical assistance. Some groups have received support from state governments but usually have not worked under the direction or auspices of the regional ETA office.

[5] Examples of PIGs are the National Conference of State Legislatures, National Association of County Officals, and U.S. Conference of Mayors. Whether such organizations represent the "public" is not an issue we will consider; we will simply label such organizations as PIGs because that is how they are referred to among themselves and by those working with them. For a short discussion of the major PIGs and a bibliography of recent work, see Deil S. Wright, *Understanding Intergovernmental Relations*, Duxbury, North Scituate, Massachusetts, 1978, pp. 61–63.

Many prime sponsors see DOL's demands for information increasing all the time despite the fact that initially reporting requirements were less under CETA than under MDTA. Frequently, the time period granted to produce the information is unrealistic. Particularly for small cities and consortia, the normal reporting to DOL places a burden on staff, especially those without a sophisticated information system. In addition to the difficulties involved in putting the information together, prime sponsors feel that there is virtually no feedback to them. They see the information used by the regional office as a means of comparing sponsors. Although this is one valid use of information, it does not appear a sufficient reason for gathering so much information. Prime sponsors see this as another instance of the agency's lack of understanding of their limited resources and need for feedback.

One of the most commonly heard complaints from prime sponsors revolved around changes in the regulations and the concommitant burden of paper work that accompanied those modifications. One prime sponsor indicated that he had once put on a presentation for the regional office showing the evolution of CETA regulations: The first-year regulations were a small stack; the second year the stack was a taller one; and by the third year, the stack had grown to an overwhelming 2-foot tower of constraints on local government's CETA programs. As angry DOL regional people were walking out on his presentation, he ended with "Thanks to you, local government can spend most of its time filling out forms." Many sponsors feel that the proliferation and growing specificity of regulations point to a common agency reaction to every new situation—write a guideline to fit it. This can create a kind of agency inertia that sponsors feel kills innovation and response to regional variation. The National Academy of Sciences study came to similar conclusions:

> The unfamiliarity of many local governments with manpower programs, requests for clarification and specific guidance, and the belief that there is a need for uniformity have occasioned a steady stream of written instructions from DOL. With continual changes in legislation, policies, directives, and regulations, *the stream has become a torrent*, and some prime sponsors complain that excessively burdensome regulations restrict their flexibility to design and conduct local programs.[6]

DOL Tightens Up

Along with the trend toward increased reporting demands on the part of DOL, there is clear indication of a tightening up of the regulations for the CETA program. This effort is viewed by prime sponsors as

---

[6] Mirengoff and Rindler, 1978, p. 88, italics added.

an attempt both to pull back power granted to local governments and to limit flexibility. Sponsors believe that as requirements become more rigid, the possibilities of building a comprehensive employment and training program designed to meet the particular needs of a locality greatly diminish. ETA officials, however, see the "fine tuning" and information requests as a legitimate function of their legislative mandate to carry out oversight responsibilities.

Local officals see recent DOL actions as strong indication of the department's desire to gain more control over sponsors. In particular, DOL is pushing for a more stringent assessment of sponsors' operations prior to annual funding and the development of national performance indicators. The response of prime sponsors to the latter has been mixed. Some saw it as a strong, positive step by DOL to give clear, defined prior direction to sponsors as to department expectations for CETA programs. Others, however, believed that the development of national performance indicators will narrow the boundaries for acceptable program planning and performance. Another step in this resumption of power at the national level comes as performance indicators become performance standards. According to Robert McPherson, then director of the King–Snohomish Manpower Consortium based in Seattle, Washington:

> National performance standards will immediately affect and eventually control the mix of manpower services in state and local prime sponsor jurisdictions. Local elected officials' flexibility and power over Title I manpower programs will be effectively usurped by the National Office of the Department of Labor. Prime sponsors will be relegated to the role of the local administrative arm for a federal categorical grant program.[7]

There is little disagreement on the part of prime sponsors that DOL has been moving back to a centralized approach to manpower programs. At the same time, Congress has recategorized the way in which money will be distributed. In particular, the increased emphasis on the public employment component has cut down the flexibility sponsors had in developing a comprehensive manpower plan.

LOCAL OPERATORS' PERCEPTIONS OF PRIME SPONSORS, ETA REGIONAL OFFICES, AND CETA

The major power shift under CETA to the prime sponsor has brought problems for local operators. Under MDTA, these operators,

[7] Robert McPherson, "CETA—the Basic Assumptions and Future Prospects," a paper prepared for a Conference on Manpower Policy sponsored by the Employment Studies Program, San Francisco State University, San Francisco, October 1976, p. 24.

either personally or through national organizations, had developed effective channels of communication and influence with the federal government. Many experienced operators complained bitterly of the new group of local government bureaucrats, many of whom were new to manpower administration and had little knowledge of manpower needs in their communities or of appropriate programmatic responses to those needs. Particularly in the first year of CETA, almost any group that developed a project could become a manpower operator. This resulted in a number of questionable projects absorbing limited funds.

Prime sponsors can and do choose to operate their own programs. This may be in part because many of the CETA administrators had been program people who wanted to stay involved in actual operations. However, local operators felt a pinch in terms of the number of contracts available. Operators representing community organizations believe that this trend indicated a centralization of power at the prime sponsor level rather than at the regional office level. That is, decentralization at the national level has brought recentralization at the local level. It also serves to dilute the impact of combined deliverer–citizen representative organizations such as the National Urban League.

In the eyes of some program operators, especially the established ones, prime sponsors added a damaging naivete about manpower politics to their lack of experience in manpower programs and administration. Many program operators, particularly those affiliated with strong national organizations, would have much preferred to continue the tried and true interaction with DOL they had enjoyed under MDTA rather than enter the uncertain relationships existing with local officials. Before, they had known the actors and had established procedures to obtain their piece of the action. Prime sponsors were not necessarily cognizant or impressed by some of the time-honored pressure points that had been exploited previously to bring home the funds from Washington or concessions in program guidelines. Project operators often faced frustration and a sense of powerlessness in dealing with the new political realities of CETA funding.

These new political facts have had a major influence on the allocation of CETA resources. The local decision-making process came to determine which operators received what share of the manpower pie. Local operators, who previously had their connections with the federal government and their own national offices, soon discovered that local pressures were the key to funding decisions. We found this was particularly true in cities where contracts traditionally have been awarded to "old established" ethnic organizations. These groups found themselves competing against newly emerging ethnic groups now able to harness local political power. The National Urban League could offer little help on the local scene under the present system where much is dependent on sudden shifts of allegiance. Elected officials tend to be more accessible and more vulnerable than federal administrators to an array of politically strong groups that have their own interests to protect or advance.

The development of a kind of "ethnic funding" system has meant that more groups may be competing for a fixed pie with less assurance of a share of the monies. The effectiveness of program at times is an irrelevant factor in awarding contracts. In addition, program operators have found that they must concentrate an unreasonable amount of energy and resources on the politicking process.

At least part of what is happening would probably have occurred had the categorical programs continued. In the Great Society days, the term *minority* basically meant blacks in most cities. But other groups now demand their share, sometimes claiming that black officials are discriminating. This development would have come without CETA, but the shift of responsibility seems to have speeded up the changes.

One positive aspect of the prime sponsor role in local administration of the CETA programs has come in the area of monitoring. Although some project operators might not see this as an improvement from their own perspective, it appears that checking on projects by prime sponsors is performed far more frequently and more carefully in some regions than it was under MDTA, when the regional office was responsible for project monitoring.[8]

In addition, and this holds true especially for smaller, local operators, we observed that prime sponsors have a tendency to be more responsive than the feds to requests for advice and information when they have the capacity to give it. For this we have no clear single explanation. One reason seems to be the closeness of the prime sponsors, who find it difficult politically to ignore the operators. Also, at least in some larger cities, the operators view the prime sponsor staff as more able than the regional office people.

WHERE ETA DECISIONS ARE MADE

As the CETA legislation was being developed, there was much talk in Washington that responsibility for the success of programs would be shifting to the local governments charged with the administration of the program. Commensurate with this shift in responsibility, there

---

[8] For a similar view, see Mirengoff and Rindler, 1978, p. 110.

was to be a shift in decision-making authority both to local governments (decentralization) and to regional offices (regionalization). However, things did not work out exactly that way.

The National-Regional-Local Power Distribution

On paper, the RETA has the power to accept or reject CETA grants to prime sponsors for Title I and the public employment titles (II and VI) without consulting the national office. This power is delegated by the secretary of labor to the regional administrator, who in turn is allowed to redelegate to a number of subordinates. RETAs have the authority to sign contract agreements, to shift Employment Service money from state to state based on their estimation of which states are doing the best job, and to approve or disapprove grant modifications. In other words, the regional administrator theoretically has a good deal of discretionary authority over all manpower activities within the region.

Having said this, however, it is necessary to point out that there have been two major obstacles to this power shift to the regions. The first one has to do with how much actual discretion the national office grants to the regions. The direction coming down from the national office both through the field memoranda and at the monthly meetings of regional administrators in Washington has usually been quite specific and explicit. There is some room for the regional staff to interpret regulations and decide on methods of implementation with the approval of the RETA. However, it seems unlikely that a regional decision would differ markedly from a national office directive. DOL regional staff simply do not see themselves in the role of policymakers. In practice, the veteran ETA staff takes orthodox views of national policy and readily accepts the standard DOL top–down authority pattern.

It would be a mistake, however, not to recognize that RETAs and their staffs do have real influence on headquarters. The best characterization would seem to be as follows: *Headquarters encourages regional office advice and uses it to make policy, yet is uncomfortable with field autonomy.* Regional administrators review policy decisions made at headquarters and feel they have a significant influence on regulations, formula questions, and legislation. In addition to comment by the RETAs, the regulations are reviewed by other regional and area office staff.

ETA has also organized national planning meetings where selected CETA prime sponsor administrators have participated by giving advice on the development of programmatic models. These nonfederal advisors have had long experience in developing and operating manpower programs. Federal administrators seem receptive to regional input and review and increasingly appear to accept such advice. However, the national office in seeking comment from their own field people may feel quite secure knowing that the majority of field staff are well-indoctrinated career persons who are unlikely to suggest radical changes in manpower training programs.

Regional discretion is gradually being restricted. Headquarters staff in "tightening up" regulations have claimed this was not an attempt to regain decision-making authority but rather a "fine tuning" to adjust and rework regulations that had been introduced during the hurried, error-prone early days of CETA. However, to the outside observer, it appears that the time of greatest field discretion may have been in the early implementation period, when haste to get CETA into the field brought confusion.

In the three regional offices where interviews for this project were carried on, there was strong agreement that despite the original decentralized, decategorized, regionalizing thrust of CETA, power is gradually being drawn back to the national office. Some regional office staff see this as a very specific move to deregionalize decision making. ETA seems uncomfortable with too much authority in the field at either the regional or the local level. In part, this thrust reflects growing congressional discontent with the decategorized block grant approach of CETA. Congress likes categoricals, and the departmental bureaucracy likes centralization. Regional and local government people felt that the clear direction at the end of the Ford administration was toward increasing recentralization and recategorization.

Mirengoff and Rindler in the National Academy of Sciences study point out in regard to recategorization that only 34% of the original CETA appropriation went to titles authorizing categorical programs (Title II, public employment; Title III, Indians and migrants; Title IV, Job Corps). After the enactment of Title VI (another public employment program) in December 1974 and an earmarked appropriation for a summer youth program, 58% of CETA funds were for categorical programs.[9] It is worth noting that the growth of the new categorical programs was in response to unusually large unemployment rates, especially for youth. But then categoricals almost always are for special problems that Congress or the executive branch identify and do not trust others to meet. So Mirengoff and Rindler's comment is apt: "Thus,

___

[9] Mirengoff and Rindler, 1976, p. 5.

before CETA was well off the ground, it was turned back toward a prescribed system of specific programs for special problems."[10]

Power and discretion was originally shifted to local government from the federal government under CETA. As McPherson observed: "[T]he elected official became the focal point of the local manpower program system—responsible for performing the basic functions of local policy determination, planning, and program delivery."[11] With that shift of power has come a growing capacity to administer programs and use information. This storing up of power and capacity complicate any federal government attempt to pull back and tighten up the control they released at the time of the block grant enactment.

It should be clear that we are seeing a real struggle. McPherson has put forth such a view in its strongest terms:

> With CETA, the Congress and the national bureaucracy had, for a variety of reasons, increased the flexibility and power of state and local governments. Almost without a pause, they immediately began actions to effectively reverse that decision and regain the power they had just given up. CETA was not being singled out for discrimination; it was simply being subjected to a common practice observed throughout intergovernmental relations. Under whatever heading one cares to choose, be it "carrying out the provisions of the Act," "meeting national goals, priorities and standards," "protecting the prime sponsors," or "in order to meet the informational needs of the Congress," the erosion of block grant flexibility under CETA was inevitable. . . .
>
> The institutional constraints of modern federalism do present the opportunity for development and experimentation with a block grant approach. However, these opportunities will be limited to a few well-defined functional areas, and the Congress will share a minimum of powers and flexibility with state and local governments. If CETA is a specific case from which one can generalize, there will be an immediate reaction attempting to withdraw the flexbility previously given. The realities must be recognized—block grants and general revenue sharing represent major threats to the Congress and to the national bureaucrats. Power and control are not readily given away.[12]

We may debate whether such a statement goes too far, but the direction of federal movement appears clear. It also is clear that local governments will not give up power easily. Although Mirengoff expects greater cooperation over time between the feds and the locals, he has observed pointedly: "[I]f it comes to a critical struggle, I think the political clout of the local prime sponsors would probably prevail."[13] It

[10] Ibid.

[11] McPherson, "CETA—The Basic Assumptions and Future Prospects," p. 20.

[12] Ibid., pp. 22–23 (first paragraph), p. 26 (second paragraph).

[13] *Block Grants: A Roundtable Discussion,* Advisory Commission on Intergovernmental Relations, A–51, October 1976, Washington, D.C., p. 15.

is a classic struggle between federal and local government going far beyond CETA. We will treat this issue at length in a later chapter.

The Local Level[14]

CETA changed markedly the local power arrangements among local officials, the United States Employment Service (USES); community action agencies (CAAs); public vocational educational institutions, which generally provided classroom training under MDTA; and community-based organizations (CBOs), including those with national bases such as the Urban League, Opportunities Industrialization Centers (OIC), and Services, Employment, Redevelopment (SER). To see how power shifted under this new arrangment, we need to look at what happened in the decision-making process and in terms of the deliverers of services.

Prior to CETA, DOL had established a number of planning councils to advise about local manpower issues, but generally these councils had limited power. Under the CETA legislation, the local planning council was envisioned as a significant factor in the local decision-making process. It had important power implications as Mirengoff and Rindler indicate

> The [National Academy of Sciences] study found the composition of councils little changed from that of their predecessors. The key differences are in the control of council activities and the participation of council members. New alignment in the power structure and rearrangements of the patterns of influence are surfacing. The dominance of the traditional manpower service agencies is on the wane and is being replaced by the CETA administrator and staff. Elected officials are also taking a greater interest in planning and decision making.[15]

Clear losers were USES, which had been the presumptive deliverer of manpower services and often staffed the councils, and the CAAs, which had been a prime sponsor in major cities. Further, as Mirengoff and Rindler point out "In several areas, CBOs are not on the planning council because of possible conflicts of interest; in another they serve only in a nonvoting capacity. The most widespread complaint is the belief of CBOs that they have little actual influence even if they are on the council."[16]

[14] For a more detailed account of what transpired in particular prime sponsor areas, see William Mirengoff (editor), *Transition to Decentralized Manpower Programs: Eight Area Studies, An Interim Report*, National Academy of Sciences, Washington, D.C., 1976. A good brief review is found in Mirengoff and Rindler, 1978, pp. 79–82.

[15] Mirengoff and Rindler, 1976, p. 53.

[16] Ibid., p. 115.

There can be no question that local-level power had been altered visibly. As the National Academy of Sciences study observed: "CETA administrators and elected officials are the primary decision makers; the extent to which others participate reflects the attitudes and philosophy of these two groups."[17] Of the 24 prime sponsors observed in the NAS study, CETA administrators were rated as very important in planning in all cases, far more so than elected officials, who often seemed willing to let their CETA administrators take the lead or else simply did not find time to exert continuing leadership.

The community-based organizations experienced financial gains under CETA.[18] At the same time, the CBOs felt their power base eroding as the local CETA organization and a planning council that may exclude them became a more and more dominant force. As Mirengoff and Rindler pointed out

> [Sources of irritation are] the imposition of performance standards that community-based organizations consider unrealistic and reporting requirements that they find excessive. Some are also unhappy that the prime sponsor insists on their serving a broader client group. This they believe may undermine their attachment to a specific ethnic or racial group.
>
> Although funding of community-based organizations has increased significantly, there is a general uneasiness about their new role and their difficulty in adjusting to the prime sponsors' new institutions. They see in the trend toward consolidation a threat to their identity and to the rationale for having separate organizations to deal with specific client groups.[19]

The planning councils are made up primarily of institutional representatives—business, agriculture, and so on. Mirengoff and Rindler observe

> With their new CETA role, many elected officials are becoming aware of manpower problems and programs in their communities. But there is no evidence that the public at large is becoming more involved in the planning process, either indirectly through elected officials or directly through participation on councils.
>
> The attention focused on unemployment has made manpower programs, particularly the amount of funds available for Title VI jobs, front page news, yet CETA administrators report virtually no reaction or participation in the planning process by the community at large. All prime sponsors complied with federal regulations regarding publication of Title I plans or summaries of them, usually by notice in local newspapers. In a few cases the public was invited to attend meetings of the advisory

[17] Mirengoff and Rindler, 1978, p. 79.

[18] For a discussion of financial changes, see ibid., pp. 145–147 and Mirengoff and Rindler, 1976, pp. 112–115.

[19] Mirengoff and Rindler, 1976, p. 115.

council while it considered the plan. Observers report little response to these formal steps. Few people attend the public hearings, and rarely did anyone ask to see the plan.[20]

Unlike CDBG, as we will see, CETA has provided little or no real opportunity for participation by the general public.

ADMINISTRATIVE AND SUPPORT DOMAIN FUNCTIONS UNDER CETA

The next several sections will examine the way in which the regional office in particular, but also to some extent other elements of the administrative and support domain, responds or fails to respond in terms of the particular functions set forth in Chapter 1.

Approval Function

Regulation and guideline writing are carried on primarily at the national level, although there is some input from the regional level. As also discussed, there has been a tendency by headquarters to tighten up through more detailed specifications. However, review of the regulations by the regional office is considered an important function, and comments at the regional level appear to influence final regulations.

Every time the regulations are revised, the regional office is sent a copy with the changes underlined. The regulation changes are reviewed in detail mainly by top-level regional and area administrators. Efforts are made both by the regional field desk officer in his tours of the region and by regular input through the area office to find out field representatives' views on potential regulations changes. But field representatives are usually under time pressures in dealing with their prime sponsors, so their opportunity to contribute to discussions on the regulations tends to be limited. Without major input from the field reps, who have the greatest firsthand knowledge of actual field problems, the kinds of practical problems sponsors are likely to encounter with new regulations frequently are not addressed in their development.

In theory, the views of the regional staff are considered of greater importance than those of the field reps, because it is assumed that these people have an overview, whereas the field reps have specialized insight into the workings of the regulations. Also regional staff are the trained technicians who should be able to analyze the impact a revision of the regulations would bring. The process is quite tidy and pro-

---

[20] Ibid., p. 60.

fessional. However, there is grave question that comments from the top of the regional office level can yield as valuable information for the national office as that provided by field representatives.

Nor is there much indication that prime sponsors' views on the regulations are regularly elicited. Moreover, on the occasions when opinions are sought, they usually come from friendly, cooperative prime sponsors and not from those who are seen by the regional office as "thorns in DOL's side." Too often, both prime sponsors and field representatives confront regulation problems head-on after the regulations are in final form. This can precipitate another revision, with the attendant flurry of activity at all levels and probably real inconvenience to prime sponsors.

The way in which grant or plan approval is performed at the regional level by the RETA and his staff might be described as the following: fairly consistent; too oriented toward relatively low level, nonprogrammatic issues; and, on balance, not extremely demanding. Comment is limited by the usual lack of substantive progammatic knowledge by regional staff. In general, a strong emphasis on performance is missing. DOL asks sponsors to set performance goals. When goals are not reached, DOL does not punish but rather adjusts goals downward. As the National Academy of Sciences report observed: "[T]he regional office places a greater premium on accurate guesses as to what will happen than on a challenging blue print for what should happen. Through successive modifications, planning comes to reflect rather than guide program operations."[21]

Regional office grant approval so often is a pro forma activity in which the plans of sponsors and expectations of ETA are juggled until a satisfactory political–bureaucratic mesh is produced. Comment: are restricted mainly to procedural and compliance issues, with little focus on the larger questions of program substance and organizational viability. Indeed, the tendency in regional offices is to smooth over problems of inadequate or misleading guidelines from headquarters and poor local performance without necessarily trying to bring real improvement. Such action well may keep bad practices, procedures, and performance going to maintain political–bureaucratic peace.

Information Development and Analysis Function

DOL does a poor job of developing information to aid either national or local governance. The National Academy of Sciences Committee of Evaluation of Employment and Training Programs put the infor-

---

[21] Mirengoff and Rindler, 1978, p. 73.

mation problem forcefully observing: "The study finds that the data system does not provide adequate information for national policy purposes or for local management."[22]

The regional office has an evaluation unit in the Office of Program and Technical Services. The unit, however, does not carry out field evaluations that yield *primary* data on effectiveness or efficiency.[23] Rather it reviews information coming from ETA data systems and reporting requirements for sponsors. This is sometimes labeled "desk evaluation" or "desk monitoring," which means that the regional office staff itself almost never sees a program or project.

Regional offices do not conduct major field evaluations in which sample survey methods are used to assess the extent to which projects benefit participants. "On-site" monitoring is performed by the field representatives and generally is restricted to prime sponsors. Generally, DOL field staff do not observe individual projects directly to determine compliance with regulations or organizational viability. Rather they look at another administrative unit—the prime sponsor. Before CETA, the regional office monitored operating projects to make sure they were running smoothly. Now that responsibility rests with the prime sponsors.

Overall, DOL's assessment effort has been limited and seems to follow a "don't rock the boat" approach. The best example we found of this was in the 1976 CETA assessment of prime sponsors carried out by headquarters DOL Office of Field Operations, which relied upon the regional offices' own assessments. In one region, which our interviews indicated was "easy" in regard to prime sponsors' performance, all prime sponsors received a satisfactory rating by headquarters for both Titles I and II. Despite this good showing on paper, our interviews with regional and area staff as well as with CETA people in a particular city pointed to constant indications of that city's problems both in administering the program and with the regional office. On more than one occasion, there were federal threats to defund this prime sponsor. In another region, considered to be "tough" on prime sponsors, headquarters gave only seven prime sponsors satisfactory ratings as well as two prime sponsors unsatisfactory marks out of 23 prime sponsors. Needless to say, both regional office staff and prime sponsors were furious at this result, which represented a sincere effort by the regional office to push for improvement and in some cases by the prime sponsors to carry out the improvements.

[22] Ibid., p. 265.

[23] DOL does not restrict the term *evaluation* to effectiveness as we have but uses it generally to cover any kind of assessment, including monitoring.

Policy analysis and research are not viewed as regional activities by ETA, so regional offices have not developed analytic shops as have other agency field operations. Only the evaluation unit in the Office of Program and Technical Services bears a vague resemblance to an operation concerned with the examination and use of information. Essentially, the RETA receives technical policy advice from the assistant regional administrators (ARAs) heading up the Offices of Program and Technical Services and Administration and Management Services. In most regions, these people are career civil servants with extensive experience. Their efforts and their counsel are based upon their own knowledge and intuition developed over years of experience working with manpower programs. DOL does not see a role for or the necessity of systematic analysis and expert information in fulfilling the regional mission, but rather it regards specific manpower experience as the key factor in effective implementation of CETA programs.

Technical Assistance Function

In general, the ETA offices have provided only limited kinds of technical assistance that have not begun to approach the point on the spectrum where capacity building starts. However, the National Academy of Sciences study did find some progress, arguing that "the effort by the Department of Labor to assist sponsors in installing adequate program management tools appeared to have paid off, since sponsors were clearly improving their capability of judging contractor performance."[24] How much the increasing prime sponsor capability that both our work and the NAS study observed is due to DOL effort and how much to prime sponsors' growing experience cannot be determined. But we found few in the field who praised the DOL technical assistance performance.

On paper, the specialist staffs in regional offices have responsibility for technical assistance in such areas as program planning, monitoring, contracts and data processing, and administrative management. However, in most of these areas, we found that prime sponsors, particularly those with extensive manpower program experience, consider the technical assistance given individually or in group training sessions to be low in quality.

We should reemphasize that part of the problem comes from the information flow itself. Headquarters does a poor job of developing the information inputs it requires and seldom demands the kind of evalua-

[24] Mirengoff and Rindler, 1978, p. 70.

tive or monitoring information that would push field units toward a concentration on programmatic substance. Concomitantly, regional office checking efforts, generally speaking, do not reflect a concern with program substance matters as such. So along with limitations of technical capacity, there is a deficient information base and insufficient incentive to move toward improving the system.

Training has been the major component of CETA technical assistance, because CETA required inexperienced local administrators to set up and run complicated management and information systems. Approaches to training differ from region to region. Despite the fact that training has become the prime function of the regional role under CETA, a major part of training (particularly the TTT or Training the Trainers to Train program) for most regions has been contracted out. Professional firms are hired to train the field reps, who in turn train the prime sponsors to train their local operators, or the firms train prime sponsors directly.

In some regions, there is a greater degree of centralization, with much of the technical training being provided "in-house." Region I's Manpower Training Institute was the most defined and articulated example we saw of attempts to provide in-house training for field representatives, who will then train prime sponsors. The RETA in that region had recognized early the need for responsiveness to the different administrative demands of decentralization. He saw the growing need for the regional office to provide technical assistance and training. Previously in Region I, these services had been provided by outside consultants, and much time was spent in training these consultants. This administrator decided that the regional office should organize the information for itself, putting aside one day each week in which instructional material could be prepared for field reps.

There seems to be a greater mix now between in-house and outside training. Also, many regions are showing a tendency to bring prime sponsors into the regional office on a one-to-one basis for training in order to meet their individual needs. This would seem to indicate an obvious awareness of the limitations of the generalist field representative in trying to deal with prime sponsors' problems. In addition, area-wide training sessions have not proved successful, because prime sponsors are at different levels of experience and sophistication. However, on-site training for prime sponsors on a one-to-one basis by the field representative is still a common device for assistance.

A major share of training given to prime sponsors is in the areas of management information systems, fiscal and grant management, and general administration (various housekeeping activities). For the inexperienced prime sponsors, the administrative technical assistance clearly was needed. So was, and is, substantive technical assistance, including advice on planning the appropriate mix of manpower services and on the organizational problems of managing complex social service delivery programs. Also, prime sponsors need help in improving both their oversight capacity in monitoring and evaluating operating projects and their ability to provide technical assistance to projects.

Even the most sophisticated prime sponsors are well aware of their need for technical help. But what the regional offices offer is not of high quality and seldom of any real assistance to relatively competent prime sponsors. Moreover, the advisory effort in the administrative and support domain infrequently provides substantive technical assistance or continuing support to raise programmatic or oversight capabilities over time.

THE NATIONAL ACADEMY OF SCIENCES' ASSESSMENT OF CETA

The National Academy of Sciences Committee on Evaluation of Employment and Training Programs has assessed CETA based on 3 years of that program's operations. Several aspects of the assessment merit separate discussion.

The first concerns the extent to which a local project made significant program innovations. Our study did not investigate local projects in any depth, and the NAS study looked at a limited number. But their evidence showed that prime sponsors did not use the greater power and discretion granted from the federal government to make major program changes. The NAS study observed

> Although the balance among programs has changed, there has been little change in basic program design. Sponsors were inclined to continue the kinds of programs they inherited. Few of the sponsors had the necessary expertise to improve existing models.[25]

We will comment on this failure to innovate after the next paragraph.

The National Academy of Sciences committee proffered an overall assessment based on outcomes after first indicating how limited was its information base because of DOL's poor reporting system that provides only limited proximate outcomes. On this limited evidence, the commit-

[25] Ibid., p. 253.

tee points out the case is mixed and difficult to interpret because of changing economic conditions:

> There are various ways of evaluating the success of a training and employability program, including increasing proficiency of skills and enhancement of ability to compete independently in the labor market. In the final analysis, however, the primary criterion of success is the extent to which enrollees are able to obtain suitable long-term employment as a result of their CETA experience. The Department of Labor reporting system does not provide information on the duration of employment. However, placement ratios—the percentage of terminees who find jobs either through the sponsor's efforts or on their own—have been lower in the first 3 years of CETA than for comparable pre-CETA programs. The Committee recognizes the special difficulties of placement in a period of high unemployment.[26]

Striking program innovations or big gains in program performance were not forthcoming. There also are a number of explanations—beyond technical capability—for the lack of programmatic change, as will be discussed in later chapters. Indeed, a major theme will be that there have been far too high expectations in terms of the capacity of institutions to adjust. Still, it must be underscored that any hope that giving local governments more power would bring forth rapid positive changes was not fulfilled in the New Federalism experience.

The NAS committee, however, did perceive amid all the turmoil an improving local capability. It argued that on the whole "CETA, in terms of organization, delivery of service, and local participation, is a more effective way of handling the nation's employment and training programs than earlier centralized and categorical arrangements."[27] In the final chapter of its report, the NAS committee brought together the conflicting pulls in the field with this judgment:

> [The NAS study] has found that local control of programs has resulted in tighter program management, greater accountability, and more rational delivery systems. Local manpower planning, though still weak, is more meaningful than in the pre-CETA period, and grass roots participation in the planning process is greater. *However the shift of program control scrambled the relationships among government jurisdictions and among the local institutions that deliver manpower services.*[28]

We believe these to be reasonable assessments of CETA based on the first 3 years of implementation and administration.

[26] Ibid., p. 11.
[27] Ibid., p. 8.
[28] Ibid., p. 279, italics added.

4 | THE IMPLEMENTATION OF CDBG

This chapter dealing with the implementation of CDBG follows the same basic format as the previous one, with several sections on issues of organization and of government and community interrelationships and a final section on functions. We will use the present tense in this account also, even though we restrict ourselves to the New Federalism period.

HUD AT THE TOP

Let us start with the main actors in HUD's implementation of CDBG during the New Federalism period. Figure 4.1 depicts the relevant portions of HUD's three-tiered structure existing during that period. In order to avoid confusion both in the figure and in the listing below, we have left out completely elements of HUD at all levels that did not have a major impact on the implementation of CDBG. The primary CDBG actors are

Headquarters

Secretary/Under Secretary—has authority over the Housing and Community Development Act of which CDBG is Title I. The secretary alone has the power to reject CDBG grants.

Deputy Under Secretary for Field Operations—staff position to the under secretary responsible for coordination and liaison with field operations.

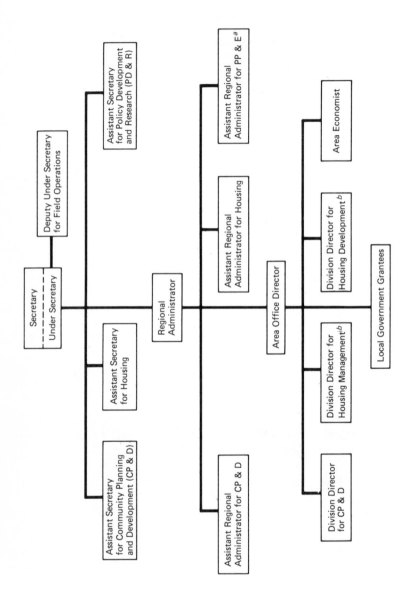

Figure 4.1. The main actors in CDBG (New Federalism period).

[a] Program Planning and Evaluation—equivalent to headquarters PD & R (only in some regions).
[b] In many area offices, the housing section is still divided into two parts.

Assistant Secretaries for

> *Community Planning and Development* (CP&D)—responsible for developing policy to implement CDBG (Title I).

> *Housing*, which now incorporates Housing Management (HM) and Housing Production and Mortgage Credit (HPMC), separate offices until 1976—responsible for developing housing policy under Title II of the Housing and Community Development Act, which policy is to be coordinated with Title I.

> *Policy Development and Research* (PD&R)—responsible for overall policy analysis and research for the agency.

Office of the Regional Administrator—has overall responsibility for interpreting policy and for monitoring the area office. This office is also responsible for providing training and technical assistance to the area office. It carries responsibility for the actual administration of other HUD programs. The majcɪ actors are

> *Regional Administrator* (RA)—has line authority over all regional and area activities.

> *Assistant Regional Administrators* (ARA)—have responsibilities corresponding to headquarters' assistant secretaries: CP&D, HM, and HPMC (sometimes consolidated into an ARA for Housing), and a unit responsible for program planning and evaluation (comparable to PD&R).

Office of Area Operations—is responsible for the implementation of the CDBG program. The office is also responsible for monitoring and evaluation of local jurisdictions as well as providing them with training and technical assistance. The main figures are

> *Area Office Director*—has sign-off authority on CDBG grants.

> *Assistant Area Office Directors*—corresponds to both headquarters and regional office positions: CP&D, HM, HPMC.

Chief Elected Officials—responsible, with their CDBG staffs, for preparing community development comprehensive plans and Housing Assistance Plans (HAP). They are responsible for the operation of the CDBG program.

HUD's Major Organizational Problems

Our efforts in this study have been concentrated as much as possible on CDBG and CETA activities in the field. In the case of ETA, the DOL structure and ETA's dominant position in delivery programs permitted us to focus exclusively on CETA and ignore other DOL activities. HUD offers no such neatness. CDBG cannot be isolated. We cannot concern ourselves with a single assistant secretary but rather must consider several top political executives who get into the CDBG act. This in turn forces us to look at HUD's top-level organizational structure beyond CDBG.

A major study of HUD organizational issues by the accounting firm of Coopers & Lybrand was carried out during the same time period as our field efforts.[1] Their findings starting and concentrating at the top and working down parallel ours, which are concerned mainly with activities in the field. This section on overall organizational problems relies heavily on the Coopers & Lybrand study.

DUAL SPAN OF COMMAND

HUD's organizational problems are captured in this Coopers & Lybrand statement:

> [HUD] is characterized by a dual span of command in which general line authority and programmatic line authority are delegated differently. As a consequence, no rigid chain of command for HUD Headquarters to the Field is adhered to, despite the fact that the Regional level is to be a conduit for communications to and from Headquarters. Moreover, although the intent of the Department is decentralization, the fact is that authority for many decisions was either not decentralized or there has been creeping recentralization.[2]

HUD has tried to combine staff and line functions in the same position so that assistant secretaries operate in both spheres. Figure 4.2 gives graphic illustration of this convoluted chain of command. Regional administrators and area office directors find themselves dealing with many-headed hydra when looking to Washington for direction. The Office of the Deputy Under Secretary for Field Operations provides the general line policy directives. But at the same time, assistant secretaries speaking directly to their counterparts at both the regional and the area office level can give conflicting policy statements based on their own particular programmatic orientation. Rather than one liaison staff in headquarters dealing with the field (as we saw in

---

[1] Coopers & Lybrand, *Recommendations for Near Term Field Organization Structure* (January 1976) and *Recommendations for HUD Organizational Structure* (March 1976), both published and distributed by the Office of Organization and Management Information Systems, HUD, Washington, D.C.. Hereafter we will cite the studies as the January and March reports.

[2] Coopers & Lybrand, March report, p. 78. For a more extended discussion of the dual span of control, see pp. 53–57.

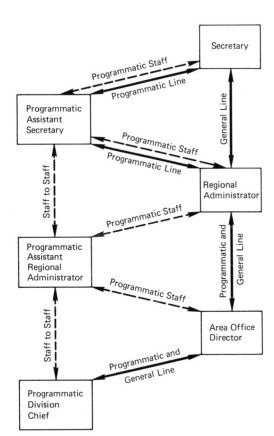

Figure 4.2. Coopers & Lybrand's depiction of HUD lines of authority (From Coopers and Lybrand, March report, p. 57).

our discussion of DOL), HUD has liaison staff in each of the programmatic areas at the national level, and each staff has a continuing relationship with its regional and area counterparts. Added to this confusion is the fact that each assistant secretary represents a specific interest (i.e., community planning and development or housing management), and often policy developed by one assistant secretary directly contradicts that of another, leaving field staff in the unenviable position of trying to implement conflicting directives. Coopers & Lybrand report in their study:

> Functional demands are made of Field staff by their programmatic counterparts at higher levels. Yet in a "genezal line," they report to Office Directors who may have conflicting priorities. The effect of this conflict on morale is significant.
> Much of the duplication of reporting required of the Field staff is caused by this dual command. . . . The coordination problem starts with the Headquarters Assis-

tant Secretaries. Throughout our interviews with HUD staffs and public organizations, we often heard the comment that it appears that the Assistant Secretaries do
not speak to each other.[3]

Interestingly enough, our more limited research on headquarters relationships also turned up the same phrase in several different interviews: "the assistant secretaries don't speak to each other." Under
these circumstances, the possibility of consultation or directive com-
patability has been remote.

THREE-TIERED STRUCTURE

HUD is unique in having three separate organizational levels mir-
roring each other as to functions. On paper, headquarters formulates
policy, standards, and procedures for all program activities of HUD;
the regional office is held responsible for policy interpretation and for
the coordination, support, and evaluation of the area and insuring offices,[4] and the area office is responsible for the actual implementation
and administration of HUD programs. But as Coopers & Lybrand point
out: "The three-tiered managerial structure and associated 'through
and to' authority delegations have resulted in confused authority relationships, declining morale, and a system of management prone to the
swings of personality."[5]

Decentralization was a major part of the rationale for this unusual
structure. Area offices were set up during the Romney administration
with the hope that they would achieve greater responsiveness, flexibility, and service to communities by decentralizing operations beyond
the regional office level. The role of the area office expanded further in
1974 after the enactment of the Housing and Community Development
Act. The bulk of the review and decision-making functions related to
the CDBG grants was going to be carried on by HUD's area offices.

HUD released an area office realignment plan that reorganized the
area offices so that they mirrored the regional and central offices. The
new structure was seen as a way to further administrative decentralization by increasing the field office's accountability. In addition, the area
office operations were to be simplified because certain of the functions
performed by this office earlier were being transferred to local com-

---

[3] Coopers & Lybrand, January report, p. 14.

[4] Insuring Offices are responsible for administering HUD–FHA programs in the
field.

[5] Coopers & Lybrand, March report, pp. 77–78.

munities under the provisions of the new act.[6] But the result within HUD appeared to be confusion.

In the section discussing the structure and functions of the regional and the area offices, we will go into more detail about the problems associated with HUD's three tiers. It is sufficient to say at this point that the problems mentioned earlier in regard to confused lines of authority and information flow are magnified and complicated with each move through the layers.

COMMUNICATIONS

No consistent, standardized channels of communication have been established between Washington and the regions. Information usually moves poorly from headquarters to the field, and sometimes not at all. This means that the field may not learn directly of changes in functions and roles of the regional staff, changes in legislation, shifts in head-quarters policy, and changes in delegations of authority. Because information may not be sent to the field, or if it is, because the possibility of miscommunicating the content is high, the regional and area staffs are often forced to make decisions independently of HUD's national policy direction. Regional and area staffs are by default allowed wide discretion in interpretation but often suffer from this latitude when their decisions are countermanded by later word from Washington. As Coopers & Lybrand have observed

> Another bottleneck in the work flow process is the apparent inability of Head-quarters to provide procedural manuals or guidelines concurrently with the implementation of new programs. Regional and/or Area Office staffs spend a great deal of time developing interim procedures which may be completely opposite from the final guidelines developed in Headquarters.[7]

In an attempt to allow for variation during the move toward decentralization, HUD did not provide consistent program interpretation in all regions. This approach, however, made allowing for legitimate variation extremely hard. That is, more consistent interpretations are needed so that equals can be treated equally before one has a basis for determining real differences that may warrant (establish the legal basis

---

[6] *Community Development: The Workings of a Federal–Local Block Grant*, Advisory Commission on Intergovernmental Relationships, Washington, D.C., A–57, March 1977, pp. 36–37

[7] Coopers & Lybrand, March report, p. 47.

for) variations from the prescribed (standard) treatment. Instead, HUD's lack of a consistent base has led to litigation over compliance enforcement and to complaints of biased enforcement.

Without clearly established channels of communications and chains of command, HUD is particularly prone to the bypass phenomenon. Headquarters frequently goes around the regional office and deals directly with the area office. Regional offices will skirt the area office and carry on direct relations with local government, placing the area office in an awkward and impotent position in dealing with local CDBG administrators. In a west coast city the regional office requested information directly from the city CDBG people in regard to the racial makeup of a series of citizen participation meetings held over a year's time as part of the CDBG planning process. The area office had not even been informed that the region had contacted the city.

Another variation of the bypass, which we will discuss later, involves HUD area office personnel working very closely with local government administrators in a kind of quiet conspiracy against the regional office. In these cases, the area office will work around the regional office to assist the local people in pushing a particular position with headquarters.

Often local governments, especially ones with political power will bypass both area and regional offices, going directly to a member of their congressional delegation or even to the HUD secretary for special treatment. In another west coast city, officials told us during interviews that they rarely talked with the area office, hardly knew the name of the area representative, and did not have dealings with the regional office. Problems were taken by the mayor directly to the secretary or by various staff members to their counterparts back in Washington. Often these staff members relied on old friendships developed during model cities days to gain information or to try and bring about accommodation in problem areas.

This bypassing technique is certainly not unique to HUD. But it is uncommon to find an organization that appears to have built into its structure the stepping over and around of the usual channels of authority and communication. Needless to say, bypassing has important implications for decision making at HUD, which we will discuss later. In terms of the field's relation to the national office and relationships between the regional and the area offices, the lack of determined, predictable channels means that messages are misconstrued, miscommunicated, or often simply lost in the system.

National-Regional Relationships

The general "on-paper" task of HUD headquarters is to make and interpret policy. It is supposed to establish priorities in the areas of housing and community development and develop the standards, criteria, and procedures for all levels of the field operation. The central office is responsible for overseeing program administration and executing program evaluations. By statute, the secretary has control over all programs, resources, and activities of HUD. This authority under a decentralized system is delegated by the secretary to assistant secretaries, who in turn redelegate it through the regional administrators to area office directors and their staff. The assistant secretaries are responsible for the administration of programs and for the development of policies in their individual programmatic areas.

Regional administrators have regular contact with the HUD secretary, allowing strong administrators to have some impact on policy deliberations in Washington. Further, regional administrators are expected to act as the secretary's representatives in the field and as such can play an important political role within the region. Assistant regional administrators also have regular contact with headquarters. The ARAs and the programmatic division chiefs in the area offices deal with counterpart assistant secretaries in Washington. Informal memos are sent from headquarters to RAs, ARAs, and staff in the area office giving policy directives to different levels of the organizations. This programmatic line contact is carried to the point that there are official liaison staffs in each assistant secretary's office.

As depicted vividly in Figure 4.2, regional and area offices are forced to follow two different lines of authority. The problem is particularly difficult for the regional administrator. On the one hand, he serves directly under the secretary and under secretary in the "general" line of authority. On the other hand, the various program assistant secretaries are the senior HUD officials responsible to the secretary in the "programmatic" line of authority so that all field staff, including the regional administrator, come under their authority.

The dual line has led to the need for an Office of the Deputy Under Secretary for Field Operations. This headquarters-based office plays a role in field relationships apart from the other programmatic and line organizations we have already mentioned. The deputy under secretary works as staff to the under secretary for coordination and liaison with the field. Desk officers in this office work on a one-to-one basis with an

assigned regional office. They act as one source of field input into
headquarters and are generally seen as the friend and ally of the
regional administrators. But this liaison office cannot solve the regional
administrator's dilemma in which he appears to have great power in
the general line but ends up far more often under the assistant
secretaries because of "their" programs in the field. As Coopers &
Lybrand observe

> The existence of this office is reinforcing evidence of the absence of a true line rela-
> tionship between Regional Administrators and the Secretary and Under Secretary.
> Since the more meaningful relationship is between the Regional Administrators and
> the Program Assistant Secretaries (who in turn relate to the Under Secretary and
> Secretary), a high-level coordinating staff position evolved to support the ad-
> ministrative interfaces required, particularly in light of the number of Assistant
> Secretaries involved.[8]

HUD IN THE FIELD

In the next two sections, the description of what regional and area
offices are supposed to do represents a kind of "on-paper" accounting.
Because such a description deals mainly with intent (wishes) rather
than reality, it is a generous picture. The third section looks at actual
problems in the field.

Regional Office Structure

Regional administrators are responsible directly to the secretary
for all HUD activities in the regions and oversee the operations of
regional staff, as well as area and insuring office directors. They also
serve as advocates for state and local governments. The regional administrators receive both specific authority and direction from and are
accountable to the appropriate program assistant secretaries on program matters and to the assistant secretary for administration on administrative matters.

The HUD regional office is expected to meet headquarters demands for information and oversee all office administration in the
region. In addition, the regional offices are responsible for administering Section 701 grants.[9] These grants are designed to assist state and
local governments in improving policy planning and management

---

[8] Ibid., p. 58.
[9] This function was previously performed by the area offices, a point we will return
to shortly.

capability and in phasing out the categorical programs that were folded into the CDBG program.

The HUD regional office has the following assistant regional administrators, whose functions parallel those of assistant secretaries in the central office: community planning and development; housing production and mortgage credit; administration; equal opportunity; and program planning and evaluation. (There are additional assistant secretaries at the national level, whose jobs are peculiar to central office needs.) The assistant regional administrators serve as staff to the regional administrator and have a GS–15 rating. The area office directors and insuring office directors (who usually have a GS–15 rating as well) are line officers and report directly to the regional administrator. The ARAs have no general line authority over the area and insuring office directors or their staffs. However, the same arrangement discussed earlier in relation to the national office applies equally in the field. ARAs in the regional office receive directions from their Washington counterparts, and their programmatic decisions affect the implementation efforts of the area office directors as well as the corresponding programmatic components within the area office.

Regional administrators are likely to have close personal contact with the assistant regional administrators who serve as their staff, seeing them frequently and relying on them for advice and counsel on policy direction, technical assistance, and staff organization. This regular interaction between the regional administrators and their staff varies from region to region, but the potential for such interaction exists. The line personnel (area and insuring office directors) usually meet with the regional administrators on a less regular basis, in large part because of geographic distance from the regional office. For many reasons, including questions of authority delegation, there appears to be tremendous strain and conflict between the regional administrators and their ARAs, on the one hand, and the area office staff responsible for implementing the CDBG programs, on the other.

Structure of HUD Area Offices

HUD's area offices are the units primarily responsible for the implementation and administration of the CDBG program. Unlike DOL where regional and area offices are coterminous, HUD locates its area offices in several cities (including the headquarters city) throughout the region. They form the constant source of contact between HUD and the units of local government that administer CDBG. Day-to-day operating authority is delegated to the area office, and the level of decentralization is such that approval—but not disapproval—of specific projects takes place here without referral to either the regional office or head-quarters. Disapproval can come only from the secretary.

Area office directors act as representatives of the regional administrator and of HUD for their areas. They supervise and direct the programs and activities carried out within the jurisdiction of their office. The area director's staff is a general duplication of the regional office, with area division directors responsible for most of the same programmatic areas found in both the regional office and headquarters.

In their charge to carry out the implementation and administration of HUD programs, the area offices have the responsibility on paper to (a) disseminate program information; (b) assist local government in completing application forms; (c) provide advice on how best to "get the money" in terms of meeting all eligibility requirements (the area office is expected to negotiate with cities and counties at an early stage of the application process so that ineligible activities will not appear in the plan and eventually create funding problems); (d) interpret regulations primarily in terms of eligible and ineligible activities; (e) review applications using national criteria; (f) monitor cities and counties to make sure that the law is being followed and to spot programs with potential problems; and (g) respond to complaints.

HUD area offices also have responsibility for providing technical assistance and training to local governments—but only upon request. Although the detailed discussion of technical assistance and training will be deferred until later in the chapter, a comment is needed at this point. Some of the area office responsibilities, for example, (b), (c), and (d), are what we label procedural technical assistance. In reality, then, HUD continued to provide much of the technical assistance of the past. But HUD's view of technical assistance as a commodity available only on request implies certain things about the way the agency perceives field relationships.

Problems in the Field

A major complaint of regional offices in regard to the central office has been that not enough authority was delegated to the regions. In turn, there has been even greater conflict between HUD's regional and area offices over authority in the field. This has been particularly true of the large area offices coincident with the location of the regional office itself. In our interviews, we heard area office staff characterize regional offices as "redundant," as "nuisances," or as "stumbling blocks," the view being dependent primarily upon the personality and administrative style of the regional administrator. Area offices generally believe that not enough authority is delegated by the regional office to the area, while the regional office feels that the area has all the flexibility it needs to do its job.

A strong complaint we heard during our spring 1977 interviews concerned the consistent pulling back of responsibility from the area to the regional office. For instance, the area offices had originally administered the 701 grants. The assistant secretary for community planning and development wanted to have more direct control over these planning grants and so removed the function to the regions. As one disgruntled area director of CP&D said: "Here's a program which needs to be coordinated with our CDBG program and we've got two reps—one from the area office and one from the regional office—working essentially the same problems. These programs are related and have to be looked at together."

Another factor that has frustrated the area offices is that the regional office has complete control over staff allocation for the area office. Only the region has a personnel office, and so the determination of how staff is allocated according to function is made by the region. The areas would like more freedom in developing their own staffing patterns so that they can respond more appropriately to local needs.

Area offices complain further that much staff time is required to complete forms and answer inquiries from the regional office but that they receive virtually no feedback as a result of this information gathering by the regions and by headquarters. Delays on the part of the regions in responding to requests by the area office, compounded by the duplication of review and processing functions, rub salt into the wounds of the area staff. One area office division director commented that he felt the regional office presented the main barriers to getting his job done effectively.

Generally, area offices appear to have been understaffed in light of the fact that the major responsibility for HUD implementation rests with them. This bottom tier of the three-tiered HUD structure might be likened to the tip of an inverted triangle supporting top-heavy regional and headquarters staffs. The regional office, which is the tier in the middle, seems to have the least reason for being and only adds more weight. The overlapping and confused authority patterns, delays in response to local governments, and breakdowns in communication have produced a situation where an area office staff person commented: "If they [the regional office] dropped through the floor tomorrow, it wouldn't make any difference in the implementation of CDBG, except that it would make our job easier."

The source of much of this confusion comes from the fact that authority is delegated to the area office through the regional office. This "pass through" function at the regional level speaks to HUD's inability to develop effective means of delegating authority. Coopers & Lybrand comment "[T]he Regional level does not seem to fit into the accepted reasons for a managerial level: to solve span of control problems or divide an organization into logical components such as production, inventory, etc."[10] And even more strongly, they say

> From the standpoint of service delivery, there exist few structural constraints to the elimination of the Regional level. HUD can provide its services without that middle tier. Indeed, it is the existence of the Regional level that is at the base of much of the role confusion and process inefficiency at HUD. Both in formal documentation and in actual practice, the tasks of the Regional Administrators and the ARAs are managerial impossibilities.[11]

Regional offices are not actually repositories of authority but instead serve as "pass throughs" for that authority on its way from headquarters to the field. This status has brought a search for a job usually centering on efforts to expand regional office duties into the operations of the area office. This often confusing and demoralizing duplication of efforts means that both offices sequentially are performing identical processing and review activities. Although grant approval resides in the area office, disapproval authority is carried out by the secretary. The area office makes recommendations for disapproval, but frequently the regional office feels that it must review and reprocess the recommendation before it is sent on to Washington. The lack of efficiency through such wasted efforts within the organization is matched only by the frustration of the local government official who may be paralyzed while waiting for HUD's response.

LOCAL OPERATIONS PERCEPTIONS OF CDBG AND HUD'S FIELD OPERATION

Unlike CETA, CDBG did not add another administrative layer. Many of the local governments that received CDBG grants had operated community development projects prior to CDBG and continued to do so under the block grant. But there were differences. First, the administration of housing and community development programs in large cities prior to CDBG was often executed by a fairly autonomous

---

[10] Coopers & Lybrand, January report, p. 8.
[11] Coopers & Lybrand, March report, p. 117.

quasi-governmental agency, such as a housing authority. Second, new governmental units—mainly urban counties—were added. But the key point is that CDBG did not create the DOL situation of removing the federal field staff from direct contact with project operators.

The First Year

The first point to make about the first year of the CDBG implementation is that HUD had a smaller role than under the categorical grants. Power visibly was shifted from the agency, including the field staff, to local grantees. The second Brookings report[12] indicated that in the 44 communities in which there had been significant prior grant experience research associates found HUD's role was smaller under CDBG in 86% of the cases.[13] For the remaining communities, there was no change for three and a somewhat greater HUD role in three communities as compared to during the categorical period. The rush of a new program may have explained part of the shift, but the concerted effort to "decentralize" power would appear to be the big factor.

CLARITY, CONSISTENCY, AND
COMPLIANCE ISSUES

During the early stages of the CDBG implementation, the rush to get the program in the field had serious effects. Forms and regulations coming from the central office were unclear, and field staff often were able to give only limited help in interpretation. Time deadlines for local government were unrealistic. Sudden changes in regulations brought chaos both to federal field staff and to local government.

As discussed earlier, HUD, in an effort to avoid charges of federal interference in the new decentralization thrust, instructed its field staff to provide no technical assistance. This move did not rule out procedural assistance, however it was labeled. *But HUD's implementation*

---

[12] Richard P. Nathan and others, *Block Grants for Community Development*, First Report on the Brookings Institution Monitoring Study of the Community Development Block Grant Program, U.S. Department of Housing and Urban Development, Washington, D.C., January 1977; and Paul R. Dommel and others, *Decentralizing Community Development*, Second Report of the Brookings Institution Monitoring Study of the Community Development Block Grant Program, U.S. Department of Housing and Urban Development, Washington, D.C., 2 June 1978. The study, which concentrated mainly on HUD–grantee–local citizen relationships, used research associates in over 60 communities. See the second report, pp. ii–vi and 6–9 for a listing of research associates and communities and a description of the sample. The reports are particularly useful in terms of what grantees actually did with funds.

[13] Dommel and others, *Decentralizing Community Development*, Table 3-3, p. 72.

*strategy amounted to a conscious decision to give no assistance in
substantive areas.* Cities and counties were told to put together
whatever they felt capable of doing with limited staff and experience.
The major kind of help provided by the regions was handholding of the
specific eligibility advice variety. This "do your own thing" stance of
HUD in relation to cities and counties has had important repercussions.
Because the legislation itself was often contradictory, there were differing expectations at all levels of government as to its intent. This, not
surprisingly, led to tremendous variations in the ways in which CDBG
has been implemented.

National intent was perhaps the first thing lost in the shuffle.
Moreover, HUD's "noninterference" and lack of direction left cities in
a vulnerable position as they determined how their CDBG funds would
be spent. During the first year of CDBG's implementation, field and national staff of HUD were willing to accept virtually all proposals from
communities, even when national intent was patently in question. By
the second year, litigation had started against the cities and against
HUD on the grounds that the legislation's intent was being violated.

Litigation was mounted either against local governments or against
HUD, contending that CDBG's intent of helping low-and moderate-
income people was not being met. The day our interviewing team arrived in Los Angeles, the evening news carried the story of a suit
brought by local legal service attorneys representing three citizens who
had gone to court to try and stop the city of Alhambra from using
CDBG funds to expand the local golf course from 9 holes to 18.[14]

Having found it difficult to justify the golf course expansion as
directly benefiting low- or moderate-income families or helping to pre-
vent blight, the city of Alhambra had allocated $100,000 (half of its
CDBG entitlement) for the golf course under the provision of the statute
that allows a community to meet needs of "particular urgency."
Frieden and Kaplan argue that Alhambra's own first-year application
did not support this claim of special urgency, having ranked the goal of
improving existing parks as eighth in priority needs of the city.[15] The
suit filed by the legal services attorneys was not against the city of
Alhambra but against the HUD secretary, because the statute gives the
secretary the authority to decide whether there is actually justification
of "particular urgency." In this case, HUD was charged with having a-
bused its discretion.

[14] *Garcia et al.* v. *Hills*, U.S. District Court, Central District of California, CD No.
76–1014, dated 29 March 1976.

[15] Bernard Frieden and Marshall Kaplan, "Community Development and the Model
Cities Legacy," in David C. Warner (editor), *Toward New Human Rights*, Lyndon B.
Johnson School of Public Affairs, University of Texas, Austin, 1977, p. 304.

A second problem arose from HUD's lack of uniform interpretation of CDBG. Responding to the vacuum at headquarters, field staff provided their own interpretations of the most troublesome issues—for example, the determination of eligible activities and the eligibility of social service projects. Most staff, left to their own devices, resorted to the old categorical guidelines and regulations. And at the top, HUD appeared to be saying that anything done in the past could still be done. In its first annual report, HUD stated

> [CDBG] consolidated seven existing grant-in-aid programs . . . each with its own limiting focus, grant formula, and distinct program requirements. . . .
>
> *Generally, activities eligible under the categorical programs can be carried out with CDBG funds,* and some new activities can be undertaken. To further increase the locality's flexibility in carrying out community development activities, these funds may be used anywhere within the local government's jurisdiction to serve principally the needs of low- and moderate-income people, to aid in the prevention or elimination of slums and blight, and/or to meet urgent community development needs.[16]

The quotation, if not inaccurate, was surely misleading. The legislation sets forth certain objectives that marked distinct changes from the earlier categorical legislation. The main legislative objectives of CDBG speak specifically to the prevention of slums and blight and the conservation and expansion of the housing stock. The principal beneficiaries of the CDBG programs, according to Title I of the legislation, are intended to be persons of low or moderate income. Conceivably, a city might be within the law if a golf course was built in a blighted area and used mainly by moderate- and low-income people. But clearly, there were new directions in CDBG that made some of the categorical activities suspect.

Some cities have been able to smooth over possible conflicts between the prime legislative objectives and their own determined priorities by addressing themselves to issues that have some effect on the elderly or the handicapped. For example, Bellevue, a wealthy satellite city of Seattle, with a minority population of .6% and with few pockets of low-income people, has been able to use CDBG monies for senior citizen centers and for curb cuts. The aged and the handicapped might be presumed to be of low or moderate income and, despite the affluence of the community, could hardly be viewed as Alhambra golfers.

This kind of situation points up the problems of distribution built

[16] *Community Development Block Grant Program: First Annual Report,* Department of Housing and Urban Development, Washington, D.C., December 1975, p. 1, italics added.

into the legislation. During the drafting and negotiation stages, the pressure of urban counties (read suburbs) and the growing number of congressmen representing these areas meant that the funds were spread more thinly, going for the first time to localities that had to work hard to figure out legitimate ways to spend the money. HUD, in its second annual report, indicated some of the results of these distributional changes:

> Fiscal Year 1976 funding has gone to many communities not involved in the first year CDBG program or in previous HUD categorical programs. Over the first two years of Title I, the number of different localities receiving HUD funds has climbed to a total more than triple that of the pre-block grant era. Within entitlement communities funded under CDBG, specific neighborhoods receiving community development assistance also have shown nearly a three-fold increase compared with the number receiving assistance prior to enactment of the block grant legislation. These newly-assisted areas are generally of higher income than those assisted before 1975. Continuation of that trend into 1976 is one reason why funds going to low- and moderate-income areas decreased by approximately 10% from 1975 to 1976.[17]

Although CDBG superceded the categorical programs, the old regulations were often used to determine eligibility by area staff who were more comfortable with programs they knew and who were at sea in interpreting CDBG. Even though HUD field staff did not take the initiative in offering help under the new block grant approach, when asked, they would often slip back into their categorical hats and advise accordingly. Not only did this practice produce confusion for local officials because of conflicts between the categorical objectives and those of CDBG, it also produced a restrictive, limiting quality to the planning being done by communities.

The combined problems of HUD ignoring congressional intent in the rush to put a program together and of the conflicting readings in using the old categorical standards for eligibility, left many local governments confused and often angry at HUD's "nonimplementation" of its major legislation. Because of the unusual demands on local staff resources and the frustrations faced in trying to ensure the eligibility of activities, some smaller communities seriously considered dropping out of the CDBG program after the first year. There was just not enough money in it for them to make the effort worthwhile. For this and other reasons, "28 entitlement communities chose not to apply for funds in Fiscal Year 1976, compared to 16 in the first year."[18]

Large cities also had their problems. Despite the surface generosity

---

[17] *Community Development Block Grant Program: Second Annual Report*, Department of Housing and Urban Development, Washington, D.C., December 1976, p. 6.
[18] Ibid.

of the hold harmless provisions, the big cities recognized that CDBG was a major step backward in efforts to deal with problems of urban renewal and housing assistance. No city was willing to commit funds to major housing and community development projects, because they feared that once the hold harmless provisions ran out in 1980 local governments would have to pick up the remaining commitments of the projects with their own money.

HOUSING ASSISTANCE PLAN

The single provision of CDBG that undoubtedly caused the most problems for communities during the first year was the drawing up of a Housing Assistance Plan (HAP). HUD was determined to integrate its community development and its housing programs into one grant. The HAP was the key to this integration, because no community regardless of size was eligible to receive CDBG funds unless it had mapped out the housing needs of low- and moderate-income people within its jurisdiction. Other provisions of CDBG could be waived if the community were below a certain size, but the submission of a HAP was essential to a grant of CDBG funds.

Two factors complicated the carrying out of this provision. The kinds of information required to develop such a plan were not readily available to many communities. Large cities might have an adequate data base, but HUD on occasion would not accept their numbers. Communities that were too small to maintain detailed population information but were too large to carry out "windshield surveys" had the most serious problems in assembling their Housing Assistance Plans. Further, this very sophisticated document required expert staff to interpret the information and use it in developing a comprehensive housing assistance program. HUD's field staff in some cases was not willing and in other cases not able to provide local communities with help in their efforts to comply with this CDBG requirement. Many cities and more particularly the urban counties simply did not have the staff resources to produce a plan that had any relation to the community development program or was a true assessment of housing needs.

The second major factor complicating preparation of the HAP was the requirement that jurisdictions assess and plan not only for the needs of its present population but also for the needs of those who might be "expected to reside" there. The first Brookings report, in its comments on the expression "expected to reside" and the controversy that surrounded it, pointed out that the problem was partly statistical in terms of the data collection difficulties but also observed

The reluctance of some jurisdictions to pursue this issue and perhaps assemble their own survey data could in some cases also be a reflection of a lack of support for housing programs for low and moderate-income persons; some jurisdictions avoided this aspect of the HAP requirement or complied only perfunctorily. . . . Of the eighteen entitlement jurisdictions that chose not to participate in the CDBG program, most decided upon this course of action because of the HAP requirement.[19]

HUD made little effort to enforce the HAP provisions of the legislation during the first year. In a memorandum dated 21 May 1975, area offices were instructed that "when applications were submitted lacking a complete assessment of housing needs, the applicant involved could either adopt estimates provided by HUD, adopt its own estimates, or indicate what steps would be taken to make a more complete HAP presentation in its second year's submission."[20]

The "expected to reside" (ETR) issue came to a head when the city of Hartford sued HUD in August 1975, enjoining HUD from releasing community development funds to seven suburbs of Hartford, charging that their applications did not comply with the law, particularly the HAP provision. A court decision handed down in January 1976 ruled that HUD had acted illegally when it approved applications from the seven suburbs "without requiring the towns to make any assessment whatsoever of the housing needs of low and moderate-income persons who might be 'expected to reside' within their borders."[21] On 15 August 1977, the U.S. Court of Appeals for the Second Circuit reversed the Hartford decision for three suburban towns involved in the suit. The city of Hartford appealed the decision to the Supreme Court. As the second Brookings report observed: "No matter what the eventual outcome, however, the Hartford case apparently sensitized HUD officials to the ETR issue."[22]

There are serious implications in HUD's treatment of the HAP provisions during the first two CDBG program years. The second Brookings report indicated that local officials consider the HAP as a "necessary evil" and observed: "It's like eating your spinach in order to get your dessert."[23]

The problems go deeper. As one HUD area staff person told us: "We have the gall to look at a mayor and say 'when the hell are you going to coordinate?' It's embarrassing when we can't even get our own house in order." The staff report of the Subcommittee on Housing and

---

[19] Nathan and others, *Block Grants for Community Development*, p. 65.

[20] Ibid., p. 66.

[21] *City of Hartford et al. v. Carla Hills et al.*, Memorandum of Decision, U.S. Court District of Connecticut, Civil No. H-75-258, p. 28.

[22] Dommel and others, *Decentralizing Community Development*, p. 95.

[23] Ibid., pp. 80–81.

Community Development of the House Committee on Banking, Finance and Urban Affairs, notes much the same feeling:

> [T]he resulting failure to make the HAP effective is viewed by some local officials as testament to the inability of the federal government to get its "act together" in accordance with the Act's purposes and objectives. In this respect, it was often cited by local officials that the Act was a step beyond model cities in achieving a coordinated federal approach to the nation's urban problems and "the feds failed to perform." They then go on to say, that despite this failure, the federal government is requiring that local governments have their "act together" in order to obtain CDBG assistance.[24]

In addition to this cynicism on the part of local government toward federal efforts, an even more serious result of the HAP failure lies in the lack of attention cities have paid to the housing needs of families. Again, according to the House subcommittee report:

> The success of the HAP concept depends largely on the availability of federal housing subsidies in amounts sufficient to at least begin to address low- and moderate-income housing needs set forth in a community's statement of annual goals. The fact is that these subsidies were not made available in most communities. While Section 8 housing assistance was mainly relied upon for meeting these subsidy needs, HUD had considerable difficulty in making this program operational. . . . In general, Section 8 allocations fell far below the amounts needed to address the housing assistance needs of most communities.[25]

If the HAP process had been effective, local governments would have been forced to consider the question of housing assistance as a basic part of policy planning in preparing the CDBG program. The HAP proved to be a main stumbling block in the implementation of CDBG. After a time, it was generally ignored by the area staffs and filled out in a pro forma way by the cities.

SOCIAL SERVICES

A final problem for communities, particularly those that had had model cities programs, revolved around the question of social services. The model cities projects had leaned heavily toward meeting social service needs. CDBG was designed as a public works approach to community development. The CDBG legislation emphasizes "hardware" by

---

[24] *Community Development Block Grant Program*, Staff Report prepared by the staff of the Subcommittee on Housing and Community Development of the Committee on Banking, Finance and Urban Affairs, House of Representatives, 95th Congress, First Session, U.S. Government Printing Office, Washington, D.C., February 1977, p. 29.

[25] Ibid., p. 27.

limiting social service monies to be used only if they relate to physical development activity in the same area and only if the community had been unable to get support for service projects from other federal programs. In many cities CDBG funds have been funneled into the general fund essentially supplementing the public works budget.

Second Year

The first year of CDBG for many communities was consumed in setting up to operate the program. Staffs were preoccupied with process and HUD field people were deliberately not intervening so that numerous programs thrown together by communities and accepted by HUD were inadequate and in some cases blatantly contrary to national intent. Then HUD sought to tighten up in the second year. For the 61 areas in the Brookings sample, research associates reported a greater HUD role in 32 jurisdictions, no change in 22, and a smaller HUD role in only 7.[26]

HUD TIGHTENS UP

The second-year round of applications was tighter, and HUD was tougher in determining eligibility. Once HUD became more active in the field, its organizational problems became more obvious and more troublesome. As the previously mentioned congressional staff report says

> Many local officials and some HUD Regional and Area Office officials are seriously questioning the effectiveness of HUD's field office structure. This centers on whether or not a highly decentralized program, such as the CDBG program, can or should be effectively administered through a highly decentralized HUD structure. In some HUD regions, there was a preponderance of local opinion that the Area Offices were largely superfluous insofar as CDBG application review function is concerned. And in almost all instances local officials voiced some criticism about the Area Offices. Often, however, they reported that Area Office staffs were cooperative and helpful. They believe that the Area Offices and to a lesser extent the Regional Offices do not have sufficient operating guidelines to carry out the responsibilities they have been vested with under the CDBG program. Frequently, the recipients could not obtain definitive decisions about major program policies from the Area Offices. Many local officials reported that they by-passed the Area Offices and sometimes even the Regional Offices to obtain firm decisions. Several Area and Regional Offices reported that they were often unable to meet their responsibilities because they were not provided essential policy guidelines from Central Office. Often HUD's regulations were not workable according to these HUD officials because they provided little more than the language in the Act. This often led to conflicting interpretations and impaired Regional and Area Offices.[27]

[26] Dommel and others, *Decentralizing Community Development*, Table 3-4, p. 75.
[27] *Community Development Block Grant Program*, pp. 46–47.

Local officials thought the CDBG application process was to be streamlined with more flexibility for comprehensive planning in contrast to the myriad requirements of the categorical days. Under the categoricals, the grant approval process was a long and onerous one, requiring months of front-end work. However, once the approval came, the decision was final and the money belonged to the cities. CDBG reversed things. Applications were approved promptly. But after that point, the area office pressed local officials for detailed compliance. With the second year, there came a flood of requests for long and complicated reports. Far greater attention was focused on compliance with certain procedural elements of the plan such as affirmative action and citizen participation. These procedural issues had received little notice during the first round in part because of time constraints. Smaller communities were hard hit by some of these reporting demands and by some of the problems of compliance. They did not necessarily have the machinery set up to meet certain requirements of the legislation such as the environmental review process. The Housing Assistance Plan was a particular burden for many communities.

HUD's tightening up on its regulations pleased many people at the local level who welcomed this new willingness on the part of HUD to be more specific at the front end of the application process. Better for HUD to speak up initially rather than to say nothing until a local government's plan was well under way and then slap them with a noncompliance charge.

Sophisticated local officials and administrators recognize the shaky base from which regional and area office staff have operated. They know that the regional and area offices are supposed to have limited policymaking authority and that directives from the central office are often unclear and conflicting. They also recognize, however, that it is the area office that either approves their grants or else recommends disapproval to the seceretary.

HUD does have power in the field, and the locals know it. The main problem has been that decisions made by the area office have been dominated by the organizational conflicts we have discussed earlier. Often the area office has been the last to know when changes were being made in Washington. Sometimes a regional office has held back information. Sometimes the regional office has not received any word from headquarters. Sometimes a decision is nullified by a contrary one from Washington. Perhaps because of these circumstances, one does not see as much animosity leveled against area office staffs in HUD as was seen in DOL. Rather, the locals and the area office seem on occasion to be allies against the Kafka-like organizations above. At any rate, bureaucratic confusion in HUD seems less resented by the locals than the better organized bureaucratic heavy-handedness in DOL.

THE FLOW OF INFORMATION

Mayors, city council members, and county executives and their staffs often know what is happening in Washington in regard to housing and community development legislation and policy before staff in the regional and area offices. One highly placed regional official granted this was true and said that a major part of the problem was the fact that the information Washington was using in making decisions was a year old. When relations between HUD field staff and the local government are good, the CDBG administrator or his boss is usually willing to share information with federal staff. The administrator of a major city's CDBG program said that he hears regularly from his congressional delegation about legislative action and usually provides "one-day service" to the HUD area director, keeping him up to date.

Nobody feels more frustration about this somewhat topsy-turvy information flow than the competent field person who knows that one of the most important functions the federal government should perform in a decentralized system is getting information to decision makers. Ironically, another important source of information for CDBG administrators comes through informal contacts with friends and colleagues working in HUD's central office. This is especially true for local people who have had experience in model cities or other categorical programs where programmatic linkages throughout the country were fostered. In addition to congressional and agency contacts, the public interest groups and various housing industry publications and meetings are an important information source for local operators.

BLOCK GRANT POLITICS

Besides highlighting the information flow problem, the second year of CDBG implementation has pointed up certain political aspects of the block grant approach. Elected officials are prone to take CDBG money and use it for showy projects that will have an impact on the official's political base. This is not to say that the public works emphasis of CDBG is purely political. There is certainly justification for the belief that the heavy social service stress of model cities produced a flood of money into services that had little lasting effect other than the jobs provided for low-income people. Curb cuts and the other so-called hardware of public works can be seen and used over time. The motive for using CDBG funds in "concrete" ways can be manifold. However, there is also reason to feel that, particularly in localities where a city or county council determines the allocation of CDBG funds, the motivating force has been to spread the money around so that each official gets some of the pot to show to his or her constituency.

Much discussion has centered on the effectiveness of dispersion versus concentration of CDBG resources. HUD has always favored the targeted population and targeted area approaches used in model cities. In the subcommittee's staff report, the findings indicate

> According to local officials, the limited funds available, the broad nature of eligible activities, the extensive citizen participation involved in developing local programs, and the political desirability of demonstrating widespread and immediate impact, all contribute toward scatteration. . . .
> From its survey, the staff learned that local community development programs which constitute the scattered approach may be as desirable as those that constitute the concentrated approach. In fact there are sound reasons for programs to include both approaches depending on the nature and extent of the conditions in communities.[28]

As communities moved farther from the mind set of model cities during the second year of CDBG, dispersion became a more common policy of local governments. HUD field people have consistently attempted to focus the attention of locals on the targeted approach, but local officials have tended to go their own way, dispersing resources throughout a jurisdiction for whatever motive.

We are not arguing here that the locals always know best. Rather, the point is that an issue such as resource allocation offers the clearest kind of example of the inherent contradictions between national intent as represented by HUD and local initiative as practiced by local governments.

Another political aspect of CDBG has been the direct link that exists between local elected officials and members of the decision domain. As mentioned earlier, where a city or county has enough political clout of its own, the area and regional offices may be ignored and action will move directly to Washington either to the congressional delegation or to the agency leadership, even to the secretary level. This is a natural tendency wherever local elected officials are helping to make allocation decisions, but it becomes particularly noticeable in HUD, where the bypass problem reaches major proportions, as we discussed earlier.

A clear example of this happened when a major west coast city with close ties to Secretary Carla Hills bypassed several layers of the federal government to take its complaint directly to the secretary. Not only was the problem resolved favorably for the city, but city officials came home with a special $1.5 million discretionary grant. This phenomenon of a powerful city mayor with strong ties to a powerful

[28] Ibid., pp. 33–34.

senator or the secretary can have a distorting effect on field activities through the most obvious kind of political influence. On occasion, the scissoring approach to bureaucratic red tape can be viewed as beneficial to a particular locality. But in addition to providing an inequitable way to circumvent the system, this direct political link tends to perpetuate a "smoothing" effect that compensates for and prolongs a bad system.

GROWING LOCAL CAPACITY

Local operators see a number of positive effects of CDBG now that the program has gone through its second year. The block grant approach at least initially cut red tape by consolidating the application process for the former seven categorical programs into one streamlined application form. It has increased local authority as to how funds will be used. Chief executives of a local jurisdiction and their direct staffs under CDBG have gained a notable amount of power in the area of housing and community development, which under the categoricals and model cities was held by housing authorities, model cities directors, and community agencies. Although this is the general rule, it does not hold in all localities; for example, in Boston, the Boston Redevelopment Agency still has important power despite the fact that nominally the mayor has authority over CDBG funds.

With more years of operation under the belt, city and county staffs have gained valuable experience in running the complicated management and information system that CDBG requires. The experience has been extremely valuable for many localities, especially those that had not operated large sophisticated programs during the categorical days. Some local officials have indicated that city government was forced to move into the twentieth century in terms of data gathering and comprehensive planning in order to implement CDBG. Those cities are unlikely to be content to return to the days of a much heavier federal hand. Staffs and officials have gained confidence in their own abilities to run programs.

Under CDBG, there is greater predictability of funding, which allows for more comprehensive long-range planning. This ability to plan ahead with a relatively stable source of funds has led to increased dialogue at the local level and in some cases attempts at integrated planning. In Seattle, for example, the city used the procedure developed for CDBG implementation to produce an integrated CDBG and Capital Improvement Plan. The block grant program in King County, Washington, has become a forum for discussion of long-term land use planning.

WHERE HUD DECISIONS ARE MADE

In this section, we will first consider decision making within HUD itself and then move to the local setting. We skip over HUD–local community relationships initially, because their nature is determined so much by HUD organizational problems that complicate communications and intensify the within-agency struggles. Unlike the DOL case, where we found fund recipients angry at federal field staffs, the locals seem to get along fairly well with HUD area office staffs as both tried to figure out what the national office wants. CDBG decision making in communities also presents an interesting contrast to CETA. While CETA decisions were confined mainly to planning councils where citizens, as opposed to long-standing groups that may represent the citizens, had almost no involvement, local CDBG decision making is much more likely to involve both individual citizens and neighborhood groups, some of which were formed expressly to participate in the community development and housing activities. These differences appear to stem in part from the already established citizen participation tradition under model cities. Also important has been the fact that cities operate their community development programs directly, rather than using intermediary community-based organizations as in CETA, and are providing funds for capital improvements that might be useful in any part of a community. The benefits of public works kinds of projects are more obvious and more easily understood than the community effects of a CETA program. But whatever the reason, the available CDBG experience provides a picture of involvement by citizens and citizen organizations in the local decision-making process.

HUD Organizational Decision Making

HUD delegates the authority to approve applications down to its area office directors who can approve applications and can make recommendations that they be disapproved. Only headquarters, at the secretary level, has disapproval authority. Area offices are able to exert a kind of disapproval function by simply refusing to approve certain portions of the grant that they find unacceptable. If it is not willing to bypass the area office or try for congressional pressure, the local government usually modifies its grant to the area office's specifications.

As we have mentioned before, the area office would like to see more authority delegated to it by the regional office. Rather than so much direct supervision where the regional office may dictate the operations functions of the area office, the area office would like to see more substantive technical assistance provided by the region. According to Coopers & Lybrand:

> The Department's Regional Offices have become more than a coordinating, supervising, and evaluating tier of management. It is charged that several Regional Offices are involving themselves directly with, or are taking operational decisions away from, the Field [Area] Offices. . . . Some decisions, particularly those of an administrative nature, are not decentralized. Personnel staff exist in Regional Offices but the personnel function exists only informally at even the larger Area Offices. . . . The formal delegations of authority down to the Area Office levels are not always adhered to. Many applications or forms that are processed at the Area level are reviewed and reprocessed at the Region and often reviewed and reprocessed again at HUD Headquarters.[29]

Relationships between the regional and an area office, particularly where the latter is responsible for the geographic area in which the regional office is housed, often become strained because each is vying for political power in that locality. The duplication of structure and of function means that there are two entities dealing with a mayor and/or city council trying to establish individual turf. In cities with sophisticated staff, one well may find these local governments playing the regional and the area offices against each other.

Both area and regional offices do agree that the central office has not delegated enough authority to the field in general. They feel even more strongly that there is a growing tendency for headquarters to take back previously delegated authority—so-called creeping recentralization. Less and less attention appears directed toward particular local conditions or to the judgments of the federal people on the spot.

One of the main concerns felt by the regions is that regulations do not take into consideration regional variation. Many people at the regional and area level believe that comment from the field is a futile activity, because criticisms on draft regulations do not appear to act as a stimulus for change in the national office. Regulation changes in draft form are sent out to the regions for comment. But the review process often appears hurried and incomplete. Area offices recall in local government officials to review the draft regulations, but in some cases, complicated information that may be of considerable significance to a local government will be read aloud to a large group of local people with no opportunity to study the changes and their effects in writing. Regulations are published with few if any of the changes advanced by the regions, and usually the regions receive no response at all from

[29] Coopers & Lybrand, March report, pp. 78–79.

their input. On those occasions when headquarters does ask for input, the timing of the request is such that even the least cynical staff persons realize that their comments cannot be effectively incorporated in changes. If the schedules are disturbed and the time frame has to be revised, the promised reviews for the regions are the first items to be deleted.

In addition to a growing trend toward a closed system in terms of inputs from the field, the actual arena where decisions are made is rapidly constricting. Despite the apparent power existing in the area office where grant applications are approved, the amount of discretion in the field in terms of staff and resource allocation is dwindling. The Coopers & Lybrand report underscored the phenomenon of authority within the agency being drawn back to headquarters:

> There has been a trend, noted several Office Directors interviewed, for the Assistant Secretaries to take back the powers that have been previously delegated to the Field. The result has been that too many routine decisions are made at Headquarters and too few Assistant Secretaries are easily accessible to their subordinates. . . .
>
> Some long-time HUD observers noted that the decision-making process was gravitating closer and closer to the top. Rather than making policy and procedure decisions, the Assistant Secretary level decisions were becoming more operational in nature.[30]

HUD had tried to decentralize but never had gone through the hard chore of deciding what decentralization meant in terms of distribution of power and functions or what structural components were best suited to that system of organization. John E. Rouse, Jr., discussed this problem:

> The decentralization experience at HUD also verfied Louis C. Gawthrop's premise that with the increase in delegations of authority in the executive branch, the more likely that the power to control organizational behavior will become increasingly fragmented, dispersed, and unequal. This fragmentation, dispersion, and unequal allotment of power for controlling organizational behavior occurred at HUD and in its field structure after decentralization of authority to the Area and Insuring Offices.
>
> Decentralization should allow top levels of administrative echelons to devote more of the central office's time to planning and policy activities. There is no significant indication that HUD's decentralization has provided its central office with more free time to develop new policies.[31]

HUD already had problems built in to its organization structure before

---

[30] Ibid., pp. 43 (first paragraph), 50 (second paragraph), italics in the original.

[31] John E. Rouse, Jr., entitled "Administrative Decentralization as a Complement to Revenue Sharing: A Case Study of the HUD Programs," as cited in Coopers & Lybrand, March report, p. 59.

it began its efforts to decentralize. The unresolved conflict between assistant secretaries over fractionalized and overlapping authority in programmatic areas made it difficult for decentralization at HUD to work well. Because no one is accountable for all phases of a particular program, there is no clear line of responsibility or authority. Potential power instead becomes power to obstruct and in reality represents powerlessness. In the long run, things do not happen because nobody is responsible to see that they happen.

Nowhere are the repercussions felt more than in the field. Field people believe that decisions made at headquarters are not transmitted to the field in a timely fashion. First, area staff must operate in response to local government even with a vacuum at headquarters. Then, area people make decisions of both a programmatic and administrative nature only to see those decisions remanded by tardy directives from Washington.

Regional offices set their own priorities without clear direction from the top, and the area offices implement CDBG programs according to those priorities only to find that an assistant secretary has made a programmatic decision that contradicts the regional priority. Local government's bitterest complaint is that area and field people cannot or will not make decisions, and this translates into long delays on eligibility and grant modification questions. Probably none is more frustrated by this limp, unresponsive chain of command than the person in the area office who must talk to local officials without any clear direction from headquarters. HUD staff at all levels and local government see little else but confusion and chaos when trying to pin down the patterns of responsibility and authority within HUD.

HUD and the CDBG Grantees

Although HUD applied a much lighter hand under CDBG than under the categorical programs, clashes still occurred between the agency and local communities over what the latter wanted to do. The second Brookings report, in looking at 61 communities, provides useful summary data on what happens when there is a HUD–grantee controversy over issues. The report observes

> To restate the findings, overall we found that local governments tended to prevail more frequently on substantive—strategy and program—issues, whereas HUD was

more assertive and successful on procedural and compliance questions. In terms of jurisdictional types, central cities were more successful than other types of jurisdictions.[32]

The general rule seems to be that experience—and experience is generally related to size—is critical in disputes. Thus, the Brookings study found that cities with model cities' experience usually came out on top in any controversies.[33]

If we go beyond clashes over particular points to the more general notion of influence, size and experience again were the critical factors. The second-year Brookings study reported ratings of their research associates in 61 communities on levels of influence exerted by HUD in the first 2 years of CDBG. Most of the respondents (45) reported minor or no HUD influence. In two communities the local programs were actually determined by HUD, and major influence was reported for 14 communities. The Brookings study then observed

> HUD's influence tended to be greater in smaller communities. Nine of the fourteen jurisdictions where HUD's influence was classified as major have populations under 100,000, and the two cases in which HUD determined the local programs involve jurisdictions with populations under 25,000.[34]

The findings are consistent either with the hypothesis that HUD concentrates the little help it gives on the neediest (small, inexperienced grantees) or with the notion that HUD was a bit of a bully in pulling out against the tougher communities but hammering on the smaller ones.

Two comments about the Brookings findings are warranted. First, the Brookings report, as already indicated, points out less HUD influence and direction than under the categorical programs. What is being reported on here is relative HUD influence or success in controversial issues during the block grant period. Second, the Brookings sample, which had a much larger and more diverse group of observation points than our own study, dramatizes the existence of variability in any large-scale program such as CDBG. Our study and the Brookings studies for the first and second years may indicate trends, such as less HUD influence compared to the categorical period for much more HUD influence on procedural rather than substantive issues, but we should not lose sight of the fact that some area offices may be exercising far more influence than before and pushing hard on and winning on substantive issues.

[32] Dommel and others, *Decentralizing Community Development*, p. 108.
[33] Ibid., p. 91.
[34] Ibid., p. 69.

CDBG Decision Making at the Local Level[35]

Congress intended that there be a significant amount of citizen involvement under CDBG, but it chose to allow local governments wide discretion in deciding the procedures for such involvement. And basically, Congress got what it wanted, at least in broad terms—lots of citizen involvement under a variety of circumstances that seemed to fit local needs. The first Brookings study reported that 52 out of the 62 localities studied "viewed citizen participation as an important part of the application process and not merely a formality"[36] and went on to observe

> On the whole, the large number of jurisdictions in which local officials were judged to have taken the citizen participation requirements seriously must be viewed as one of the surprising features of the first-year CDBG program. It is especially so in view of what was widely regarded, at best, as a widespread uneasiness among local officials with comparable requirements under previous federal programs. This generally supportive attitude under the CDBG program can be attributed to several factors; the one that appears most frequently in the observations of [research] associates is the fact that the program permits local officials to shape citizen participation to fit their own objectives and preferences, both substantially and procedurally. . . . [L]ocal officials were supportive of citizen participation because they had the opportunity to control it and use it as they saw fit.[37]

The first Brookings study sought to determine how effective citizen participation was in the CDBG decision-making process. Specifically,

[35] In this section, we rely upon two already cited efforts to study CDBG at the local level: the two volumes of the Brookings study reporting on years 1 (Nathan and others, *Block Grants for Community Development*) and 2 (Dommel and others, *Decentralizing Community Development*) of the CDBG effort; and the House Subcommittee on Housing and Community staff report (*Community Development Block Grant Program*). Because of the similiarities of titles in these and a number of other cited references, we will refer to these two as the Brookings (first or second) study and the Subcommittee on Housing and Community Development study. The Brookings study, supervised by a Washington-based group, employed research associates who were located in the communities studied to investigate 62 of the 2484 localities receiving CDBG funds in FY 1975. The Brookings study in the first year included 30 cities, 12 satellite cities, 10 urban counties, and 10 nonmetropolitan areas. Brookings dropped one locality in the second year so comparison may be for 62 (first year) or 61 (second year localities). The Subcommittee on Housing and Community Development study was based upon staff interviews in 133 CDBG recipient communities located in 36 states and the Commonwealth of Puerto Rico. The Brookings effort has extended over 2 years and provides far more detail. For their detailed discussion of citizen participation, see first Brookings study, pp. 416–496 and the second, pp. 132–152. The congressional study is summarized in Subcommittee on Housing and Community Development Study, pp. 35–36. The two studies are in general agreement in terms of their findings on citizen involvement.

[36] Brookings study (first), p. 420.

[37] Ibid., pp. 424–425.

Brookings research associates were asked whether this statement applied in the first-year application process: *"Citizen participation was influential in terms of the final outcomes contained in the CDBG application."*[38] The associates rated citizen participation as influential without qualification in 18 jurisdictions, as influential to a limited extent in 24 localities, and as having no influence in 18 communities.[39] Clearly, there was a strong effort by communities to have citizens involved in the CDBG decision-making process, and at least to some extent citizens were listened to.

One of the first Brookings report's findings about the influence of citizens is both important and interesting. The study considered various procedures for citizen involvement, including combinations of public hearings, neighborhood meetings, and citizens' advisory committees. The Brookings staff had thought that either stronger requirements, such as advisory committees, or several requirements would make for greater citizen influence. What they found was that "the attitude of local officials, and not so much the procedures set up for citizen participation, was the key factor in determining whether or not citizens' views were significantly reflected in the block grant application."[40] The attitude of local officials was shaped either by an area's past history (e.g., extensive citizen involvement under earlier elected officials) or by the official's own preferences. In the first year (and also in the second year), purely procedural devices did not seem important.

Citizen influence may be exerted on both (a) how CDBG funds are allocated to geographic areas and groups (distribution); and (b) how projects are developed and run, including the basic issues of efficiency and effectiveness (program substance). Citizen involvement in the first year of CDBG was concerned almost exclusively with the distribution issue. This was hardly surprising, since CDBG funds could support projects in the entire locality, whereas model cities and urban renewal had been targeted on specific areas.

Both Brookings studies found that various neighborhood organizations, some of which were established to get funds from CDBG, were important factors in determining fund distribution. HUD monies did not flow automatically to the disadvantaged groups previously favored under the categorical programs. Moreover, the elaborate structure of model cities that supported participation by citizens in the targeted areas was done away with. The outcome was as we might have expected: Model cities neighborhoods and the disadvantaged in general

[38] Ibid., p. 481, italics in the original.
[39] Ibid., Table 11-11, p. 483.
[40] Ibid., p. 495.

had to share power and funds with other citizens. As the Subcommittee on Housing and Community Development observed

> [The] National Urban League, the National Association for the Advancement of Colored People and the Center for Community Change [criticized] the procedures used by particular localities to provide an opportunity for lower income citizens to participate and the extent to which the views of lower income citizens resulted in their obtaining desired activities for their direct benefits.[41]

The new competitiveness raised serious questions. First was the possible conflict with national intent. The House subcommittee pointed out: "Local officials tend to agree that as the citizen participation process becomes more effective it will strengthen the tendency to spread limited CDBG funds across a wider segment of the community and tend to divert funds from the most needy areas."[42] The competitiveness also posed a threat to comprehensive planning. The first Brookings report observed

> [I]n responding to the varied demands of citizens, local officials (especially) elected officials) gained increased prominence and this, in turn, led to an overall increase in the level of citizen interest and involvement in local affairs. At the same time, the first-year experience suggests that extensive citizen participation may work at cross purposes with the objective of broader, more comprehensive planning for community development. A general pattern that emerges is that the greater the number of citizens or groups participating, the more varied their demands and the more fragmented the effort necessary to satisfy these demands.[43]

The second Brookings report put matters succinctly in stating that "at the level of program benefits, field analyses continued to show the tendency of citizens *and* legislatures to *spread* program benefits."[44]

Citizen influence with local officials is highly dependent on the political power of citizens in general and the relative distribution of power among various citizens groups. But other factors may also be important. Two critical ones—the stages of the planning process where citizens are involved and the level of the citizens' knowledge—well may be related to or support political power. As to the former, the second Brookings study observed

> An important aspect of the approach local governments took to citizen participation involves the number of stages in the application process at which opportunities for participation were provided. In the first year we identified three such stages: (1)

---

[41] Subcommittee on Housing and Community Development study, p. 35.

[42] Ibid., p. 36.

[43] Brookings study (first), p. 487.

[44] Brookings study (second), p. 113, italics added.

prior to preparation of a draft application, (2) during the drafting process, and (3) in connection with consideration by the local legislature. In the second year timing-of-involvement patterns remained largely the same as in the first year. . . . The primary pattern was that of participation before and after, but not during the drafting phase itself. There are implications for citizen influence in this finding. We found that when citizens were able to participate on an ongoing basis, especially during the critical drafting process, they were often more influential than might otherwise be expected. When participation consisted of making suggestions before the draft was prepared and/or commenting later on the finished product, the citizen role tended to be advisory. According to the associates, this advisory capacity was a preference expressed by many local officials. The comment of the associate for St. Louis County is typical. "The citizen participation component was taken seriously by local officials and the citizens advisory committee went through all the necessary motions, but *advisory* is the watchword. The buck stops at the supervisor's office and he and his staff—especially the community development staff—had the last word."[45]

Technical assistance may play a role in either distributional or substantive issues. As to the former, some groups will simply have more technical resources than others so that it may be necessary to help the deficient groups if there is to be a fair exchange in the distribution process. However, the first Brookings study found that only 6 of the 62 jurisdictions provided technical help to citizens.[46] The second year report claimed more technical assistance but did not elaborate.[47]

It is on questions of program substance that technical assistance looms even larger. As the Subcommittee on Housing and Community Development has observed

Adequate technical assistance was said to be essential to the success of the citizen participation process. According to local officials interviewed, this was often insufficient in the first CDBG program year. Many communities have taken steps toward improving this and have designed programs wherein paid technical staff is provided to neighborhood groups in addition to printed materials describing the community development program. Local officials reacted positively to the suggestion that HUD should take a more active role in providing information and guidance for CDBG recipients and potential recipients in carrying out effective citizen participation programs.[48]

Once the issue turns to program substance, citizens may be at a distinct disadvantage in terms of technical issues in trying to influence both the local officials responsible for CDBG funds and the HUD field staffs who administer local government activities.

The 1977 CDBG legislation provides more support for citizen par-

---

[45] Ibid., pp. 149–150.
[46] Brookings study (first), pp. 446–448.
[47] Brookings study (second), pp. 150–151.
[48] Subcommittee on Housing and Community Development study, p. 36.

ticipation by "requiring recipient communities to submit a written citizen participation plan and by expanding the citizen's role to include participation in program evaluation as well as the development of the application."[49] We have no information on the effect of these changes. But clearly, they reinforce the seriousness of direct citizen involvement in CDBG and make the need for technical assistance even more important.

ADMINISTRATIVE AND SUPPORT DOMAIN FUNCTIONS UNDER CDBG

The next several sections will look at the particular functions set forth in Chapter 1 and examine the way in which field staffs in particular, but also to some extent other elements of the administrative and support domain, respond or fail to respond to these needs. As in the DOL chapter, the larger headings of approval, information development and analysis, and technical assistance functions will be used. Again, the uneven treatment of functions reflects the extent to which certain functions were considered earlier in this chapter not an assessment of their relative importance.

Approval Function

Regulation and guideline writing in HUD is highly centralized. The agency does not provide institutionalized channels for field input and has shown little concern for problems stemming from regional variation. At the same time, HUD's organizational problems, which have produced poor headquarters' control over field staffs and ineffective communication with them, have made for a goodly amount of field discretion in interpretation of headquarters' directives.

In part, discretion was forced on field staff. Because regulations often were not interpreted by the central office when the region or area office requested clarification, the field staff was backed into the position of providing its own interpretation for regulations and guidelines. The headquarters weaknesses also allowed strong regional offices to exercise discretion when they wanted to. This lack of uniformity in applying regulations has led to the major problem HUD is facing in the courts as localities are in effect forcing HUD to clarify and standardize its operating rules.

[49] Brookings study (second), pp. 111–112.

The grant or plan approval function is the responsibility of the area office. However, the authority is not a direct delegation from the secretary to the field to approve applications or modifications, but must "pass through" the regional office. This extra layer in the decision-making process produces delays, duplication of efforts, and distortion of messages.

Information Development and Analysis Function

HUD focuses much attention on monitoring its own operations. One of the regional office's main responsibilities is to monitor the area office to ensure that it is effectively carrying out its implementation activities. Also, teams from headquarters regularly go out into the field and look at both the regional office and the area office operations, checking both directions in order to find out an area office's perceptions of its regional office and vice versa. The area office has the responsibility of monitoring the local governments. Having adopted an extremely laissez faire attitude toward local governments during the first year, HUD later tightened up particularly in procedural requirements. However, attention tends to settle on minor compliance questions still disregarding some of the major confrontations that increasingly are leading to litigation.

Monitoring by the area office involves checking local governments on a regular basis to make sure that activities included in the grant application are eligible and that citizen participation, affirmative action, equal opportunities, and environmental review requirements are being followed. There is great variation among area offices as to the methods used in monitoring. Even within a region, different area offices may show some differences in their checking approach. Within Region IX, for instance, the San Francisco area office monitors through area representatives who have regular contact with local CDBG administrators. The area representatives are generalists who look at all facets of the CDBG program in their monitoring capacity. The Los Angeles area office, on the other hand, sends out a team of monitors representing the various programmatic emphases of the area office divisions on regular visits to the local government units. Area offices generally feel that monitoring is built in by their continuing contact with program operators so that a representative is always in a position of knowing if a particular program is in danger of a compliance error.

The regional office is responsible for checking on the area offices and generally overseeing their administration. The task is sometimes referred to as supervision, and many area offices, as we have indicated, feel that the regions consistently try to expand their super-visory activities. The regional office checks on the operation and ad-ministration of the area offices and recommends corrective action when it finds problems within the area office domain but has no check-ing contact with local government.

Unlike DOL, HUD encourages evaluation by field offices. During the New Federalism period, a regional administrator in Region IX and his ARA for program planning and evaluation led the way in attempts to lend credibility and sophistication to HUD's evaluative process. Relying on the assertiveness and initiative of the administrator, Region IX reassembled its regional office staff resources by pulling people from programmatic offices and from the area office in order to build a relatively high-powered evaluation effort. Since the beginning of the CDBG program, Region IX's PP&E office has conducted major surveys each year to determine how effectively the program is working in its entitlement cities. The personal style and motivation of the Region IX administrator and his staff were a key component in developing an ef-fective evaluation unit. However, HUD headquarters has been respon-sive to the building of strong evaluation units in other regions and has even provided special funds to carry on evaluation studies to examine specific areas, such as rehabilitation and relocation.

HUD has increased greatly the program and financial data report-ing burden on local government with the advent of CDBG. Under the categorical programs, the complaint from the operators was the stag-gering amount of front-end work required to produce a grant applica-tion. Some of these complexities have been ironed out for the grant ap-plication, but in their place, HUD has managed to develop detailed and complicated reporting forms.

However, these reporting demands appear to yield information that is generally of limited importance, and what is of value is not well used. For example, there is virtually no feedback for cities and coun-ties. This poor development and use of reporting information in the field is part of a larger HUD information problem. As Coopers & Lybrand report

> Several respondents expressed concern about the fragmented and generally manual system for delivery of management information at HUD: no comprehensive status reports, no historical record, and no managerial control. *The feeling is that the Head-quarters makes no effort to assemble information that will allow it to gain an understanding of what goes on programmatically in the Field.*[50]

The effects of this information breakdown at the regional and area of-fice are obvious. Perhaps the most common complaint leveled by local

---

[50] Coopers & Lybrand, March report, p. 42, italics added.

officials is that information is impossible to come by through HUD sources. In summary, Coopers & Lybrand observed

> One of HUD's major difficulties in both program management and control and overall management at the Headquarters level is the lack of management information. *Although there exists a large volume of data flow from the Field to Headquarters and a great number of HUD personnel are engaged in the gathering, coding and compilation of data, there is generally insufficient information on which to base managerial and policy decisions.*[51]

In the area of policy analysis and research, as in the other information functions, HUD has consistently moved toward the development of regional capacity for analytic work. HUD mandates both program planning and evaluation offices at the regional level. However, in some regions these offices are focused on the internal management of the region not on external program analysis and evaluation. Again, a marked exception has been Region IX, where the regional administrator saw the use of expert information as of such importance to his operation that he developed a strong policy analysis–evaluation unit. There seems to be an increasing encouragement on the part of the central office for development of this kind of regional capacity either on an ongoing basis or for specialized studies.

Technical Assistance Function

When HUD started putting its housing and community development legislation into the field, area offices were not delegated any technical assistance role. The regional office, to be sure, had certain assisting functions, but they were strictly limited to helping the area office rather than local governments. There was a strong "hands-off" emphasis in the federal mission. At the point of our last interviews, the provision of technical assistance and training for local government was still not viewed by HUD as a major function. Area offices provided assistance only when it was officially requested. This does not mean that there is not informal help given by responsive area representatives, but the normal course of action appears to be to wait until the local government has gotten itself into some predicament, is desperate, and comes to HUD for help.

There are some aggressive area offices that have taken the initiative in providing technical assistance and training. However, even in an area office noted for its assertiveness, the head of CP&D indicated that his office had not offered cities alternative strategies they might consider in trying to address their community development needs. This

---

[51] Ibid., p. 61, italics in the original.

staff member felt that his office had been more responsive during the categorical days in giving technical assistance and now was doing very little in the way of training, particularly in regard to helping organize rehabilitation programs and affirmative action programs.

Many people both in local CDBG administration and in the regions feel that HUD is making a mistake with this approach. A number of the areas that are involved in the CDBG legislation, particularly in regard to housing, are extremely complicated and local governments could well use advice in handling these areas to their advantage. Those cities that have had experience in model cities or other categorical programs may have the expertise on their staffs to deal with housing associated programs and comprehensive, integrated planning, but many others do not. There seems to be a growing desire on the part of both HUD and local staffs for HUD to take the initiative in offering assistance and preventing serious problems before they develop.

In many regions, however, the level of assistance and training that HUD could provide is considered grossly inadequate by CDBG administrators. The lack of competence combined with major deficiencies in regard to up-to-date information leaves big-city people asking HUD: "What can you possibly do for us?" Some of these more capable, experienced administrators would rather see HUD facilitating an exchange of information and advice among local governmental units than trying to do the training themselves. Many cities and urban counties have developed very sophisticated systems for administering their CDBG grants, but most of them have devised these on their own without any help from HUD. In terms of useful technical assistance, training, and capacity building, with few exceptions, HUD receives low marks from local government.

5 AGENCY STRUCTURAL REORGANIZATION: THE HUD EXAMPLE

The incoming Carter administration underscored Harold Seidman's observation that "reorganization has become almost a religion in Washington."[1] Reorganization in these terms is being used most broadly to include major efforts at overall government redirection or reform. Rufus Miles has noted "Organization is especially important at the federal level in expressing the nation's priorities, in allocating resources, in attracting its most competent leader–executives to key positions, and in accomplishing the purposes of the President, the Congress, and the body politic."[2] Here organization sets the power distribution and hence the direction of commitment and policy. Thus, the creation of the new Department of Energy or the establishment of a separate Department of Education crystallizes national intent.

Reorganization may also aim at broad reform, such as attempts to cut back overall federal staff or restructure the federal civil service. Such reforms affect the entire executive branch or at least major portions of it. These broad uses of the term *reorganization* have led Kauf-

---

[1] Cited in David S. Brown, " 'Reforming' the Bureaucracy: Some Suggestions for the New President," *Public Administration Review*, March–April 1977, p. 165. The discussion will be restricted for the bulk of this chapter to public sector reorganizations but corporate structure (and strategy) will be considered briefly in the final section in terms of the relevance of the concepts to government structural changes.

[2] Rufus E. Miles, Jr., "Considerations for a President Bent on Reorganization," *Public Administration Review*, March–April 1977, p. 155.

man to claim that "the calculus of reorganization is essentially the calculus of politics itself."[3]

But with such breadth, reorganization becomes a cover word for any agency change. We use *structural reorganization* more narrowly to describe efforts within a single agency that alter functions, responsibilities, or staff assignments but that do not change the agency's overall mission or reduce personnel on board. This means existing staff may undergo status and location shifts, but there will be no reduction of existing staff.

Either structural reorganization alone or that associated with minor staff reductions have tremendous appeal. First, they are direct. It is the agency's own organization—on its own home ground. Moreover, structural changes usually do not require congressional approval and may raise little or no White House interest. Second, organizational flaws are easy to find. Over any reasonably long period of time, bureaucratic compromises of internal battles, arrangements to satisfy Congress, and personal efforts to move ahead (e.g., the creation of another administrative layer to accommodate a promotion) seem certain to produce an "attackable" organization chart, one that can be criticized as illogical or irrational. Third, there is a continuing belief that rational organizational design will help management and staff do better. If only the organizational structure made more sense, management and staff would be able to improve agency performance.

Structural reorganization alone or that associated with minor staff reductions is the typical kind of federal agency reorganization. Incoming political executives (particularly when there is a change in administration or agency head) or existing management decide to improve agency performance and look for means to do it. The agency's overall mission is set out by Congress, so it is taken as given. Then the executives discover, if they do not already know it, that (a) major staff cuts have inordinate bureaucratic and political costs; and (b) replacing staff by firing one person and hiring another in any significant quantity is virtually impossible. The option of firing the bottom 10% of the staff and replacing them will not be an available option. A few new people may be brought in, but most, if not all, of the career civil servants there at the start of the reorganization will be there at its conclusion. So concern turns toward structural modifications that leave mission alone and do not fire the staff on board.

Structural changes, however, are not necessarily cosmetic. They

[3] Herbert Kaufman, "Reflections on Administrative Reorganization," in Joseph A. Pechman (editor), *Setting National Priorities: The 1978 Budget*, Brookings Institution, Washington, D.C., 1977, p. 406.

can involve reallocations of staff, functions, and responsibilities; alterations in the way functions are performed; a recasting of job descriptions; modifications in personnel procedures, including performance and promotion standards; and a redrawing of organizational charts that alter bureaucratic layers and relationships. In part because staff is so hard to fire, structural changes may bring a goodly amount of staff movement, including shuffling people around to get them out of the way. The structural reorganization also is likely to redistribute power among agency bureaus and between headquarters and the field, including changes in how and where functions are executed.

The structural changes that appear deceptively easy to make on paper can open a Pandora's box of problems. The magnitude of an overall structural reorganization is almost overwhelming, even in the medium-sized social agencies. HUD or DOL administer billions of dollars of funds each year in a wide array of programs with thousands of employees located in Washington and in the field. Both agencies operate through a "tall" hierarchy with countless layers stretching between the political executives at the top and the field. Implementing a major structural reorganization requires the same kind of effort needed to put new legislation in the field.

The agency organizational structure sets out in formal terms the activities to be done, who is to do them, and what resources will be made available to execute the assigned activities. Turf and status are both at stake in any structural reorganization that shifts people and power. As Havemann has observed about President Carter's reorganization efforts across agencies:

> In its baldest form, turf is the desire to exercise power for its own sake. . . . If it's not always clear when turf is the real force behind an argument for or against a particular reorganization, the President's Reorganization Project has learned one lesson: substantive arguments rarely fail to coincide with self-interest.[4]

The issues of turf as an organizational and status as a personal phenomenon apply whether or not the reorganization is among agencies or within a bureau in a single agency. Organizational units do not like to give up resources; people in those units do not yield personal power easily. *An agency may face no more difficult kind of implementation than that of a reorganization where it must deal with its own bureaucracy, which has both inside knowledge and power, including the staying power of the career civil service.*

---

[4] Joel Havemann, "Carter's Reorganization Plans—Scrambling for Turf," *National Journal,* 20 May 1978, p. 788.

There is an even more basic problem: Agency deficiencies that appear to flow from an inadequate organizational structure often come from management and staff weaknesses. In such cases, structural changes can end up as poorly directed searches for sound governance—a scarce commodity not necessarily conjured up by a "rational" organizational design. In the case of management versus structure, causality is likely to flow from management to structure. That is, sound structure per se does not produce either good management or better staff performance and may have little or no effect upon a weak management or on a weak staff that has been moved around but not changed in composition.

Structural reorganization, however, presents itself as a general means available to agency management for trying to gain greater control or to increase agency efficiency and performance. Obvious flaws in the existing institutional structure impel managers toward change—especially if they had no hand in building that structure. Wholesale structural reorganization provides the most immediate device for new political executives to establish power and to show their intent and commitment. New directions can be most directly reflected by reallocating, redefining, and redirecting the responsibilities and functions of the staff and management resources in an organization.

This chapter discusses a major reorganization of HUD in the early Carter administration. The reorganization provides information that supplements the materials presented in the New Federalism case studies in two ways. The Carter administration efforts in effect indicate what was perceived as wrong with the organizational approaches used during the New Federalism period. For example, HUD's *Report on Organizational Assessment*, a document by an agency task force rationalizing the early Carter administration agency reorganization, reveals most clearly the task force's perception of misgovernance occuring during the New Federalism period.[5] Second, the Carter ad-

---

[5] *Report on Organization Assessment*, Department of Housing and Urban Development, Washington, D.C., 1977. The Republican administration, of course, had leaped to the call of reorganization, too. As Downs observes pointedly in discussing the period 1968–1974 after he has introduced the notion of the "Law of Compulsive Innovation" (the desire of new managers to change their predecessors' programs so as to claim credit for their innovative successes): "A corollary of the 'Law of Compulsive Innovation' had an even more drastic impact upon HUD's behavior: *Whenever one party replaces the other in the executive branch, the newcomers have a compulsive desire to reorganize nearly every agency.* Since all human organizations are imperfect, and large bureaucracies are especially subject to inertia and malfunction, it is always easy to justify reorganization as 'required' to improve performance. HUD and FHA were subjected to several overlapping reorganizations that involved both reshuffling functions in

ministration reorganization effort allows examination of structural changes not associated with legislative changes. *This is important, because the New Federalism legislation itself created enough disruption that it is difficult to consider the impact of changes in organization alone.* The Carter administration experience provides us with a broad base for considering major issues of structural reorganization and staff allocation.

One final note before turning to the HUD reorganization: No effort was made by us to follow the reorganization to "final implementation" since that required a longitudinal study extending well beyond the closing date of our fieldwork. In large-scale reorganizations, there generally is a formal announcement of reorganization (a document signed by the secretary) and a timetable for making the proposed changes. When the changes in the timetable have been made, the reorganization will be "in place" in the eyes of the agency. But we conceive of this as the initial implementation effort. Final implementation occurs after working through the organizational problems and some modifications just as is the case with the new legislation.

THE NEW ADMINISTRATION AND
THE OLD ORGANIZATION

The HUD organizational changes that started in 1977 provide an almost classic example of an overall structural reorganization combined with some staff reduction. The HUD structural problems treated in detail in Chapter 4 were well known. Everyone we talked to believed the existing HUD structure stymied communication and control and inhibited performance in the field. Probably if President Ford had been reelected, HUD would have undertaken a major reorganization. With a number of study efforts already completed on organization problems, the base had been laid for major changes in a continuing Republican administration. However, the coming of a new Democratic administration provided more flexibility, because criticisms of past efforts would seem less threatening to the new political executives.

Early in the Carter administration, HUD established an Organization Assessment Group composed entirely of agency headquarters and

---

Washington and creating a whole new decentralized layer of regional offices. The internal confusion generated by these reorganizations had a devastating impact upon HUD's capabilities." Anthony Downs, *Urban Problems and Prospects*, Second Edition, Rand McNally, Chicago, 1976, pp. 98–99, italics in the original. This reorganization effort got confounded in the New Federalism program changes as discussed next.

field staffs and chaired by the under secretary. The group issued a
Report on Organization Assessment dated October 1977. Secretary
Patricia Harris sent out a 12 October memo on reorganization based on
that report.[6]

The Harris memo was the basic decision document that made the
reorganization official. It and the attachments spelled out the initial
details of the restructuring and provided a timetable labeled the "Implementation Schedule." The initial implementation phase was to run
almost 6 months from 10 October 1977 to 20 March 1978. During this
period, new organizational manuals had to be written, new job descriptions spelled out, and people moved physically.

Staff changes were not discussed explicitly in the Harris memo and
attachments, although it was clear the restructuring would involve
significant movements of staff. Beyond this but without elaboration,
the Implementation Schedule at four places used that most dreaded of
all terms to the bureaucrat—reduction-in-force (RIF). People were to be
fired. Since the Carter administration was so reorganization oriented,
RIFs became a problem across much of the executive branch. Although
staff reductions have been defined as outside the scope of structural
reorganization per se, we cannot avoid considering them to some extent.

The *Report on Organization Assessment* is of particular interest for
our purposes. First, it is unusually candid in its criticism as it discusses
how agency deficiencies were perceived from the inside, at the point of
transition from one administration to another. Second, the report
presents in detail both the rationale behind agency reorganization decisions and the expected organizational behavior envisioned after the
restructuring.

There are two main themes in the report. The first and most prominent concerns deficient organizational structure. Later, the second
theme of management weaknesses emerges. In it, we find a clear ar-
ticulation of the basic issue of management versus structure that asks if
organizational structure changes alone make a difference.

BASIC STRUCTURAL CHANGES

The HUD organizational restructuring effort focused most explicitly on lines of communication and authority, a particularly pressing
problem for a tall hierarchical organization with extensive field offices.

---

[6] The work by the HUD task force is a 51-page document, hereafter generally referred to as the *Report*. The 12 October three-page memorandum (Harris memo) signed
by the secretary also had several attachments.

Good communications back and forth between headquarters and the field raises issues both of adequate administrative and technical design for the communications network (e.g., routing procedures, reporting forms) and of clear lines of authority. HUD in the period under study provided a prime example of deficiencies in both. The three-tier organizational structure, which had one management level too many, often made basic communication between top and bottom difficult if not impossible. But even when technical problems did not block the message, conflicting and counteracting messages from different program assistant secretaries or other headquarters elements could leave those in the field, including the federal field staffs, with no clear idea of what headquarters wanted. The bulk of the reorganization effort was aimed at these deficiencies.

Strengthening the Program Assistant Secretaries

No message in the *Report on Organization Assessment* is more clear than that of the need to strengthen the hand of the program assistant secretaries over the regional administrators. Although the Coopers & Lybrand study indicated a mismatch between the program assistant secretaries and regional administrators with the latter being at a distinct disadvantage, the HUD Organization Assessment Group either saw the imbalance going the other way or else felt that direct headquarters control outweighed other considerations. The report states: "The authority of Assistant Secretaries to override the direction of Regional Administrators should be clearly published. This should indicate that Headquarters may take over management and direction of poorly performing field offices when determined by Assistant Secretaries."[7] There is no specific statement to this effect in the Harris memo. But the clear intent of writers of the report was to produce "Assistant Secretary control of performance"[8] with unambiguous accountability for the field effort lodged with these people.

The Harris memo reflected the report's thrust. It granted program assistant secretaries the following authority: (a) to make personnel selections for key area office vacancies; (b) to determine program training needs and attendance; (c) to receive requests for waivers directly from the field; (d) to deal directly with area offices without the interference of assistant regional administrators; and (e) to set out "program policy, objectives, priorities, and operating procedures [from which] deviations will not be permitted without headquarters ap-

---

[7] *Report*, p. 32.
[8] Ibid.

proval."[9] The main direction of these is to link the program assistant secretaries much more directly to the area office's housing and community planning and development divisions without regional office involvement.

Changes in Regional and Area Offices

If there was one point of agreement among almost all HUD critics, it was that the regional office created major—probably *the* major—problems of communication and authority in the period before the 1977 reorganization. The report observed: "The Department's three-tier organization includes an unnecessary layer (the Regional Office) which causes delays in processing and creates confusion in lines of authority."[10] The Coopers & Lybrand study went even further to point out that the regional office could well be eliminated, since (as quoted earlier) "the tasks of the Regional Administrators and the ARAs are managerial impossibilities."[11] That study claimed that over time "there is a strong argument for reducing the Regional function to ministerial" which would "[remove] the Region from the interpret, monitor, and evaluate role."[12] This would leave the regional administrator functioning mainly as HUD's ambassador to the region without major operational or managerial responsibilities.

To reduce the regional office to a ministerial role, Coopers & Lybrand recommended that evaluation and monitoring be made a part of the HUD headquarters activities and that the bulk of other activities then in the regional offices be put in strong area offices. The HUD reorganization goes in this direction by reducing the scope and staff of the regional offices and by increasing the size and activities of the area offices while tieing them much more explicitly to the programmatic assistant secretaries. The restructuring is intended to "*remove Regional Offices as an operational 'layer' in the program process.*"[13]

The most significant changes in the regional offices involved the assistant regional administrators. Before the reorganization, the ARAs for housing and for community planning and development had responsibilities for technical and program guidance and interpretation and the technical evaluation of area offices. Those activities interposed

---

[9] Harris memo attachments, p. 1.

[10] *Report*, p. 29.

[11] Coopers & Lybrand, *Recommendations for HUD Organizational Structure*, Department of Housing and Urban Development, Washington, D.C., March 1976, p. 117.

[12] Ibid., pp. 133, 117.

[13] Harris memo attachments, p. 2, italics in the original.

them between the program assistant secretaries and the housing and CP&D division chiefs in the area offices. Technical and programmatic activities now "will be handled directly between subordinate field offices [housing and CP&D divisions in the area office] and headquarters."[14] Authority flows straight from the program assistant secretary to the area offices. ARAs no longer have any line responsibilities or authority. They are the big losers of turf and status.

The regional offices in the old organizational arrangement appeared much overstaffed. The excess staff ended up involving itself in routine operational issues that should not have concerned them. The reorganization shifted significant numbers of regional office personnel, particularly from the housing and community development activities, both up to headquarters and down to the area offices.

Area offices were materially strengthened in the restructuring, with their heads now being called area office managers "to reflect their increased responsibilities for management of programs in the new pattern."[15] The Harris memo attachments go on to say that "Area Offices have final sign-off authority on almost all program operations. They are the focal point for program integration at the operating level."[16] According to our interviews with HUD officials, the area office managers were expected to be able to handle most of the program and technical issues that come up in the field. The direct ties to headquarters for technical and program guidance are intended to facilitate rapid turnaround time when questions arise so that the area offices can give quick answers and responses in the field. In these terms, HUD describes the area offices as highly "decentralized" in being able to treat most matters in the field.

At the same time, the area offices, particularly the housing and the community planning and development divisions, look much more like clear extensions of headquarters. The implications of the power shift to the program assistant secretary becomes clear, since it is he or she, rather than the area office manager or the regional administrator, who appoints the heads of the key program divisions in the area office. The direct line for technical guidance extends from headquarters to these divisions, with the program assistant secretaries establishing policies, priorities, and operating procedures from which, as the Harris memo stated, "deviations will not be permitted without headquarters approval."

In sum, the changes discussed thus far appear to strengthen (a) the

---

[14] Ibid.
[15] Ibid., p. 3.
[16] Ibid., no page number.

authority and capacity of the program assistant secretaries to make all major decisions about program objectives, priorities, and operating procedures, to communicate them directly with area offices, *and* to enforce these decisions on federal field staffs; and (b) the capacity of the area offices to *execute* these decisions.

The structural reorganization then interjects the regional office into this clean line authority relationship. As the Harris memo attachments observe

> *Regional Offices will provide managerial supervision.* . . . The elimination of routine program operations from Regional Offices will permit increased emphasis of Regional Administrators on their functions of monitoring and evaluating program management, carrying out Secretarial policy in the region, meshing HUD functions in the field, and balancing social and program goals in the administration of HUD programs.[17]

In the HUD hierarchy, there is direct management authority flowing from the secretary to the regional administrator to the area office manager. At the same time, the regional administrators, and to some extent the area office managers especially on housing matters, seem to be expected to keep their distance from program and technical questions, which are the domain of the program assistant secretaries and the area office division chiefs.

However, a goodly amount of the confusion and potential conflict between the programmatic and general line authorities discussed in Chapter 4 seem to have remained in (or crept back into) the new organizational structure. In discussing this phenomenon, one of our headquarters interviewees offered management of housing production as an excellent example of the potential problems. Housing and Urban Development has placed a great deal of emphasis upon housing production, with responsibility for such production in the field running from the area office manager to the regional administrator directly to the secretary. Or at least, this is the linkage for general line management. But programs belong to the assistant secretaries. In the face of low housing production, either the regional administrator or the area office manager can say, quite legitimately one might observe, that he or she really cannot do much about the head of the area office housing division, since that individual was appointed by the program assistant secretary and takes directions from headquarters. Responsibility and authority remain difficult to tie together in HUD.

---

[17] Ibid., p. 1, italics in the original.

What Is the New, Improved Regional Office Expected to Do?

What are the regional administrator and the regional office really intended to do in the new organizational structure? Early in the reorganization effort there was speculation that the office as a major entity would soon wither away. In the first go-around, deep reductions were made in regional staff, and the forecast was that the next one would go to the bone. The regional administrator would then be responsible for ministerial activities and certain housekeeping functions for which there are economies of scale (e.g., supplies, travel, and so on).

However, the detailed guidelines that elaborate upon the decision documents yield a quite different picture. The *Regional Office Organization: A HUD Handbook* issued in January 1978 sets out 12 responsibilities for regional administrators, giving them a host of activities including these:

> Ensuring that programs are functioning in accord with policies, criteria and procedures established by the Assistant Secretaries and that quality results are achieved while production targets and objectives are met.
>
> Taking immediate corrective action wherever problems are found, Headquarters' policies, standards, or procedures are not being followed, or the quality or timeliness of work is sub-standard.
>
> Evaluating, reporting, and making recommendations with respect to the effectiveness of overall management performance of HUD program within the Region. Making recommendations to Assistant Secretaries regarding the short-term and long-term need for changes in program structure.[18]

Anyone reading these responsibilities for regional administrators would have a great deal of trouble detecting that they are now not to be concerned with programmatic issues.

The argument concerning the continuing regional office role that came from our headquarters interviews conducted shortly after the reorganization announcement was that the retention of regional administrators in the authority line was mainly for span of control reasons. The 50 plus area offices would be difficult to administer without an intermediate layer. However, it should be noted that such an intermediate layer of managers could be headquarters based, possibly with such managers in both housing and CP&D to serve the

---

[18] *Regional Office Organization: A HUD Handbook*, U.S. Department of Housing and Urban Development, Washington, D.C., January 1978, p. 2–1.

program assistant secretaries in supervising the area offices. This straightforward administrative justification hardly seems sufficient.

Another explanation is that the regional administrators and their offices are intended to be buffers between the program assistant secretaries and the area office managers and perhaps to some extent between the secretary and the program assistant secretaries. As to the former, despite a great deal of rhetoric, particularly in the *Report on Organization Assessment*, about program assistant secretaries spelling out clearly their policies and objectives, the problem of clashes between housing and CP&D assistant secretaries seems endemic in HUD. No reorganization per se is likely to end the conflicts that made for headquarters battles and field confusion. Relatedly, the basic power problems in HUD go all the way up to the secretary so that the regional administrator can also be seen as the secretary's independent voice in the field with capacity to "break the circuit," when necessary, between the program assistant secretaries and the area offices.

There is another explanation that fits well both with our notions on the effects of history and with the often noted staying power of bureaucracy. In our interviews with mid level staff at headquarters, we found the strong view that top agency officials really wanted to do away with the regional offices completely. They did not because of potentially high political–bureaucratic costs. Such costs could occur both because the regional administrators are seen as political plums and because lopping off an entire layer of an agency can devastate morale, as will be discussed later.

Given life, the regional administrators took steps to try to increase their scant power, including banding together to gain the advantage of speaking as a cohesive group. HUD's usual bureaucratic problems, including the infighting among assistant secretaries, continued to plague the early implementation activities. The regional administrators were relatively free of this taint, and arguments for their buffer role surely were strengthened.

What happened with the handbook entitled *Regional Office Organization* issued in January 1978 well illustrates the bureaucratic fluidity in which the regional administrators regained some of their lost power. According to our interviews, the early draft of the handbook circulated within the agency was based upon the beginning perception of the weak regional administrator. Comments on that draft, however, reflected the shifting view that the regional administrator should play a more prominent role. So the rewritten final version of the handbook from which we have quoted revives the regional administrator's role. Even if we discount the tendency of those writing government guidelines or handbooks to overstate responsibilities, the handbook surely evidences a regional administrator far stronger than the one depicted in the *Report on Organization Assessment* and the Harris memo and attachments. As one staff member in a regional office said: "If the Regional Administrator has less power, he doesn't know it." We see in short a good example of the ability of the "wounded" segment of an organization to fight back at least toward partial restoration.

Perhaps the "best" explanation for what has happened in HUD is that we are seeing the result of the agency's groping toward a resolution of its basic conflicts. The search for a viable role for the regional administrator and his office is part of this larger search. There is no question HUD wanted the regional office out of daily operations and moved toward this goal in word and deed. HUD documents state repeatedly that the reorganization "deletes Regional Office operational and technical program guidance functions."[19] That message is brought home most dramatically in taking the ARAs completely out of the line of authority and by cutting the staffs. At the same time, as will be discussed later, HUD wanted better management and the regional administrator, as cut back, offered a possible place for such improvement. The dilemma is that management cannot be separated entirely from programs. As the quotes from the regional office handbook make so clear, the regional administrator as manager must have some authority to get into programs. HUD is seeking a delicate balance that includes a viable role for regional offices in social agency governance.

MANAGEMENT VERSUS STRUCTURE

At the heart of the *Report on Organization Assessment* is the recognition of the central need for better management in HUD. Admittedly, the organization of that report is curious in that managerial concerns that are so basic are not set out explicitly until a final two-page appendix entitled "Organization Assessment Group's General Comments on HUD Problems."[20] But then the extent of mismanagement is summarized in no uncertain terms. It is worth quoting entirely the statement entitled "Management Considerations":

> Many of the problems that have surfaced are more managerial than structural in nature and these problems should be addressed along with any structural changes.

[19] The quote is found under a heading "Significant Changes," on the transmittal page dated 16 January 1978, which accompanied the regional office reorganization handbook cited in footnote 18.

[20] *Report*, p. 50.

Correcting these managerial problems may be of equal, if not more, importance in improving the total effectiveness of the Department.

This emphasis on better management certainly does not argue against necessary organization change. Nonetheless, reorganization is no panacea, and without improved management no organization will achieve the performance desired.

A critical management problem affecting the Department in its recent history has been a shortfall in leadership, competence and timely policy decision-making by many of its key managers at all levels.

As missions changed and the Department's roles vis-à-vis the clientele it served were altered under the previous Administration, these shortfalls have been perceived as largely organizational. We believe that strong, competent leadership at all management levels along with timely and lucid delineation of operating policies and procedures, will go a long way towards alleviating these problems.

It is also vital that channels of communication throughout the organization be clarified. Fully open and candid communication up and down the organization should be strongly encouraged.

Another significant problem is the Department's staffing of management positions. Selection should be made on the basis of integrity, demonstrated ability and experience. There is also a need for an effective personnel performance evaluation process which is used to remove managers who fail to perform as office heads or in other key positions, and to nurture and reward high level performance.[21]

Seldom do we find stated so sharply the basic issue of whether changes in organizational structure such as those in HUD will have much impact on agency performance in the field *without better management.*

HUD wanted both better structure and improved management. It made little sense to leave HUD in organizational disarray. The report recommended and Secretary Harris endorsed structural changes aimed at reducing obvious organizational blockages and strengthening the lines of authority and communication. Both the heads of the regional and area offices were recast as managers. (The latter even got the word in their official title.) However, it was far from clear that much thought had been given to what the newly designated managers were to do. Simply calling them managers in the decision documents and spelling out a number of tasks in the region and area office handbooks that require managerial skills for their successful performance did not transform new or continuing regional and area office administrators into the managers that HUD desired.[22]

Again, the Organization Assessment Group made the case most vividly when it observed

The Department has never definitely set forth the management principles and practices that it expects its supervisors to follow. . . . The lack of a set of principles and practices for HUD managers manifests itself in the following ways:

[21] Ibid., pp. 50–51.

[22] Regional administrators are political appointments who must answer a number of political demands. Managerial skills hardly are uppermost in the minds of the various politicians and interest groups concerned with the appointments.

—Managers who tend to by-pass the "chain-of-command."
—Supervisors with weak human relations skills.
—Rewards to managers and supervisors for "doing their own thing" instead of working constructively within the organization.[23]

When it comes to recommendations, however, the report is limited to comments about developing a management philosophy as a basis for selection, training, and evaluation.

We may recall that the DOL–ETA structure that emerged during the New Federalism period is similar to the newly reorganized HUD. Moreover, not only does ETA look fairly good on paper, DOL lacks the tension and conflict of competing assistant secretaries since ETA is the dominant activity in the field. But DOL has had severe problems of implementation and administration in the field, too. Interestingly enough, in our interviews we found that local staffs were much more critical of DOL than of HUD in terms of field operations.

A sound organizational structure moves the agency to a starting point for reasonable performance but itself does not bring better performance. In the case of communications, for example, a decent communications network and relatively clear lines of authority provide a basis for sending and receiving messages with an acceptable degree of accuracy. Whether communications will flow both ways or whether the messages sent will be useful is not a question addressed by organizational structure per se. Such a statement simply recognizes that organizational structure is the servant of management, not the opposite. Given reasonably competent managers and a commitment to management, organizational changes may provide critical help, a point addressed shortly.

STAFF MORALE

Structural changes that do not bring staff reductions sometimes appear simply as orderly rearrangings of organizational boxes to foster better performance. But, except in the rare case where everybody benefits in an expansionary move, changes that shift personnel and redistribute power threaten turf and status. Even without actual reductions in force, the specter of such cuts permeates the atmosphere of an agency. After pointing out that "staff morale is at an extremely low level," the report goes on to observe

Since 1970 there have been frequent reorganizations in the field. Following the 1970 decentralization, which was extremely traumatic, there have been further

---

[23] *Report,* p. 23.

reorganizations including regionalization of some functions, the realignment of the Area Offices and the creation of full service housing offices. These have resulted in RIFs [reduction in force], forced relocations and changes in job status, all of which have had an adverse effect on morale.

Frequent changes in the overall philosophy of the Department, unrealistic goal setting, program procedures that appear geared more to assuring failure than success, rapid turnover in top staff (particularly Housing), downgrading actions, and Inspector General audits perceived as searches for intentional personal wrongdoings have also affected morale in a negative way.[24]

Indeed, reorganizations had come so fast in HUD and agency morale was so low, that Coopers & Lybrand recommended postponing major changes in the near term to avoid continued trauma for agency staff.

In 1977–1978 HUD reorganization, which went beyond structural changes to actual staff reductions, raised severe morale problems. A 30 January 1978 *Washington Post* article by Kathy Sawyer entitled "Federal Staffs are Fearful of Shake-up Plans," which treated the administration-wide reorganization efforts, quoted a HUD employee as saying: "We keep saying around here that things can't get any worse—but things keep getting worse. . . . The gloom is so thick you can almost see it, and people are walking around like zombies." Overall morale within the executive branch became such a problem that President Carter moved to end all firings and demotions stemming from reorganization. Mike Causey reported in a 15 December 1977 *Washington Post* article: "President Carter has approved a plan that would prohibit federal government agencies from firing any employee as a result of efforts to reorganize the bureaucracy. The plan would also restore grade and pay levels to thousands of employees who already have been demoted this year in various routine shifts."

Even if a reorganization states that there will be no RIFs and no demotions in grade, few restructurings will not involve people being shifted around, with power and status being lost. But unless the political executives are willing to promise only cosmetic shifts, there is little they can say to convince people that personnel actions will not hurt. This would appear to be especially true in an agency such as HUD where repeated reorganization has already made for low morale.

The recommended solutions for the problem of extremely low staff morale made in the HUD report bring out another aspect of the dilemma of structural reorganizations: When an organization is in trouble, what appear to be problems of organizational structure may be breakdowns in the most fundamental kinds of staff or management behavior. Consider these recommendations:

[24] Ibid., p. 33.

Staff should be made to feel they are retained for their knowledge and ability, that they are part of a team, that they will be evaluated fairly on their performance and then they, and their colleagues, will be rewarded or penalized based on that performance. . . .

Assistant Secretaries should visit field activities more frequently and should be available to and consult with more employees during such visits. . . .

Highlight accomplishments of the Department and various field offices in a more positive way by various methods including increased coverage in HUD publications.[25]

The intriguing thing about this list is that these recommended actions were already encouraged either implicitly or explicitly by established agency procedures. But staff morale problems demand leadership and good management—scarce commodities structural changes pari passu do not carry with them.

LIMITS OF STRUCTURAL REORGANIZATION

This final section seeks to put into perspective the potential of structural reorganization as a vehicle for improving an agency's capability to carry out its responsibilities. How good a means of enhancing capability is it? In Donald Warwick's penetrating study of a Department of State reorganization that failed, he warned in the final chapter, entitled "Is There Hope?":

It would be fashionable to end this book on a ringing note of reform: "Cut positions—slash hierarchy—abolish rules—merge overlapping units—streamline the bureaucracy." Such pieties make good copy, but they would be totally insincere as policy recommendations from this study. If there is a single conclusion to be drawn from our observations, it is that a reorganization plan pegged only to considerations of rationality is doomed to failure. Even worse, it will often aggravate the very maladies it was designed to cure.[26]

It should be emphasized that all of Warwick's pieties, save that of cutting positions, fall within our definition of structural reorganization.

Warwick argues that two kinds of change are almost always counterproductive. The first is to make deep cuts in staff—what he labels provocatively "debureaucratization by decimation."[27] The second mistake is to try to impose the changes from the top.

---

[25] Ibid., p. 33. Again, we quote the *Report* extensively because it is such a revealing "insider" discussion.

[26] Donald P. Warwick, *A Theory of Public Bureaucracy: Politics, Personality and Organization in the State Department*, Harvard University Press, Cambridge, Massachusetts, 1975, p. 205.

[27] Ibid., p. 206.

What Warwick has to say about major personnel cuts, we believe applies both to much smaller cutbacks (the "minor" staff adjustments that so often attach to a structural reorganization) and to shifts of people that do not involve actual staff cuts but do decrease the power and status of appreciable numbers of staff. That is, the reaction to just a little bloodletting through staff reductions or the shipping of some employees to undesirable positions seems to elicit much the same bureaucratic behavior as deep cuts. Warwick describes this behavior as follows

> [Such cuts] will lead to even less risk-taking and to a search for organizational defenses against a hostile environment. A reduction in risk-taking will mean that more and more decisions are referred to superiors for approval, with a consequent strain on their information-handling ability. At the same time the battered bureaucrat will seek out other means of protecting himself against the threat of dismissal. One might be more sharply defined rules about "proper" behavior. Another might be a heightened demand for management positions, on the hypothesis that managers or administrators are more durable than ordinary bureaucrats.[28]

Warwick believes that the most basic strategic error of the State Department structural reorganization was to impose the changes from the top. The structural reorganization should be sold to the internal constituencies affected by it. To do this requires that the people be brought in early, consulted about what to do, and finally convinced that the changes are in their interests. As Warwick observes "This may seem an odd suggestion given the earlier documentation of the self-protective tendencies within the State Department. Nevertheless if change is to be made and, more importantly, if it is to endure, it must have strong roots within the agency."[29]

The reorganization needs to make sense both to the agency employees all along the line who must implement that reorganization and to external actors who have a stake in the outcome. The latter may include Congress, employee unions, fund recipients, and anyone else who sees the reorganization as a threat and has power to do something about it. But it is the internal actors who are likely to be the most dangerous, and the ones who draw in the external constituents.

Reorganization must make sense in terms of substantive field implementation issues. But the recommendations must also meet the needs of various internal and external constituencies. Here we might

[28] Ibid., p. 208.
[29] Ibid., p. 210.

speak of internal and external validity of the structural changes, not as statistical but as political–bureaucratic concepts.

Bringing people in early can create problems. The kinds of significant changes that disrupt people's lives and lessen status and power simply may not be saleable. Early negotiating may allow staff to build up defenses or result in endless wrangling. In the long run, however, it might be better to abort the structural reorganization than to spring it on the agency and have it bring endless disruption. Various constituencies in the agency must be sold on reorganization, and working with them before the change appears in final form will aid in the selling.

All that has been written thus far in no way denies that poor structure may inhibit performance. However, sound structure alone does not produce either better management or better staff performance and may have little or no effect upon a weak management or on an inferior staff that has been moved around but not changed in composition. Poor structure may well be a symptom of poor management rather than the cause of problems. As Anthony and Dearden observed "Good people can overcome the defects in a management control system, but even the best management control system will not lead to satisfactory results without good people to operate it."[30] Competent managers may be able to make structural changes over time that speak more directly to problems and are not as disruptive as the large, rapid ones.

It is well to keep in mind the dangers of structural reorganization. There can be a numbing effect when reorganizations threaten either the organization itself or the turf and status of its members. Complex organizations such as social agencies and their subunits generally exhibit both strong resistance to structural changes and a susceptibility to prolonged disturbances when experiencing significant organizational change. Further, frequent reorganization appears to increase problems geometrically. Survival well may drive out almost any other concerns for staff members who feel threatened by current changes or expected future ones. Here we may see the most excessive forms of bureaucratic and organizational pathology.

At the same time it also must be recognized that organizational structure can be an important resource—a critical factor available to management for solving problems that inhibit reaching the objectives of the organization. Indeed, an organization has little chance of high performance if its basic structure is not compatible with what the organization wants to do and how it plans to do it. This notion has been developed in depth in the work on corporate strategy and structure.

[30] Robert N. Anthony and John Dearden, *Management Control Systems*, Third Edition, Richard D. Irwin, Homewood, Illinois, 1976, p. 19.

Chandler in his major work *Strategy and Structure* defines the two key terms of his title as follows

> *Strategy* can be defined as the determination of the basic long-term goals and objectives of an enterprise, and the adoption of courses of action and the allocation of resources necessary for carrying out these goals. . . .
> *Structure* can be defined as the design of organization through which the enterprise is administered. This design, whether formally or informally defined, has two aspects. It includes, first, the lines of authority and communication between the different administrative offices and officers and second, the information and data that flow through these lines of communication and authority.[31]

Chandler through an in-depth analysis of four companies—Dupont, General Motors, Sears, Roebuck, and Standard Oil of New Jersey— shows how changes in these corporations' strategies over time brought an imbalance between their evolving strategies and the existing corporate structures. In particular, growing differentiation of product and expanding markets caused existing organizational structures to inhibit execution of the new strategies.[32] Only by major structural reorganizations could these companies implement fully their new strategies.

The critical point made by Chandler and others is that strategy precedes structure. Or, as Andrews, another major figure writing in the field, has observed

> [T]he nature of the corporate strategy must be made to dominate the design of organizational structure and processes. That is, the principal criterion for all decisions on organizational structure and behavior should be their relevance to the achievement of the organizational purpose, not their conformity to the dictates of special disciplines. . . . [T]he chief determinant of organizational structure and processes by which tasks are assigned and performance motivated, rewarded, and controlled should be the *strategy of the firm*, not the history of the company, its position in its industry, the specialized background of its executives, the principles of organization as developed in textbooks, the recommendations of consultants, or the conviction that one form of organization is intrinsically better than another.[33]

The clear message is that so many of the justifications for structural reorganization neither warrant this important undertaking nor guide it

[31] Alfred D. Chandler, Jr., *Strategy and Structure: Chapters in the History of the American Industrial Enterprise*, MIT Press, Cambridge, Massachusetts, 1962, pp. 13–14, italics in the original.

[32] For a brief account of Chandler's thesis, see William H. Gruber and John S. Niles, *The New Management: Line Executive and Staff Professionals in the Future Firm*, McGraw-Hill, New York, 1976, pp. 5–6.

[33] Kenneth R. Andrews, *The Concept of Corporate Strategy*, Dow Jones-Irwin, Homewood, Illinois, 1971, p. 181, italics in the original.

very usefully. Social agency structural reorganizations may seem so fruitless, so destructive of the organizational fabric in good part because they do not flow from strategy in the broad meaning of that term. And surely the typical public sector reorganization to underscore the coming of a new management team (Downs' Law of Compulsive Innovation) or to gain more control for these new managers so often falls in this category.[34] Only a well-thought-through strategy that speaks to major organizational objectives and how to reach them is likely to orient either the private corporation or the public organization toward successful reorganization. But when do we find social agencies trying seriously to lay out broadly where they want to go and how to get there so as to guide organizational behavior, structure, and processes?[35]

That structure follows strategy should not be read to indicate that developing a new structure, once strategy is determined, is a simple, straightforward activity, or one of little consequence. As Andrews points out after observing that some students of organizational behavior have claimed structure is of no importance: "On the contrary, progress in a growing organization is impossible without substrategies for organizational development. *Restructuring the organization becomes a goal in itself to be worked toward over a period of years.*"[36] Structural reorganization, then, can be an extremely important factor—a potentially effective vehicle for moving the agency toward its desired objectives. However, such structural changes appear to demand both a coherent strategy to shape them and a period of time sufficient to confront many of the problems discussed in this chapter. This surely is a difficult message for the agency political executives with their short tenure in government and their lack of knowledge which makes developing a coherent strategy difficult at the time they enter the government.

Strategy and structure are key notions for us. But first we need to set out some intervening concepts before they are addressed directly again in Chapter 10. Then, a primary task will be to indicate the nature of an agency management strategy and the implications of that strategy for agency structure and processes.

---

[34] Downs, *Urban Problems and Prospects*, pp. 98–99.

[35] About the only place that one hears of strategies being developed in government is in the defense and foreign affairs areas. For a discussion of this point, see Frederic V. Malek, *Washington's Hidden Tragedy: The Failure to Make Government Work*, Free Press, New York, 1978, pp. 118–140.

[36] Andrews, *Concept of Corporate Strategy*, p. 190, italics added.

6 MOVING ON: FROM THE CASE MATERIALS TO A BROADER ANALYSIS

The case studies of CETA and CDBG indicate the complexity in the sharing of field responsibilities as the social agencies attempted to implement and administer social service delivery programs through local governments during a critical part of the grants-in-aid era. Shown vividly are the working-level problems of shared governance. This brief chapter will (a) summarize our findings based on the analysis of the legislation, our field interviews, and a study of secondary sources; and (b) outline the upcoming analysis.

THE FINDINGS IN SUMMARY[1]

Except in the case of the first two subheadings, statements will summarize *final* observations that were made 2–3 years after the legislation passed. Two qualifying comments are needed. First, the summary will stress the negative aspects of our findings, emphasizing what needs improving as a basis for investigation and recommendations. It is not

[1] For a discussion of the experiences with the first two federal block grant programs—the Partnership for Health Act of 1966 and the Omnibus Crime Control and Safe Streets Act of 1968—see Carl W. Stenberg and David B. Walker, "The Block Grant: Lessons from Two Early Experiences," PUBLIUS, *Journal of Federalism*, Spring 1977, pp. 31–60. Both of these acts had state governments in critical roles. However, broadly speaking, Stenberg and Walker's findings are similar to the CETA and CDBG experiences discussed in Chapters 3–5 and summarized in this one.

intended to support judgments about the relative performance of DOL and HUD, which were implementing a new funding approach during a period of changing economic conditions that further complicated matters. We offer no basis for assessing whether the agencies did better or worse as compared to earlier social service delivery program implementations. Criticism after the fact is easy in general and particularly so with complex social service delivery programs where so little is understood and so much can go wrong.

Second, however useful summary statements may be in helping us see what was happening during the New Federalism period, they should not be allowed to mask the great variability among the many funded organizations. These organizations vary in terms of capabilities, political and organizational pressures, socioeconomic conditions, and their perceptions, resulting in behavior that is likely to be neither consistent nor predictable. Indeed, this variability that places such a heavy burden on social agency management is the theme of our final summary statement.

Clarity of the Legislation

Both CETA and CDBG legislation was (and still is) unclear as to overall intent and purpose as well as in terms of specific details. In particular, both pieces of legislation did not resolve, and at times complicated through contradictory statements, the basic issue of the distribution of responsibilities between federal and local governments. The confusion concerned both who was to decide what (national intent versus local initiative) and who was to do what (where responsibility and authority for various functions rested).

In the case of CDBG, there were clear incongruities between provisions of the seven categorical programs that were decategorized and those of the new legislation. However, these incongruities were not dealt with either in the legislation or in initial implementation efforts.

Initial Power Redistribution

Both CETA and the CDBG program clearly shifted power to subnational governments, taking it from the federal government including the regional offices and from nongovernmental groups and their national organizations. In particular, subnational governments gained more power over the distribution of funds to specific projects at the expense of the federal government, particularly regional and area offices. The result was a decentralization of power within the entire governmental (federal, state, and local) system in which social service delivery programs are administered and operated and a recentralization at the local level itself, bringing far more power to elected officials of general purpose governments.

An intramural shift of power occurred within the federal government from the national office to the regions. However, this gain was more than offset by the loss of power to subnational governments. The result was that regional offices were net power losers under the new legislation. This power loss confused and demoralized the regional offices at the outset of implementation, leaving them wondering what they were expected to do.

Organization

HUD's organizational difficulties made it hard for the agency to communicate either within the agency itself or with local governments. It was not structured so that the field could provide headquarters with responses on new guidelines or on emerging problems. Over time, some improvements were made in HUD during the tenure of Secretary Carla Hills so that some of the conflict and confusion was reduced at the top of the agency, but time did not permit these changes to work their way into the field by the end of our field observation activities.

The early Carter administration HUD structural reorganization did clarify lines of authority within the agency and to some extent reduced the confusion of the three-tier field structure. The changes, however, created severe morale problems in the agency. Further, the changes underscored the hard organization truth that structural reorganization does not attend to grave problems of managerial capability that plague field governance.

ETA over time improved its ability to have a regular flow of information from the field to headquarters. However, it is a strong hierarchical (top-to-bottom) system in which headquarters wants comments from the field and uses them but also seeks to minimize discretion in the field once headquarters decisions are made. DOL also has made internal organizational improvements that increased the morale of regional staffs, but these changes did not appear to have improved materially the capacity of the regional offices to administer programs.

In comparative terms, DOL has superior lines of communication to HUD. However, Labor is slow and ponderous compared to the public interest groups that service local governments. Part of the problem is bureaucratic in that communications get hung up in working their way through the organizational layers of a federal agency. But it also appears that the public interest groups are simply more competent then the federal bureaucrats in developing and working sources of information. This seems especially true in the case of regional offices, whose staffs are often forced to go to fund recipients (e.g., prime sponsors) to get the most current information.

The Approval Function

Although the change from categorical programs to block grants indicated a shift in what regulation writers and regional office staffs were supposed to do, the fact that staffs themselves did not change materially meant a carry-over of many of the categorical procedures. In particular, regulations and guidelines tended to be written more frequently and in more detail than the notion of block grants would indicate and staff often fell back upon the old categorical rules in treating grant applications.

Both HUD and DOL initially cut back on regulations and reporting demands, but such factors as congressional pressures and legislative changes, shifting socioeconomic conditions, and the apparent bureaucratic drive for order and uniformity so increased regulations and reporting requirements that one critic of CETA observed that "the stream [of regulations] has become a torrent."[2]

The agencies in general and the field staffs in particular in their grant approval activities are preoccupied with procedure, giving only limited attention to program substance. Moreover, there is a strong tendency for field staffs to try to smooth over problems with regulations from above and with grantee efforts so that inadequate guidance and weak performance are not corrected. Local officials feel that there is an unwillingness or inability of regional office staff to approve innovative approaches to problem solving, for example, leveraging or consolidation of monies from both local and federal programs to lead to more comprehensive solutions. They complain of an excessive by-the-book approach on the part of the feds that often utilizes the now superceded categorical standards. The regional office may not be able to block discretionary behavior by prime sponsors—especially the strong ones—but it seldom supports it and often inhibits it.

Compliance clearly dominates building capacity as a main concern of federal staff in the administrative and support domain. And this thrust toward compliance as defined and redefined by the social agencies with so many inconsistencies from multiple voices and shifting directions increases field complexity and confusion.

The Information Development and Analysis Function

Both DOL and HUD develop information of low quality and limited usefulness for decision making. The available federally generated information does not support the reasonable exercise of governance at either the national or local levels. In some cases, prime sponsors are developing information about project operations that facilitate their decision making.

We did not find a strong evaluative capability at any level of government. However, there are some scattered efforts to get outcome information at the prime-sponsor or local-government level.

Monitoring gets done by the regional and area offices, but poorly. The standards of monitoring compliance are not made clear beforehand so that local governments are resentful when criticized on grant applications or when they are forced to make expensive, time consuming, and difficult modifications of local procedures. Monitoring seldom addresses issues of programmatic substance or organizational management and viability but rather focuses more on narrow compliance issues often appearing nitpicking or obstructionist.

Fund recipients claim that information demands are excessive and unrealistic in terms of time constraints. Moreover, there is a lack of feedback from the information that is forwarded to regional offices.

---

[2] William Mirengoff and Lester Rindler, *CETA: Manpower Programs under Local Control,* National Academy of Sciences, Washington, D.C., 1978, p. 88.

Local governments experience information delays both in their requests for information on eligibility of activities and in getting information from Washington on changes in legislation and regulations.

In CETA, the prime sponsors add another layer to the administrative and support domain where additional information is demanded from local operators.

The Technical Assistance Function

Both DOL and HUD provide limited technical assistance, mainly focused on compliance with financial and administrative procedures. Almost no help is provided on problems of programmatic substance and organizational viability or of raising the capacity of grantees to monitor and evaluate projects. Nor is technical assistance likely to lay out possible courses of action as advice rather than as directive. That is, the agencies in the main provide procedural technical assistance aimed at compliance, not advice on substantive problems.

Local governments recognize that they need more substantive programmatic technical assistance and capacity building. They want help in better design, planning, and delivery. They would also like to know more about assessing local projects.

The federal weaknesses appeared to stem from confusion about the federal role in offering technical assistance, especially at HUD; the assignment of relatively low-level staff to the field generally and to the technical assistance function specifically; and the failure of information activities to produce extensive programmatic and organizational data to support substantive assistance.

The Emerging Power Balance

Observers and participants at all government levels stressed the growing move toward recentralization, recategorization, and deregionalization of the two block grants programs. There has been a tightening up of regulations, greater demand for information without feedback or without opportunity for input, and less willingness to keep the federal hands off.

The move toward centralization within the agencies has tended to reduce the discretion of federal field staffs. The notion of a strong regional office as a key factor in the shift of power to the field that was stressed in the New Federalism has been a victim of the agency recentralizing efforts.

Even with the growing efforts by the federal government to regain power, much of the real power that was shifted to local governments with the original legislation remains at the local level.

The trend that emerged during the categorical grants of the Great Society period whereby local governments strengthened their political, bureaucratic, and technical capability and power to administer or operate social service delivery programs has continued throughout the New Federalism period.

At the same time, the gaining of greater power by local governments—particularly power   er fund distribution—has brought greater pressures on them from local organizations and people. Under these local pressures, local governments may not perceive themselves as much more powerful than before the power shift.

Overview

A critical liability flowing from the original block grant legislation and subsequent changes has been greater confusion about responsibility at all levels of government than existed at the onset of implementation. It centers on the regional offices. Organizations above and below them seem confused as to regional office responsibility and authority. The result of the confusion about responsibility in the field is that no one can be pinned down as accountable for the performance of the social service delivery programs under CETA and CDBG.

On balance, the findings indicate that regional offices provide limited staff support and often are viewed by fund recipients and others in the field as impediments in the implementation and administration of programs.

Area offices provide useful functions, operating as line organizations having direct contact with fund recipients. However, their usefulness often is confined to relatively low-level servicing activities, such as routine question answering, forms processing, and so on.

Generally speaking, the limited program and organizational innovation found in the field is generated at the local level. Further, local governments appear more willing than federal field units have been in the past to engage in programmatic monitoring and evaluation and to place emphasis upon performance. However, the little available evidence indicates that local governments have not used their greater power to engage in significant innovations.

During the New Federalism period amid all the confusion and turmoil the process of local governance does seem to have improved. There has been an increase both in the organizational capability of local organizations and in the role of the public and nongovernmental organizations in the local decision-making process.

We find no evidence to indicate that the federal government has any real power over whether participants receive lasting benefits from programs (what have been labeled final outcomes). Moreover, the federal government appears to have less power over other outcomes and processes than it might if it were more realistic about responsibilities and more concerned with fundamental organizational issues, including information development in support of control.

Lastly, there is tremendous variability among grantees in terms both of internal factors, such as organizational commitment and capacity, and of external factors, such as political pressures and socioeconomic conditions. This variability that produces inconsistency and unpredictability of behavior and widely differing demands for resources greatly complicates agency field governance.

What can we make of these findings? It is hardly surprising that the social agencies had so many problems of governance in attempting to implement two new laws that set out in quite different directions than the legislation they replaced. To some extent, we were dealing with the epiphenomena arising from well-known start-up problems. However, the summary set out in the preceding pages indicates in the main what was happening at the end of the New Federalism period. Most of the grave problems of field governance continued as a new administration came in to start another oscillation. And there is no indication problems of implementation are withering away as the social agencies try to cope with the great variability in capability and behavior by local organizations.

The key point is that, whether or not we have dramatic changes in basic legislation, as was the case in CETA and CDBG; or within that legislation, as arose with the huge doses of public service employment both a year after CETA's passage and again early in the Carter administration; or a change in administration; or a continuing series of congressional and agency shifts; there are (over time) major and minor decisions that require implementation. Although, as in any study based on a historical period, the names and places change, the nature of the problems do not. The New Federalism period provides insights into the kinds of continuing implementation problems that complicate and bedevil federal field governance. And it remains far from clear what can be done to improve the situation. At basic issue is whether or not we can find means that make political, organizational, and technical sense to improve the implementation and administration of federal social service delivery programs funded through subnational governments.

THE UPCOMING ANALYSIS

Having inundated ourselves in the CETA and CDBG experiences, we now step back a pace for a more general and systematic analysis that will draw on theory and other evidence to extend the case findings. The next several chapters analyze how the limits, power, and resources of government generally and the social agency specifically shape federal governance.

To introduce the forthcoming chapters, it is useful to spell out the principal actors in shared governance. Star billing in our analysis goes to the political executives. This requires some explanation.

The case materials have emphasized the administrative and support domain, particularly field operations, both because we believe the agency field effort is so crucial to federal management and because other elements of governance have been studied much more fully in the past. In any detailed critique of how the agency is to improve organizational performance in the field, however, the need is to consider the entire sweep of federal governance from the executive office and Congress on down. In particular, it is the agency level where the full complement of resources, responsibilities, functions, and strategies can be considered. While a good regional office manager may improve agency field efforts, it remains true that the regional office is a creature of headquarters, highly dependent on it for direction and resources. Headquarters decides how many people the regional office will have, its other resources, its mission, its reporting requirements, and further engages in a host of relationships that impinge upon what field staff can do. Taking the political executives and the overall agency management strategy as pivotal gives needed scope to the analysis, even though the main concern is with field operations.

Other principal actors include the Congress; the White House; outside influence groups; the agency bureaucracy, of which we will later distinguish several components; and various local-level entities, including governments. In addition, we need to recognize a number of social and economic forces—labeled exogenous factors—that affect desired performance but over which political executives have little or no control.

Chapters 7 and 8 represent two different perspectives on the political executives and their potential influence on organizational and program performance. In Chapter 7, we look broadly at the basic relationships of the political executives to the other principal actors. The main concern is the extent to which the actions of these principal actors and exogenous factors constitute continuing barriers that in general reduce significantly agency power over performance.

The perspective in Chapter 8 is more sharply focused. It zeros in on the direct and indirect control devices available to top management in a large-scale hierarchical organization. Political executives are charged by major social legislation with exerting a direct impact on both their own organization, which administers funds, and other organizations, which administer and operate the social service delivery projects. They have two different control problems. The first is the exercise of control within an organization, a basic issue faced by all types of large organizations. The second direct control issue comes about when one government unit has significant managerial responsibilities, but the principal operating elements are part of or administered by other governments. Where separate political jurisdictions are involved, we face a power issue unique to government.

Finally, Chapter 8 will treat the question of indirect controls, such as competition among service deliverers or consumer action. The question is how the agency might establish these pressure points that operate like market forces to drive both the social agency itself and local organizations toward better performance.

The next two chapters treat in detail organizational resources and strategies, two issues often difficult to separate in practice. Chapter 9 concentrates on basic resources available to social agencies generally. Considered briefly is the underlying knowledge base that shows the available delivery technology for social services to be most limited. Then we turn to extended discussions of information development and technical assistance. Of central concern are (a) the kinds of programmatic and organizational information current methodologies can provide in support of control and advice; and (b) the main institutional and technical factors that shape the delivery of technical assistance.

Chapter 10 considers a number of issues—the elements of a management strategy—each social agency needs to analyze in determining the extent to which it is reasonable for it to reorient toward the field. Making the commitment and capacity of the local organizations that deliver social services the central focus of agency governance raises basic issues concerning the agency decision-making framework; its allocation of staff, other resources, and responsibilities; its mechanisms of control and influence; and its organizational structure.

The final chapter first considers how a social agency goes about assessing the implications of reorienting and restructuring itself. Although we believe that the social agencies need to adopt a field perspective if they are going to improve social agency governance, we also believe that each agency must itself engage in an extended analysis to determine whether it has the organizational capability and commitment to make the needed changes. A new agency management strategy, with the commitment and capacity of local service deliverers as its main guide, cannot be forced on the agencies from above.

In the final chapter, some concluding observations are made on the broader implications of adopting an agency management strategy that reorients the agency toward the field. Let us not mislead the readers by building up expectations that somehow we will extract from all this complexity a sure path to better field governance. Instead, we will offer two things. First, we propose what we hope is a reasonable approach for the social agency to take in considering means of improving field governance. Second, we offer some optimism based on our historical perspective of the grants-in-aid era. We do not claim that all is well or that necessarily all will be well. We will argue it is early in the game and premature to write off the federal–local partnership, since the changes in federalism that have occurred have been so rapid as to make the strains in the system a near certainty. We are not cockeyed optimists, but we do still have faith that our democratic institutions can adjust to cope better with the demands of the shared governance.

7 | THE LIMITS OF POWER: EXOGENOUS AND POLITICAL-BUREAUCRATIC BARRIERS

Fundamental power problems plague the federal social agency in its efforts to implement and administer social service delivery programs through another level of government. The top-level political executives in this large-scale bureaucracy must deal "above" with the executive office, Congress, and outside interest groups, all of which may at one time or another see local governments as prime constituents. Congress and outside interest groups may well have strong ties to the agency career staff. "Below" are the agency's own bureaucracy and the local governments that themselves are large-scale public bureaucracies also facing internal and external power problems. In a CETA vocational training project, for example, DOL may provide funds to a prime sponsor that is a general purpose government, which in turn provides funds to a school district that is a special purpose government that must deal with its own bureaucracy in order to offer vocational training. Two governments and their bureaucracies in this case stand between the final federal outpost in the administrative and support domain and the provision of training.

The question is that of agency power. In his analysis of the Cuban missile crisis, Allison argues that power "is an elusive blend of at least three elements: bargaining advantages, skill and will in using bargaining advantages, and other players' perceptions of the first two ingredients.[1] This image is of a governmental process in which the key ac-

[1] Graham T. Allison, *Essence of Decision: Explaining the Cuban Missile Crisis*, Little, Brown, Boston, 1971, p.168.

tors have various bargaining advantages, or in our terms resources, which in the gaming analogy are like the hands dealt the players. At fundamental issue in the agency power equation is the extent to which top-level agency political executives using their skill and will can gain and use resources to keep their own organization on course in pursuit of legislative goals and to induce and aid local governments in moving in the desired directions. Our systematic analysis of agency power begins with a consideration of continuing exogenous and political–bureaucratic barriers that stand between the agency and the desired results of social legislation.

FACTORS EXOGENOUS TO THE SOCIAL AGENCY

Exogenous factors affect the desired results of social legislation but are basically outside the influence of agency policymakers. A look at a DOL employment and training program aimed at increasing long-run earnings illustrates the nature of exogenous factors. Whether participants of training improve their earnings may depend far less on how well DOL administers the program than it does on various participants' innate skills, their previous work experience, and the socioeconomic settings in which they live. These factors, which are exogenous to *all* governments except perhaps in some long-run terms where government action might influence socioeconomic conditions, are beyond agency control.

Other exogenous factors in terms of employment and training programs are efforts to regulate the United States economy and work place structure, such as monetary and fiscal policy, business subsidies, and laws that regulate union membership or overall hiring practices. Individual agency programs such as CETA are expected to fit into this larger structure and complement these policies. This is not to suggest that the secretary of labor will refrain from speaking or acting on general economic or union policy. But the likelihood that the secretary can exert significant influence on these policies as they pertain to the specifics of employment and training programs seems remote.

These exogenous forces are not policy relevant in the sense that they are not resources "the policymaker can manipulate through his program or policy activity."[2] Hence, they are not a principal concern in

---

[2] Walter Williams, *Social Policy Research and Analysis,* American Elsevier, New York, 1971, p. 55.

a study of the use of agency resources. This is so even though these exogenous factors may dominate the desired results of the social legislation the agency is charged with implementing.

We do need to keep in mind one impact of exogenous factors on
the determination of social policy. Gross underestimates of the effect of
exogenous forces on the desired results of legislation can lead to
unrealistic performance expectations. Since these impacts are difficult
to calculate, the politics of program passage where high expectations
are encouraged lead to just such underestimates. This is a matter of
direct policy concern to the agency. Agency operations are served
when the executive office, Congress, and the public understand what
can be expected realistically in terms of results. Exogenous factors per
se are outside the influence of the social agency, but expectations about
program performance may be determined in part by unrealistic underestimates of the impact of exogenous factors. These expectations may
be amenable to agency influence, mainly through activities in the decision domain.

NATIONAL POLITICAL–BUREAUCRATIC
BARRIERS TO AGENCY POWER[3]

Now we turn to broad political–bureaucratic forces operating at
the national level that (a) seem likely to have an impact upon the
desired results of specific social legislation that the social agency is
charged with administering; and (b) appear, at least before extended
analysis, susceptible to social agency direct or indirect influence
through the use of that agency's political, organizational, and technical
resources. The discussion in this section will move from the decision
domain through the administrative and support domain. The main concern is with several key actors, including both those outside of the
agency, particularly Congress and the executive office, and the
agency's own bureaucracy, which can be viewed as having some external aspects. These bureaucratic forces are worth treating as partially
external because of the strong outside ties of a particular agency's own
bureaucracy and because they cut across all large-scale public bureaucracies, including those of the subnational governments with which the
agency must deal. Then, in a final section, we will look at the local

---

[3] For discussion purposes, we will separate national and local actors, in part to highlight the importance of the latter. The interaction between national and local actors,
such as congressional–local relations, will be considered in this section.

scene addressing both the administrative and support and the operations domains. Here the focus is on local governments and social service delivery organizations. A main concern is the organizational behavior of service deliverers with professional status who are seen as having significant influence on how that service is provided—those who have been labeled "street-level bureaucrats."

Federal Government at the Top

In this section, the main concern is with the "federal government team" comprised of the Congress, the executive office, and the social agencies, more particularly their political executives. At issue is what the first two do or do not do that restricts the capacity of the social agency to affect the desired goals of social legislation. The discussion of the executive office and Congress will be restricted to implementation and administrative issues arising after legislation has been enacted and has moved into the field. Such a focus does not deny that actions prior to passage of a bill or during the period before the legislation becomes effective can undercut implementation. Nor does it imply that agency efforts during legislative development to stimulate concern about implementation might not be desirable, since congressional and presidential haggling before passage often is a primary factor complicating implementation. But now we will focus our attention on field problems arising from (a) agency efforts to determine congressional intent; (b) the working relationships of the agency with the executive office and Congress; and (c) White House or congressional alliances with those groups with which the agency must deal in administering legislation (e.g., local politicians).

CONGRESSIONAL INTENT[4]

In studying implementation, probably nothing is more frustrating than trying to pin down what is to be implemented. Although surely overdrawn, what happens in the decision domain has been depicted vividly in William Greider's "The Grand Bazaar: Living with the Federal Bureaucracy," written for the *Washington Post*'s inauguration day edition of 20 January 1977:

> Congress, after all, does not really enact laws in most areas—it proposes subjects for bargaining in the bazaar. A law, one would think, tells all citizens or certain

[4] The two references we found most useful in understanding congressional intent and relatedly congressional interests and power were David R. Mayhew, *Congress: The Electoral Connection*, Yale University Press, New Haven, 1974; and Gary Orfield, *Congressional Power: Congress and Social Change*, Harcourt Brace Jovanovich, New York, 1975. Both have extensive bibliographies.

recognizable classes of citizens that they must do something (like pay their taxes) or must not do something else (like commit murders).

But so much of modern legislation doesn't do that. It declares worthy intentions. Let us end poverty. Let there be literacy. Let there be clean meat. Modern laws announce high purposes, noble goals, but they usually fuzz the crucial questions in the fine print, the language which declares: Thou shalt not.

The legislative process has become a reflexive exercise in wishful thinking. Congress concludes that too many workers are killed and maimed every year in American industry. To general applause it enacts a law that says industrial deaths and injuries are a grave national affliction and unsafe working conditions ought to be eliminated.

Then the whole mess is turned over to an agency of the Executive Branch with vague instructions to work out the details (actually, it is turned over to several agencies). Some very broad guidelines are provided on how to proceed (subject to revision if the political backfire is too great) and a new pot of money is appropriated for enforcement (though not enough to enforce this new law thoroughly since that would cost an outrageous amount). . . .

The political advantages for members of Congress are obvious. They can claim credit for attacking the great problems of the society—but they insulate themselves from direct responsibility for the hard decisions. Indeed, when they exercise "oversight" of the executive departments, this allows them to second-guess the tough choices which they could not resolve among themselves. [Reprinted with permission from the Washington Post.]

Using the work of Professor Kenneth C. Davis, Lowi in *The End of Liberalism* accuses Congress of failing to set out directions in legislation:

In 1958 Professor Davis concluded his analysis of delegated legislation with the widely-quoted observation that the typical statute was telling the agency, "Here is the problem; deal with it." Seven years later, following a period of unprecedented government expansion, Davis went further: "Sometimes [the statute] has not even said 'Here is the problem.' It does less than that. It says, instead: 'We the Congress don't know what the problems are; find them and deal with them.' "[5]

A piece of legislation represents an agreement among a majority in both houses, each of which is composed of members with diverse views and diverse constituencies pressuring them. Abstract, "high principle" language used in legislation allows substantial leeway for agreement but complicates the agency task of interpretation.

In general, programmatic detail is not important in the legislative realm. Members of Congress usually have little direct knowledge about how programs operate, scant time to obtain such knowledge, and minimal concern with program specification. As Mayhew observes "On matters where credit-claiming possibilities wear thin, therefore, we

[5] Theodore J. Lowi, *The End of Liberalism*, Norton, New York, 1969, pp. 302–303. The Davis quotes are from Kenneth C. Davis, *Administrative Law Treatise*, West Publishing Company, 1958, and the 1965 *Supplement*.

should not be surprised to find that members display only modest interest in what goes into bills or what their passage accomplishes."[6] But there is wisdom here, too. Preoccupation with these specifics can bog down legislators whose main concern is setting policy and leave them vulnerable to charges of tampering with operations.

Some members do demand specificity in legislation, and clashes result over individual provisions. True compromises do not necessarily follow, however, if we accept the dictionary definition of "a settlement of differences in which each side makes concessions."[7] The resolution of conflict may well involve putting opposing provisions in different sections of the bill. CETA is a classic example, where a call for the flexible treatment of prime sponsors is combined with a litany of specific charges to the secretary of labor that, strongly interpreted, would leave local CETA administrators barely able to buy pencils without a call to Washington.

Successful legislation demands nothing more than enough votes to pass the Senate and the House and, if needed, to override a presidential veto. As Mayhew puts it most pointedly: "The Constitution does not require, nor does political theory decisively insist, that legislative processes enshrine high standards of instrumental rationality."[8]

Several comments can be made about lack of specificity and of compromise in legislation. First, agencies charged with implementing complex social service legislation frequently have problems determining congressional intent and translating it into operational terms. Second, the lack of clarity can also be a bureaucratic opportunity. Agencies can make free translations that reflect less what Congress or the president desires and more what the agencies as bureaucratic organizations want. Third, a lack of clarity permits programmatic flexibility and innovation in social areas where there are seldom any tried and proven approaches.

Specificity is a two-edged sword. On the one hand, it is a central element of implementation and of control, since desired results need to be set out in sufficient detail to determine whether what is being done measures up to what is desired. On the other hand, premature specificity can lead in the wrong direction, overburden resources, drown out initiative, or hinder change. As McLaughlin comments "There is general agreement that a major component of the 'implementation problem'

---

[6] Mayhew, *Congress: The Electoral Connection*, p. 122.

[7] *The American Heritage Dictionary of the English Language*, Houghton Mifflin, Boston, 1969, p. 274.

[8] Mayhew, *Congress: The Electoral Connection*, p. 136.

has to do with inadequate operational specificity. There is debate concerning *who* should make project operations more specific, *how* it can be done, and *when* specificity should be introduced."[9]

An even broader interpretation to the lack of specificity can be made in seeing it as an important aspect of democratic federalism. In a strong federated system, national intent is not some independent phenomenon determined by central government authorities but represents an amalgamation of both geographic and group interests leavened by the participation of national-level actors. Political pressures and wisdom combine to render national intent a summation of interests sufficiently broad to allow diversity. National intent most often sets out a rather loose group of acceptable activities rather than one acceptable behavior. There seldom is sufficient agreement to permit a single, tight legalistic directive that allows little range in permissible action. This looseness in spelling out national intent in such a way that it is acceptable to quite different interests and can satisfy a broad coalition of the Congress and the public reflects the wisdom of democratic federalism. But this lack of specificity does place special demands on social agency governance, a point we will explore again and again.

AGENCY IMPLEMENTATION RELATIONSHIPS
WITH THE EXECUTIVE OFFICE AND CONGRESS

White House–social agency relationships concerning implementation appear to lean more toward conflict or at least a guarded stand-off position than one of cooperation. Harold Seidman has observed pointedly: "Sudden awareness of his dependency on the executive establishment and the bureaucracy can produce severe cultural shock in a President fresh from the Congress, or for that matter, from the Pentagon .... *It is the agency heads, not the President, who have the men, money, matériel, and legal powers.*"[10] Presidents may think of themselves as the commander in chief of the executive establishment with their political appointees from cabinet secretary on down lined up waiting for marching orders. But as Heclo observes

Weaknesses among political executives lead inevitably to White House complaints about their "going native" in the bureaucracy. The image is apt. To a large extent the

[9] Milbrey McLaughlin, "Implementation as Mutual Adaptation: Change in Classroom Organization," in Walter Williams and Richard F. Elmore (editors), *Social Program Implementation*, Academic Press, New York, 1976, p. 177, italics in the original.

[10] Harold Seidman, *Politics, Position, and Power*, Oxford University Press, New York, 1970, pp. 72–73, italics added.

particular agencies and bureaus *are* the native villages of executive politics. Even the most presidentially minded political executive will discover that his own agency provides the one relatively secure reference point amid all the other uncertainties of Washington.[11]

Open defiance of a presidential directive is much less frequent than a studied procrastination in the hope that the president or his staff will not follow up. A classic example came in the Cuban missile crisis when President Kennedy found to his consternation that his strong order to remove American missiles from Turkey had not been carried out, leaving the president in most embarrassing circumstances.[12] The vastness of an agency with its complicated bureaucratic structure provides protection from White House interference particularly in the far reaches of the field.

Seidman has pointed out, we think quite correctly, that "department heads remain the weakest link in the chain of Federal Administration."[13] The White House contributes to this weakness. Since presidents are much more concerned with foreign policy and economic issues than domestic policy, the White House problem for the social agencies is much more likely to be interference by presidential aides. In pointed reference to Joseph Califano and John Ehrlichman, who were the White House social policy chiefs under Presidents Johnson and Nixon, respectively, Cronin remarks "Presidents probably will not stop delegating the leadership and coordination of domestic policy matters to White House aides. But is it now enough to have a small band of staff lawyers or former public relations specialists manage the nation's domestic policy?"[14] Presidents have great trouble following Peter Drucker's advice, which says "never let the [White House] central staff get between the chief executive and the key men in his administration who are responsible for managing major activities."[15]

The important point is not that the White House is likely to dominate the agency in its implementation efforts, especially as things

---

[11] Hugh Heclo, *A Government of Strangers: Executive Politics in Washington*, Brookings Institution, Washington, D.C., 1977, p. 111, italics in the original.

[12] See Allison, *Essence of Decision*, for a discussion of the difficulties of removing the missiles in Turkey. An excellent general work on the problems the president has with agencies, including an extended bibliography, is Thomas E. Cronin, *The State of the Presidency*, Little, Brown, Boston, 1975.

[13] Seidman, *Politics, Position, and Power*, p. 135.

[14] Cronin, *The State of the Presidency*, p. 206.

[15] Peter F. Drucker, "How to Make the Presidency Manageable," *Fortune*, November 1974, p. 147.

move deeper into the field. It is rather that White House staff can cause early implementation problems. Further, the staff is not likely to understand implementation issues and so not offer much help in getting changes that might facilitate implementation over time.

In *Congressional Power: Congress and Social Change*, Orfield points out that the congressional contribution to domestic policy often manifests itself more in incremental action once legislation has been passed than in the highly dramatic passage of a bill. Over time, congressional efforts to modify programs and to alter spending at the margin may add up to a material impact on domestic policy. As between Congress and the president, Congress appears to be the far more important factor in the implementation process.[16] This is not to argue that Congress understands implementation problems or is terribly interested in general implementation issues but rather that it is more likely to take actions that impinge upon implementation and represents the most important barrier through which agency implementation concerns must pass in moving from the top of the decision domain.

DECISION DOMAIN ALLIANCES

Presidential and congressional alliances with the agency's own bureaucrats, local politicians, and national representatives of service deliverers or program beneficiaries complicate agency authority and relationships. They can establish continuing wedges between the agency political executives and the desired results of legislation.

The so-called iron triangle represents the links among an agency bureau, its related interest group, and congressional supporters, usually including key committee or subcommittee members. This alliance makes the agency's own bureau part of what Heclo labels a "subgovernment" that the agency political executives surely should view as an external force:

> The common features of these subgovernments are enduring mutual interests across the executive and legislative branches and between the public and private sectors. However high-minded the ultimate purpose, the immediate aim of each alliance is to become "self-sustaining in control of power in its own sphere." The longer an agency's tradition of independence, the greater the political controversy surrounding its subject matter and the more it is allied with outside groups, the more a new appointee can expect sub rosa opposition to develop to any proposed changes. If political leadership in the executive branch is to be more than the accidental sum of these alliances and if political representation is to be less arbitrary than the demands of any group that claims to speak for the unrepresented, then some conflict

---

[16] See Orfield, *Congressional Power: Congress and Social Change*, for an excellent discussion of this point.

seems inevitable between higher political leaders and the subgovernments operating within their sphere.[17]

The alliances of the White House and Congress with the politicians whose governments receive social service delivery program funds or with the national representatives of service deliverers or beneficiaries present another formidable barrier. The ties between Congress and local fund recipients are particularly troublesome. As Ingram has observed "Unfettered grant provisions are an attractive support-building strategy for congressional sponsors in the struggle to build legislative majorities. The cost to successful implementation of federal programs is rarely explicitly recognized by Congress."[18] But even greater problems may arise when Congress has told the agency to administer funds to local governments under quite specific conditions. When congressional members line up on the side of those receiving funds against the agency in questions concerning compliance with those conditions, the basic rules of the game become confused.

The discussion of alliances comes last in this section, because the topic leads into and continues to be discussed in the next two sections. Its briefness derives not from the lack of importance of these barriers but rather because the bureaucrats and local politicians who are prominent members of these alliances are discussed at length later.

Bureaucratic Constraints in Large-Scale Public Organizations[19]

Elmore argues that "only by understanding how [large public] organizations work can we understand how policies are shaped in the process of implementation."[20] Unfortunately, as Warwick observed

---

[17] Heclo, *Government of Strangers*, p. 225.

[18] Helen Ingram, "Policy Implementation through Bargaining: The Case of Federal Grants-in-Aid," *Public Policy*, Fall 1977, p. 525.

[19] The best examples of bureaucratic constraints come from the much studied foreign defense policy area. One of the first and most important works is Allison's *Essence of Decision*, especially pp. 67–100. A particularly useful book (we draw on it heavily in Chapter 5) is Donald P. Warwick, *A Theory of Public Bureaucracy: Politics, Personality, and Organization in the State Department*, Harvard University Press, Cambridge Massachusetts, 1975. Also, see Morton H. Halperin, *Bureaucratic Politics and Foreign Policy*, Brookings Institution, Washington, D.C., 1974; and I. M. Destler, *Presidents, Bureaucrats, and Foreign Policy*, Princeton University Press, Princeton, 1972. For a more general treatment plus an extensive bibliography, see Francis E. Rourke, *Bureaucracy, Politics, and Public Policy*, Second Edition, Little, Brown, Boston, 1976. The already cited *A Government of Strangers* by Hugh Heclo is an insightful study, focusing on the barriers established by poor relationships between political executives and the high-level civil servants working directly with them.

[20] Richard F. Elmore, "Organizational Models of Social Program Implementation," *Public Policy*, Spring 1978, p. 187.

"But as of the time of writing [1975] there is not a single general work on organization theory that pays systematic attention to the distinctive features of the public bureaucracy and makes a serious effort to incorporate the findings of the many case studies reported in the literature of public administration."[21] Not only have large government bureaucracies been studied less than private organizations, they appear far more complicated in part because of their susceptibility to outside influences. If we shut out these outside forces at this point and look only within, we find two prominent guideposts for examination—"tall" hierarchy and excessive rules.[22]

THE NOTION OF HIERARCHY[23]

Federal agency organization charts depict box after box connected from the secretary to the lowliest field office with solid lines indicating a top-to-bottom chain of command. And within those boxes, there will be a strict hierarchical pecking order with administrators over deputy administrators over associate administrators over assistant administrators over division chiefs over deputy division chiefs over branch chiefs (full blown, we would include a few deputy assistant or deputy associate administrators, and so on). However much the outside observers may find this as almost a parody on the hierarchical organization form, the agency organizational chart is to be taken seriously as indicating the agency, and the congressional, views that those above have the power needed to direct the actions of those below. As Warwick points out from the old Hoover commission study: "The commission postulates that the only way to have accountability and responsibility is the classic structure of hierarchical authority."[24]

The overriding message of recent studies of both private and public organizations, however, is that we can take as given neither that the organization is a value-maximizing entity operated along purely rational lines nor that those below will necessarily do what those above them want.[25] Even in the private corporation, getting people below to

[21] Warwick, *A Theory of Public Bureaucracy*, p. 190.

[22] Warwick's study of the Department of State, which he points out is limited by being based on a single case of public bureaucracy, stresses this tendency of large public agencies to move toward hierarchy and rules. He uses the term *tall*, which seems particularly apt to describe government hierarchies.

[23] Here we move briefly into the issue of hierarchical control that is critical to the next chapter, but in the main treating it now somewhat more broadly than in the later discussion.

[24] Warwick, *A Theory of Public Bureaucracy*, p. 70. For a discussion of this view, see pp. 69–71.

[25] Both Warwick in a *Theory of Public Bureaucracy* and Elmore in "Organizational Models of Social Program Implementation" summarize organizational findings as they

do what people above want has turned out to be an extremely complicated problem. There is no sure path to the successful implementation of decisions made at the top.

The problem of hierarchical authority is particularly difficult for the political executives who serve for such short time periods. The difficulties start at the crucial link with the top-level career civil servants who occupied key positions under the predecessor political executives and who are likely to have similar positions when another group of future political executives replace the incoming ones. In his study of the relationship of agency political executives and the high-level civil servants, Heclo observes in a section entitled "Power":

> The basis of the top bureaucrats' power vis-à-vis political executives lies primarily in the services they can provide or withhold. Straightforward as this statement seems, it is a crucial point that is frequently overlooked in the self-centered atmosphere of many top political offices. . . .
>
> Compared with the saboteur's negative acts, the top bureaucrats' power derived from withholding positive help is enormous. Unlike the "legislative veto" (in which executive actions take effect unless disapproved by Congress), the "bureaucratic veto" is a pervasive constant of government, for without higher civil service support almost nothing sought by political executives is likely to take effect. It is a power that can consist simply of waiting to be asked for solutions by appointees who do not know they have problems. . . .
>
> Because most political appointees require considerable help in government, higher civil servants normally need do little by way of harmful actions in order to prevail. All that is usually necessary is for officials to fail to come forward with their services. "That," as one undersecretary declared, "is their ultimate truth."[26]

Some high-level bureaucratic resistance arises from overt actions such as those of the bureaucratic members of the iron triangle. But more often the lack of knowledge and sensitivity or the outright ineptness of political executives permits inaction by key career staff to suffice. The high-level bureaucrats can be either a primary resource or a potential barrier in implementing legislation—or both. If political ex-

---

pertain to the public sector and provide useful citations. The Elmore work is particularly useful in its development of several models that represent the major schools of thought on organizational behavior that can be brought to bear on the implementation problem. Only one of these, labeled the "systems management" model, is based on the maximizing, rationalist framework.

[26] Heclo, A Government of Strangers, pp. 171–173. The impact of the New Senior Executive Service (SES) that provides more mobility and more incentives for certain high-level (GS-16 and above) civil servants will not be known for a long time. But SES does not have much impact on the basic problem that the political executives and the career civil servants are strangers and the latter possess special knowledge about the agency or government in general.

ecutives cannot draw on the experience of the top-level civil servants in the agency, cannot use their skills to exert within-agency power over the vast bureaucracy below, they are dead in the water. The political executives will fail in their efforts to govern.

At the same time, winning over the top-level civil servants, however necessary, is not sufficient for strong within-agency control. Vast layers of bureaucracy lie below, stretching ultimately to the administrative and support domain units in the field.

THE GAME IN THE ADMINISTRATIVE
AND SUPPORT DOMAIN

In the complex social agency organization, effective handling of the top-level careerists does not turn the mammoth hierarchy into a smooth functioning machine. The game is not simply "them" (bureaucrats) and "us" (political appointees). Games abound in the various bureaucratic layers. Throughout the agency, bureaucratic needs may be in conflict with directions from above, and each layer will have power to protect its interests.

CETA and CDBG are classic examples in that both were intended to take power from federal bureaucrats, especially those in the administrative and support domain, who were charged with too much interference under the old categorical programs. But as Jerome Murphy has remarked in regard to the Elementary and Secondary Education Act of 1965 (a categorical program enacted at the height of federal intervention):

> The nature of the bureaucratic problem in implementing governmental programs has been obscured. Blame has been placed on the inefficiencies of the federal aid delivery system, when in fact major faults associated with categorical aid appear to be general features of public bureaucracies. As long as the investigation of the problem of governmental paralysis is reduced to a search for scapegoats, at the expense of attempting to understand organizational behavior, we can expect only limited improvement in the way education bureaucracies work.[27]

Let us dwell upon the role of these federal-level bureaucrats for a minute. As legislation (a decision) moves down toward operations, it passes into the hands of a number of middle- and lower-echelon—administrative and support domain—bureaucrats both in headquarters and in the region. It is not necessary to conjure up either evil or slothful people to recognize that they can cause trouble in the change to a new

---

[27] Jerome T. Murphy, "Title V of ESEA: The Impact of Discretionary Funds on State Education Bureaucracies," *Harvard Educational Review*, August 1973, p. 385.

system. Organizations and bureaucrats have limited repertoires.[28] CETA and CDBG again illustrate the point. Under the previous legislation, which mandated various categorical programs, detailed regulations and guidelines poured forth and the writers and interpreters tended to inflate the importance of writing and interpretation.[29] Although block grants were designed to cut down on detailed guidelines and interpretations from above, these same writers and interpreters were still in place and continued to do the job they had learned to do reasonably well despite the change in the legislation.

What emerges is a kind of iron rule of bureaucratic behavior. As Sundquist has observed

> The tendency of federal officials to retain power in their own hands must be recognized as natural and inevitable. It is they who must defend their programs before congressional committees. It is they who are held accountable if things go wrong. They are experts confident that they have the best perspective of the country's needs. They are impatient for results. Rather than defer to thousands of independent community decisions on a given question, some of which by the law of averages will be wrong, they prefer to make the one "right" decision themselves and impose it by regulation. And the regulations incorporating those decisions grow ever more detailed, complex, and rigid.[30]

Given the vagueness of legislation discussed earlier in this chapter, federal agencies usually have plenty of room to justify their intrusion. Even when there is greater legislative specificity, any good regulation writer can muscle in between the lines with administrative details that simply "define and fine tune" the law.

The tremendous importance of regulations and guidelines has seldom been considered.[31] As Brown and Frieden have observed "This scholarly neglect [of guidelines] is unfortunate for it is reasonable to surmise—again at least a priori—that the guideline process constitutes the cutting edge of administrative power, the most direct legitimate and effective means by which public administrators make recipients of public funds dependent upon bureaucratic interpretations of public law."[32] Nathan's comment on the Nixon presidency reflects how impor-

---

[28] See Allison, *Essence of Decision*, p. 83.

[29] Regulations are controlled by the Administrative Procedure Act, which requires advanced publication and comments by interested parties. Guidelines are less formal, covering most other directives issued by bureaucrats to interpret the law.

[30] James L. Sundquist, *Making Federalism Work*, Brookings Institution, Washington, D.C., 1969, p. 250.

[31] A notable exception is an issue of *Policy Sciences* devoted solely to a discussion of regulations and guidelines. See *Policy Sciences*, 7, 1976.

[32] Larry D. Brown and Bernard J. Frieden, "Rulemaking by Improvisation: Guidelines and Goals in the Model Cities Program" in ibid., pp. 455–456.

tant these administrative and support domain activities are: "Nixon and Ehrlichman came to the conclusion sometime in 1971 that in many areas of domestic affairs, *operations is policy.* Much of the day-to-day management of domestic programs—regulation writing, grant approval, and budget apportionment—actually involves policymaking."[33]

Regulations and guidelines are a crucial part of regional office operations. Legislation is supposed to tell the agencies what Congress wants; regulations and guidelines are headquarters interpretation of what Congress says it wants. These headquarters directives also need interpretation and translation. Regulations and guidelines that may seem straightforward bureaucratic documents—a simple elaboration of legislative language—provide a second political arena that requires more interpretation and translation. The main interpreter of directives is the regional office. It is not a simple task. The political contradictions that make legislation vague often render directives unclear, too—a shaky treaty reflecting legislative, administrative, and "outside" special interest pulls. As Brown and Frieden observe in their insightful study of the model cities program:

> The regional role proved crucial in creatively adapting Washington's guidelines to local communities. However, it too raises some important questions: if guidelines assume operational meaning at the regional level of the federal bureaucracy, can equity (among localities within a region and among regions themselves) be properly assured? If the operational meaning of guidelines depends so heavily upon regional officials' efforts at compromise and improvisation, can accountability of these officials to their bureaucratic and political superiors in Washington be adequately maintained? If the nature of the guideline process in Washington is itself the main reason why regional officials assume the roles that they do, what are the hidden costs of such accountability? And how strongly should the public insist that they be paid?
>
> The American political system tends to settle disagreements of opinion and value by bargaining and compromise; the results (the Model Cities program, for example) may be a sort of bounded incoherence. The dilemma of the guideline process is that it is expected both to partake of this political process and to rationalize it. As tools of politics as well as of government, guidelines are open to manipulation by many actors, throughout the federal system. This is to be expected. But guidelines remain after all bureaucratic variations on this common political theme, and it is this fact that nags one on toward empirical and normative models of the process, elusive as they may seem. Guidelines formulated by compromise among political and bureaucratic actors may strike a balance between administrative discretion and political leadership. Guidelines formulated by compromise among political and bureaucratic actors also defeat the distinctive purposes guidelines are expected to serve, fragment political control beyond repair, and thereby place unintended

---

[33] Richard P. Nathan, *The Plot That Failed,* Wiley, New York, 1975, p. 62, italics in original. This and other references to the same article are under copyright © 1975 by John Wiley & Sons, Inc. Reprinted with permission of John Wiley & Sons, Inc.

obstacles in the way of the public's attempt to hold government officials accountable for the words by which we are governed.[34]

History itself plays a role. Local officials may seek clarification of
any action seen as out of the ordinary, aware that federal officials were
quite sticky about rules and regulations in the past. When the request
comes from one region, headquarters may send out the interpretation
to all 10 regions. In this process, administrative rulings rebuild the kind
of categorical structure the new legislation was designed to eliminate.
As we have seen, the block grant programs have gradually moved back
toward more federal rules and more federal involvement by
bureaucrats.

Perhaps the most insidious aspect of regulations and guidelines is
that they so often increase confusion and complexity. The problem so
often comes from a "regulatory mentality" equating agency control
with field compliance. The costs of compliance can be steep. The
regulations and guidelines designed to ensure compliance themselves
become a major source of complexity and confusion that require additional directives and more surveillance. The stream of regulations and
guidelines becomes a torrent. Guideline begets guideline. And the second one so often is needed to correct or refine a first one. Complexity
and confusion mount.

The emphasis on compliance as manifested in regulations and
guidelines can drive out more substantive concerns, leaving the federal
staff tending mainly to narrow procedural issues. Moreover, efforts to
enforce compliance with regulation and guidelines is likely to bring
harassment by the federal staff. The interaction in the field between
federal and local staffs becomes a game of wits in which the grantee
becomes the enemy. It is hardly a partnership seeking delivery capacity. As Elmore has observed

> When it becomes necessary to rely mainly on hierarchical control, regulation, and
> compliance to get the job done, the game is essentially lost. . . . Regulation increases
> complexity and invites subversion; it diverts attention from accomplishing the task
> to understanding and manipulating rules.[35]

---

[34] Brown and Frieden, "Rulemaking by Improvision," p. 488.

[35] Richard F. Elmore, *Complexity and Control: What Legislators and Administrators
Can Do about Implementation,* Institute of Governmental Research, University of
Washington, Public Policy Paper No. 11, Seattle, April 1979, pp. 27–28, italics in the
original.

THE LOCAL SCENE

The CETA and CDBG experiences underscore the loss of federal power over social service delivery programs once another political jurisdiction receives the federal funds. And CETA is particularly dramatic, with local government as prime sponsors, many without previous involvement in employment and training programs, moving rapidly to the fore in local decision making. The social agencies limited power over local governments comes partly from their own internal bureaucratic problems and partly from their bureaucratic timidity in confronting local political actors. The lack of power, however, is not merely a bureaucratic limitation. Mirengoff's earlier statement bears repeating that "if it comes to a critical struggle, I think the political clout of the local prime sponsors would probably prevail."[36]

The power gain over the federal government is not the last step for local government, however. Their capacity to exert power can be constrained severely by the constituencies they serve and the organizations they fund. We need to look at the entire local setting.

Local Power

In considering local power, two points need to be made. First, local clout does not come about because the federal government lacks the raw force to do its will. Second, local-level power did not suddenly emerge with the introduction of block grants providing funds by formula to local governments.

The "ultimate" weapons of fund cutoff and cutback are in the federal arsenal available to Congress and the agencies. Congress has clear power to determine the funding standards. These criteria can be arbitrary, unrealistic in terms of existing information, or contradictory as long as they do not violate the Constitution. Further, Congress can punish the social agencies if they do not apply these weapons. And the social agencies do not want for legal means to punish the locals. Recall that CETA goes so far as to permit a DOL takeover of a deficient prime sponsor.

Congress and the agencies can destroy with the big weapons. The federal establishment, however, sits there with a destructive power it is

---

[36] *Block Grants: A Round Table Discussion,* Advisory Commission on Intergovernmental Relations, A-51, October 1976, p. 15.

afraid to use. Hence, the actual, in the sense of likely to be used, power to force positive changes from the federal perspective may be small.

Despite the many laments about too much federal interference under categorical programs, both subnational governments and nongovernmental organizations operated under these programs with a goodly amount of freedom. Just as now, the federal power failure was sometimes bureaucratic, coming from organizational timidity, political fear, or "collusion" with like-minded professionals in the recipient organization. Also, when faced with agency coercion, fund recipients under categorical programs were adroit at playing Congress off against the federal agencies, shifting funds around to give the appearance of complying with spending restrictions, and—if all else failed—in simply "toughing it out" in defiance of legislation, regulations, and guidelines.

Local power, then, in CETA and CDBG, or in other social service delivery programs, is explained neither by the absence of strong federal weapons nor by the special circumstances of the New Federalism. Instead, as will be discussed in the next chapter, local power already existed in such areas as education and started to grow during the Great Society period in such new areas as training. Early bargaining advantages of the federal government faded as local governments gained organizational and program experience and political savvy. By the end of the New Federalism period, local governments' power vis-à-vis their federal partner was great.

Local Government: Win Some, Lose Some

How much power do local governments have? The answer may be not all that much when they deal with local constituencies and local organizations. In CETA, for example, a "lock-in effect" may occur with local funding so that local governments will have great difficulties not continuing to fund a nongovernmental organization once the initial grant is made. Inhibited by local political actors and ignored or defied by local operators, the local governments may not be able to do what federal staff desires even if they want to. Nor are the local constraints only political. Local governments face the same problems with their bureaucrats as does the federal government. All of the bureaucratic blockages hold here, too.

The power of local government will be determined primarily in the local setting. Take the prime sponsors as examples. They were the immediate big winners when CETA was enacted in 1973. Most importantly, the prime sponsors won direct power over fund distribution that in the past had been a federal function. But these funds were not unrestricted. The local government could not just figure out what it desired to do and then proceed as it wished. These were public funds, and ones with a prior history. A pre-CETA pattern of funding existed. Established project operators surely expected to go on as before even though a new distribution channel had been established.

The changing of power over distribution from the federal to the local level shifted the target of distributional pressures. Thus, CETA reshuffled the deck and dealt new hands. All eyes turned toward the winners who gained power. The funding pressures shifted from the old to the new power center. Local government prime sponsors may well have discovered that the CETA arrangements were a short-lived power trip. Gaining the power to distribute federal funds can carry a high price tag for a prime sponsor.

A piece of legislation such as CETA that makes dramatic changes in the distribution of power toward the local level creates a disturbance among political, organizational, and bureaucratic forces that sends shock waves throughout the established local system. The effect goes beyond the local administrative structure and delivery organizations into the broader community in which the delivery mechanism is embedded. It is much like dropping a stone into a pond with the initial force generating itself out to more distant points.

CETA again offers an excellent example. In the pre-CETA days, national contracts between DOL and such organizations as the Urban League were negotiated in Washington. Local Urban League units then got the funds to run their programs. Under CETA the local Urban League project—now without the benefit of a national contract—had to fight for its own funds. It well may be that local Urban League officials felt less powerful than before when forced to argue with the local government against competing claims to keep funding their project. Concomitantly, the local government itself may have wondered about its new-won power as operators of manpower projects queued up to tell it how to spend its newfound funds.

Social Service Delivery Organizations

Central to the issue of local power—and concomitantly, federal power—over social service delivery programs are the organizations and the professional staffs that actually deliver services. The social service delivery organizations are characterized by "labor-intensive technologies . . . multiple, conflicting, and generally unmeasurable social goals; and uncertain and uncontrollable environment."[37] Skilled personnel directly serve single individuals or small numbers of people in complex settings where uncertainty often dominates the interaction. Elmore has captured the essence of the situation in this statement specifically describing local school systems but pertaining generally to all complex social service delivery programs:

> The system is *bottom-heavy* and *loosely-coupled*. It is bottom-heavy because the closer we get to the bottom of the pyramid, the closer we get to the factors that have the greatest effect on the program's success or failure. It is loosely-coupled because the ability of one level to control the behavior of another is weak and largely negative.[38]

The unavoidable discretion exercised by the professional staff directly responsible for service delivery within these organizations means these bottom-heavy, loosely coupled entities are difficult to control from above and from within.

This professional staff who provides public services directly, often labeled "street-level bureaucrats," includes "[teachers], police officers, welfare workers, legal-assistance lawyers, lower-court judges, and health workers. These and other public employees interact with the public and make decisions calling for both individual initiative and considerable routinization."[39] Weatherley and Lipsky observe

> The work of street-level bureaucrats is inherently discretionary. Some influences that might be thought to provide behavioral guidance for them do not actually do much to dictate their behavior. For example, the work objectives for public-service employees are usually vague and contradictory. Moreover, it is difficult to establish or impose valid work-performance measures, and the consumers of services are relatively insignificant as a reference group. Thus, street-level bureaucrats are constrained but not directed in their work.
>
> These accommodations and coping mechanisms that they are free to develop form patterns of behavior which become the government program that is "delivered" to the public. In a significant sense, then, street-level bureaucrats *are the policymakers* in their respective work arenas.[40]

Decisions made by front-line bureaucrats concerning the services a client receives and how the services are delivered are one of the, *if not*

---

[37] Paul Berman, *The Study of Macro and Micro Implementation of Social Policy*, Rand Corporation, P–6071, Santa Monica, California, January 1978, p. 27.

[38] Elmore, *Complexity and Control*, p. 27, italics in the original.

[39] Richard Weatherley and Michael Lipsky, "Street-Level Bureaucrats and Institutional Innovation: Implementing Special-Education Reform," *Harvard Educational Review*, May 1977, p. 172. This and other references to the same article are under copyright © by President and Fellows of Harvard College.

[40] Ibid., italics in the original.

the, most powerful determinants of government policy. However, we should not conjure a vision of persons with great power who themselves control the situation. The classroom teacher and the welfare caseworker hardly appear as powerful figures. Indeed, conversations with them indicate how harried they feel. Still the fact remains that when the classroom door closes or the welfare recipient sits down at the caseworker's desk, the final service deliverer has critical unavoidable discretion.

It is discretion, however, in dealing with a final actor, the treatment recipient. That is the person who will have the last word on discretion. A treatment recipient must both be able to benefit from the treatment and be willing to receive it. This is vividly illustrated in efforts to "upgrade" children's television. As Tom Shales observed in the 19 May 1974 issue of the *Washington Post:* "A sad fact of children's TV reform is that while all the educational consulting and pro-socializing is going on, children still tend to prefer junk when they plop themselves down in front of a TV set. . . . Getting children to like what's good for them—or what some people think is good for them—could well be the hardest job ahead, then, for the children's TV reformers." The Shales article reports that when quality shows (as defined by adults) compete with such shows as a "Deputy Dawg" cartoon rerun, the score was 85% for the cartoon, 15% for the programs viewed as being of high quality. The treatment recipients whose welfare is ostensibly the main thrust of a program simply cannot be expected to accept passively what is offered. They choose.

This final discretion by treatment recipients makes the discretionary judgments of front-line professionals so central to policy. These professionals are the last institutional actors. Their reactions to the treatment recipients' discretionary behavior is the final institutional link in a long chain of social policy. Thus, the capacity of the front-line professionals to make sound judgments in the complex delivery setting is the critical policy input. Their sound judgments over time are the needed ingredient for strong programs—the positive factor that can make social policies work.

Moreover, and this is crucial, *these front-line judgments defy the development of prepackaged regulations and guidelines.* Standard operating procedures may yield compliance but are unlikely to help, and often will hinder, the needed discretionary judgments.

What does this mean for higher level managers including those in the social agency? They must recognize that they can provide needed resources or enhance the setting for the exercise of reasonable discretion, but it is the actual service deliverer, and perhaps an immediate supervisor, who must make the basic choices concerning resource use and discretionary action. It would be a grave error not to recognize this power—albeit often a negative power to block—at the bottom of the organization. The unavoidable discretion possessed by individuals and small units at the point of service delivery determines what big decisions really look like.

A FINAL NOTE

As we have moved from exogenous factors through the street-level bureaucrats, there emerges a strong case for the severe limits of social agency power over desired results. Much of the desired outcome of policy is beyond the direct power of any government. There are many more blockages. Moreover, the argument of agency limits is easily turned to support the case for the limited power of local governments. A failure to take account of this weakness and unavoidable discretion that permeates the governance of social service delivery programs can bring great confusion about responsibility and power. And this confusion itself can further limit power over implementation and performance.

Perceived powerlessness is the image that best captures the milieu of social service delivery programs generally and that of the shared governance of these programs specifically. No matter how many resources major institutional participants have, no matter how much relative power organizations have, central actors usually feel frustrated, hemmed in, unable to exert discretion.

CETA offers clear examples of this perceived powerlessness. The DOL staff, particularly in the field, so often seemed to be acting out of pure frustration when Congress or headquarters behaved as if field staff had strong control or when grantees appeared to be encroaching on the limited power field staff perceived it had. A regulatory mentality and harassment were the field staff responses to their limited real power.

Even the apparent big power winners—the prime sponsors—did not behave as if they were masters of the situation. Federal staff harassed them from above; local politicians and organizations applied pressures because the prime sponsors now decided the money flow; and below, all of the bureaucratic, organizational, and technical problems that beset social service delivery programs continued on with no magic transformation because more power and discretion came to local authorities. *Is it so surprising that innovations did not spring forth, that prime sponsors so bemoaned the pressures on them rather than racing ahead with new ideas?*

Much the same holds when we turn to the social service delivery organizations and to the street-level bureaucrats, whose roles loom so large—with so much irreducible discretion attributed to them by scholars. They end up perceiving themselves as the least powerful organizational actors in the institutional game. They bemoan their beleaguered position between regulations and bosses above and difficult clients below.

At the same time, it is critical to recognize a kind of power imbalance. There is far more power in the system for both individuals and organizations to block or veto action, or at least to harass and impede. Powerlessness is much more of a problem for organizations trying to move toward positive objectives such as better organizational or programmatic performance. This power imbalance means that an individual actor may be able to block action or undercut plans, but that coalitions are likely to be needed in efforts to effect positive changes.

Even in the best circumstances, movement toward destined objectives will be difficult since knowledge about organizational and programmatic tactics is most limited and uncertainty abounds. Generally, unpredictability rules out the preselection of tactics, and even on-the-spot decisions about what to do are both hard to make and dependent on highly variable local conditions. There is an inherent variability and indeterminacy to the performance game—not only is there no absolute monarch, but there are no clearly discernable tactics.

Mutual dependency and the need for mutual adaptation over time are critical aspects of powerlessness. The social agency may have little choice but to try to build the capacity of social service delivery organizations if there is to be a real chance of increased organizational performance. At the local level, better performance may require the search for a viable coalition of actors, a coalition that can only be put together over time. Such factors demand thinking in terms of a different style of agency control and influence and of a different use of resources than in the past. With such powerlessness in mind, let us turn to the issues of agency control and influence, resources, and strategies.[41]

[41] For an extremely broad view of the notions of limits, see Rufus Miles, Jr., *Awakening from the American Dream: The Social and Political Limits to Growth,* Universe Books, New York, 1976. Miles in this book discusses the limits to physical growth for the entire United States economy, much of which is relevant to government policy. He observes (on p. 171) that "social management is now being strained close to the breaking point"—no wonder a feeling of powerlessness.

8 | THE LIMITS OF CONTROL: COMMAND TO INFLUENCE

The last chapter treated agency power broadly in looking at a wide range of mainly external forces that can inhibit the agency's impact on performance. We now focus our concern more sharply on how the agency is managed. The central issue is what top-level agency managers—those responsible for agency governance, its leaders—can do to exert control or influence on field behavior.

In large-scale organizations with many field units, the first management problem is to find means through which those at the top can induce intermediate-level managers to do what they desire. Anthony and Dearden observe "A business company, or indeed any organization, must . . . be controlled; that is, there must be devices that insure that it goes where its leaders want it to."[1]

Control is an exceedingly complex notion. The simple image may be of a clear command followed to the letter by a subordinate who carries out that order at least in part because the superior possesses strong sanctions to punish insubordination. But as Anthony has pointed out: "The word control in its ordinary sense has unfortunate connotations . . . . [I]t often is used in the sense of 'boss, curb, dominate, enforce, forestall, hinder, inhibit, manipulate, prevail, restrain, shackle, and watch,' and these connotations are not at all realistic as descrip-

[1] Robert N. Anthony and John Dearden, *Management Control Systems: Texts and Cases,* Third Edition, Richard D. Irwin, Homewood, Illinois, 1976, p. 3. Anthony and his colleagues at the Harvard Business School have been the most prolific writers on management control.

tions of what actually goes on in a well-managed organization."[2] Management control ultimately comes down to the intangible ability of top managers to motivate line managers. "Psychological considerations are dominant in management control. Activities such as communicating, persuading, exhorting, inspiring, and criticizing are an important part of the process."[3]

The control issue is particularly pressing where top decision makers are located at headquarters, and most of the implementers and the operators are in the field. Lundquist observes "[D]ecentralization is a general problem of organizations. In all the meanings in which the term is used, there is a common denominator, namely, 'away from the centre.' "[4] The recurring question is: How much discretionary authority should headquarters grant to the field?

The notion of control gets exceedingly complex when we think of it in terms of the long, hierarchically dense process that runs from the top of a social agency through another political jurisdiction to a point where a professional person in a social service organization delivers a service to a client. In that process, what does it mean for political executives or headquarters to have control over programs in the field. Is it control over what the various organizations and their professional staff do, what benefits clients receive, or both? Our colleague Richard Elmore began to sort out this issue as follows

> When we speak of government agencies or programs being "out of control," we generally mean that they are aimless, unresponsive to policymakers and clients, sluggish, uncoordinated, or self-serving. Control, then, consists of bringing administrative actions into line with the expectations of policymakers and citizens. But this general notion of control conceals two very different meanings: One meaning is the *control that superiors exercise over subordinates* and the other is the *control that individuals exercise over their own actions*. In the first instance we're talking about *hierarchical control*—authority, supervision, regulation, coercion—and in the second we're talking about *delegated control*—individual responsibility, initiative, and discretion. A bit of common sense tells us that both kinds of control are required for successful implementation. Hierarchical control is the means by which policymakers (legislators and high-level administrators) affect the actions of subordinates (mid-level managers and service deliverers). But the administrative structure would soon collapse if individuals didn't exercise some degree of responsibility, initiative and control over their own actions. Imagine a group of policymakers presiding over a bureaucracy in which no one acted unless they were explicitly told to do

[2] Robert N. Anthony, *Planning and Control Systems*, Harvard University Press, 1965, p. 28.

[3] Robert N. Anthony, John Dearden, and Richard F. Vancil, *Management Control Systems: Text and Cases*, Richard D. Irwin, Homewood, Illinois, 1972, p. 5.

[4] Lennart Lundquist, *Means and Goals of Political Decentralization*, Studentlitteratur, Malmö, Sweden, 1972, p. 13.

something. The success of policymakers depends, to a very large degree, on the skill and initiative of policy implementors.[5]

A key issue of the chapter is the extent to which the social agency political executives can or should exercise hierarchical control over the various organizations in the social service delivery process. As we work through large-scale organizations and the complexity of intergovernmental relationships, however, we should keep in mind that the most basic question is that of social agency influence at the point of social service delivery. What can agency management do so that social service delivery professionals and their organizational superiors are more able to exercise what Elmore calls "delegated control"—to have more capacity to use reasonable discretion and so to "control" the situation in individual terms?

In this chapter, we will look first at the problem of control for the agency as manifested in regional offices. This sets the stage for looking more generally at the traditional problem of hierarchical control within an organization. Next is considered the problem of two political jurisdictions (intergovernmental relations) forced into what might be viewed as an uneasy partnership to deliver social services. Here we treat at length the critical notion of bargaining where hierarchical authority stops and the social agency attempts to negotiate with another political entity in a continuing bargaining relationship to determine how federal funds are to be used.

Next we consider the concept of fixing. The inherent difficulties of social service delivery programs mean that legislation is quickly found to have flaws, detailed plans go awry, bargains breakdown. Somebody has to step in to try to set things right. The particular situation may demand the exercise of control in the traditional sense, more bargaining, or simply some constructive help. Fixing, which has to do with adjustments, repairs and modifications, is the effort made to address these basic problems. In this sense, it cuts across traditional control and bargaining. That point needs elaboration. But for now, we can say the performance game needs a fixer along with a bargainer.

Finally, we will consider the use of some type of incentives or marketlike approaches—what can be labeled broadly as indirect controls. The question is whether such efforts can either substitute for or supplement direct agency approaches. Can the social agency increase its im-

---

[5] Richard F. Elmore, *Complexity and Control: What Legislators and Administrators Can Do about Implementation*, Institute of Governmental Research, University of Washington, Public Policy Paper No. 11, Seattle, April 1979, p. 3, italics in the original.

pact, albeit indirectly, by utilizing the unseen hand of Adam Smith to guide action?

THE PROBLEM OF CONTROL IN FEDERAL REGIONAL OFFICES

Administrative decentralization—the locating of staff outside of headquarters—has a long history in the federal government.[6] Such field offices may well be direct extentions of the central office for span of control and efficiency purposes to execute functions for which headquarters is responsible. We should not forget that one of the strongest arguments for locating in the field is to exert greater control. As Fesler has observed, "Field organizations have their historical genesis in the need of central governments to carry out their regulations and their services to citizens throughout the country. The flow may be entirely from the center to the circumference, with field agents merely executing central orders."[7] Getting into the field may permit federal officials to watch what the locals do much more closely and to regulate and supervise more thoroughly.

In considering administrative decentralization, it is important to recall that the issue in federal agencies until the last quarter century involved federal field units delivering services directly. Only with the rapid growth of grants-in-aid did the problem emerge of federal field staff as intermediaries between headquarters and organizations in other political jurisdictions. It was not a problem given much thought or planning at the time it arose. Social agency regional and area office staffs "just grew" in the wake of the rapid expansion of social services in the mid-1960s.

Then, in the mystique of the New Federalism, the notion of regionalism emerged. There was to be a intramural shift of power within the federal government that gave field offices more independence from headquarters. Regionalism, however, was also part of the larger decentralization theme in which power was to be shifted from the federal government to local governments. In a brief time period, without much thought about design or consequences, social agencies moved from small field staffs serving as simple extensions of headquarters to a new concept of standardized, relatively large regional offices with some degree of autonomy operating as an integral part of the larger decentralization effort.

---

[6] For an account of federal field offices, see James W. Fesler, *Area and Administration*, University of Alabama Press, Tuscaloosa, Alabama, 1949.

[7] Ibid., pp. 61–62.

The New Federalism combined the shifts of power to local governments and to regional offices in its decentralization efforts. However, the federal government could have given subnational governments more power without an intramural power shift from headquarters to regional offices. For example, CETA provisions establishing local governments as prime sponsors would have increased local power relative to the federal office whether or not there had been regional offices. Decentralization and regionalization are not necessarily tied. Indeed, regionalization can increase federal interference through more pedestrian and rigid behavior from federal field staff. As Nathan has pointed out:

> [A] closer analysis of the consequences of administrative decentralization reveals that it is not necessarily consistent with *policy decentralization* as outlined under the New Federalism. For administrative decentralization tends to solidify the very group that policy decentralization would weaken—the bureaucracy. At the regional level especially, career program officials, if given the power actually to make grant awards, are in a strong position to bring the viewpoint and interests of their particular program to bear in setting state and local priorities and structuring program operations. Moreover, federal officials in the field often tend to be the most rigid and inflexible of program-oriented career officials. Their more creative and innovative colleagues tend to gravitate to Washington; the old liners are the ones typically "selected-out" for field assignments when changes are sought either within the bureaucracy or from outside. For an Administration committed to strengthening the chief elected executives of general-purpose units of state and local government, administrative decentralization often had the exact opposite effect of deepening the hold of special program interests.[8]

As we saw in the case materials, headquarters through the later New Federalism period was seeking to take back power from the field. The Carter administration went further. In discussing what they saw as a "tilt" toward Washington in the early Carter administration, the Advisory Commission on Intergovernmental Relations stated "Of even greater concern to some observers was the action by the Secretaries of HEW, HUD, and Labor to strip their regional offices of any real authority over grant decisions. . . . These decisions, which for the most part were made without consultation with state or local officials, suggested a recentralization of authority at the national level."[9]

[8] Richard P. Nathan, *The Plot That Failed: Nixon and the Administrative President,* Wiley, New York, 1975, p. 30, italics in the original. This and other references to the same article are under copyright © by John Wiley & Sons, Inc. Reprinted with permission of John Wiley & Sons, Inc.

[9] *Intergovernmental Perspective,* Advisory Commission on Intergovernmental Relations, Winter 1978, p. 6. The entire issue of *Intergovernmental Perspective* bears the title "A Tilt toward Washington: Federalism in 1977." In it ACIR is pushing the thesis that on balance the Carter administration is trying to undo much of the New Federalism. As we saw in the discussion of the HUD reorganization, the quoted statement on the regional offices, though overdrawn, points to the general direction of recentralization.

We have come again to the dilemma of the duality of discretion. On the one hand, the case for clear lines of authority and communication and for unambiguous headquarters accountability pushes toward little or no field staff discretion. The argument for more headquarters power is that the agency will have the clearest lines of communication, responsibility, and authority possible. The danger exists that the message will be changed, time will be lost, and responsibility lines will be blurred when a directive from Washington must be passed through the various layers of the regional office hierarchy before it is handed down to the field representative or the area office. A tight structure that eliminates all field staff except to provide routine services or develop information needed by headquarters promises to reduce the confusion and ambiguity in the field that so plagued CETA and CDBG. It holds out the lure of putting headquarters political executives clearly in charge of what the agency does.

On the other hand, given the complexity and diversity in operating social service delivery programs in the field, a knowledgeable person from the agency who is on the spot to exercise discretion seems highly desirable. Since the tendency of headquarters is to push to uniformity in interpretation, it is important for field staffs to have the authority to allow variations more likely to improve performance. Holding too tight a rein increases the turnaround time in the field and decreases the stature of the field staffs. Local people will see little value in discussing anything with field staff when they always have to go to headquarters to get a final answer.

Even though the decentralization issue is a common problem for large-scale organizations, whether in the public or private sector, we must be careful to keep in mind a fundamental difference. In the business area, top management will be able at least to some degree to choose between decentralization and centralization in the traditional sense of only having to confront a within-organization choice. But Congress in effect rules out a direct tie to operating elements by opting for the shared responsibilities model. The complex setting of shared governance dominates. When the social agency considers the question of centralization versus decentralization for its own field staff, it is a second-order decision made *after* the political one that puts both some of the implementers and all project operators within the jurisdictions of other political entities.

Moreover, the demands on the federal social agency—particularly in the block grant legislation—are for a delicate balancing of national and local interests. As Stenberg and Walker have observed

The federal administering agency is a middleman between Congress and interest groups on the one side, and recipient jurisdictions on the other. It must provide for national leadership and direction, while allowing recipients maximum latitude in exercising discretion. While the demands are not irreconcilable, this is a very difficult—but essential—balance to strike. This is the basic reason why the block grant appears to be the least stable of all forms of intergovernmental fiscal transfers. Unless the federal administering agency takes proper steps to assure that the intent of the statute is being carried out and that federal funds are being used effectively and efficiently—such as through substantive plan approval, development of performance standards, and evaluation of recipient programs—pressures for recategorization will grow. And unless it assures that recipients have genuine flexibility in tailoring funds to their needs, disillusionment with decentralization will ensue. Furthermore, in the conversion from the categorical to block grant mode of program operations, new recipients require technical assistance and regional offices require guidance. The block grant, then, does not abrogate federal responsibility; it merely changes the nature and extent of agency involvement in program implementation.[10]

Here the complexity of the federal agency's role in shared governance brought about by within and external organizational control problems is most vivid.

To complicate matters further, the two control problems get intertwined in practice. In particular, legislation such as CETA and CDBG set out top political executive responsibilities for what social service deliverers do *as if all* administrative units and the service deliverers were segments of a single organization. The political executives appear to be expected to plan for and control implementation and operations in the same way that business managers do.

MANAGEMENT CONTROL WITHIN ORGANIZATIONS

Management control must address the basic problem for top-level executives in a decentralized organization of motivating its field managers and staff to use discretion within boundaries. Central management wants field managers to exercise discretion when the field situation is sufficiently complex and unpredictable to limit the usefulness of detailed guidelines in particular cases. Such a setting generally demands tactical choices to be made on the spot by people with more detailed and more current knowledge of the terrain than their superiors. And this need for discretion so often becomes critical at the point of service delivery, where street-level bureaucrats or their immediate superiors must confront the diversity of individual cases and situations.

The basic thesis is that discretion as to means will enhance performance leading to stated objectives. However, top management gener-

---

[10] Carl W. Stenberg and David B. Walker, "The Block Grant: Lessons from Two Early Experiments," PUBLIUS, *Journal of Federalism*, Spring 1977, p. 57.

ally wants boundaries to action. Top management seeks limits cast in terms of objectives and of means that bound discretionary field judgments. Over time, management may end up emphasizing the adherence to boundaries more than the exercise of discretion.

Centralization

Centralization is the organizational control strategy pursued by top-level managers who seek to establish quite limited boundaries for the exercise of discretion by field managers. Headquarters will try to establish set or programmed responses that fit potential field contingencies. Both rules and sanctions are constructed to drive field managers toward either following explicit guidelines developed by top management or turning to headquarters when what to do is not clear.

In a centralized system, discretion seems to be viewed as either not useful or too risky. As to the former, there may be few enough decisions requiring discretion that headquarters can act on them expeditiously and with greater skill than field staff. More likely, top management does not want to risk field judgments, even though limiting discretion may involve significant costs from lost time or lack of particular information by headquarters. They may fear that field managers will make poor judgments or purposely will go against the organizational interests as perceived by headquarters.

The choice of the centralized structure may derive from leadership style or tradition consistent with the idealized image of the classic hierarchical organization. However, centralization, which is labeled "tight control," often indicates "weak controls." That is, top management believes it must give up the benefits of field discretion because there are insufficient means to bound it. Sound performance information, powerful incentives, like-mindedness of middle-level managers—factors discussed later that may provide boundaries for discretion—are not in place. The strategy of centralization is to create rules and establish functions that constrain discretion.

Decentralized Control[11]

Even where top management sees the need for more discretionary field behavior, it is likely to yield discretion rather grudgingly. We need to consider two approaches that broaden but still bound discretion.

[11] For an interesting discussion of decentralization in broader federalism terms, see Daniel J. Elazar, "Federalism vs. Decentralization: The Drift from Authenticity," PUBLIUS, *Journal of Federalism*, Fall 1976, pp. 9–19. Note particularly Elazar's notion of

The two, as will be clear, are complementary and so are likely to be employed together.

The first seeks like-minded behavior by field managers with homogeneity of background and training, long association, indoctrination, or some combination of these. As Philip Selznick observed in his classic book on leadership:

> The need for centralization declines as the homogeneity of personnel increases. A unified outlook, binding all levels of administration, will permit decentralization without damage to policy. When top leadership cannot depend on adherence to its viewpoint, formal controls are required, if only to take measures that will increase homogeneity. On the other hand, when the premises of official policy are well understood and well accepted, centralization is more readily dispensable.[12]

Various strategies for hiring and training people to exhibit such like-minded thinking have been tried. Organizations may employ people with specific kinds of professional training or backgrounds or recruit from particular schools. Another device is to run formal training programs for managers at different stages of their careers. An organization may have a beginning training period of several months to impart special skills and to indoctrinate the new managers. A less formal route is to bring people up through the ranks, slowly building esprit de corps. Kaufman in his study of the United States Forest Service pointed out that "the Rangers want to do the very things that the Forest Service wants them to do, and are able to do them because these are the decisions and actions that become second nature to them as a result of years of obedience."[13] As we have seen, the Department of Labor fits this mold to some extent. Even though DOL seemed to be philosophically uncomfortable with field discretion, headquarters managers often could rely upon people in the field to act within self-imposed boundaries that had formed over a considerable period of time.

The second approach for supporting more decentralized manage-

---

non-centralization, which recognizes that federal and local governments are not in a hierarchical relationship. Technically decentralization comes about from a hierarchical relationship (a superior unit). However, we will employ the term *decentralization* because of its wide usage, even though *noncentralization* better describes shared governance in terms of intergovernmental relationships.

[12] Philip Selznick, *Leadership in Administration: A Sociological Interpretation*, Row, Peterson and Co., New York, 1957, p. 113.

[13] Herbert Kaufman, *The Forest Ranger: A Study of Administrative Interpretation*, Johns Hopkins University Press, Baltimore, 1960, p. 228.

ment is a formal control system. Anthony and Dearden define such a system as follows

> A control system is a system whose purpose is to maintain a desired state or condition. Any control system has at least these four elements:
> 1. A measuring device which detects what is happening in the parameter being controlled, that is, a detector
> 2. A device for assessing the significance of what is happening, usually by comparing information of what is *actually happening* with some standard or expectation of what *should be happening*, that is, a selector
> 3. A device for altering behavior if the need for doing so is indicated, that is, an effector
> 4. A means for communicating information among these devices.[14]

The basic requirements for a high level of decentralized control are (a) objectives and standards for which there are measurable control points; (b) sanctions that induce performance, inhibit the overstepping of boundaries, or preferably both; and (c) good lines of communication, facilitating clear messages flowing both up and down the organization. That is, the organization needs to be able to establish and communicate measurable boundaries and to apply sanctions that reward or punish in terms of the boundaries.

The central technical issues of decentralization concern the underlying quality of information and the organization of efforts to check on behavior. A strong empirical base of control requires both available techniques that produce sound data and an organizational structure that will yield it in a timely fashion.[15]

Solid control points can provide top management a strong empirical base for applying both the carrot and the stick. Top managers still need to motivate field managers, who in turn must be able to find the right tactics in the field. But it is no small asset to have a strong underlying basis for exerting such leadership. Good structure, good information, and strong sanctions aid in inducing high performance.

The granting of some discretion to field managers is more likely to be viewed as a means of increasing performance when top-level managers (a) know where they want to go; (b) can put objectives and stand-

[14] Anthony and Dearden, *Management Control Systems*, Third Edition, pp. 3–4, italics in the original.

[15] Another useful discussion of control systems is William G. Ouchi, "The Relationship between Organizational Structure and Organizational Control," *Administrative Science Quarterly*, March 1977, pp. 95–113. Like the work of Anthony and his colleagues, Ouchi's effort is based mainly on private sector examples. He stresses information techniques in observing at p. 99 that "the control system of an organization consists essentially of a process of monitoring, evaluating, and rewarding."

ards in sufficiently clear terms to direct and bound field managers; but (c) are unable to specify what should be done in the field sufficiently well to prescribe field manager responses and do not have the time or the detailed knowledge to determine tactics for unpredicted situations.[16]

Iron Laws of Control, Congress, and the Social Agencies

We need to consider both how Congress treats the control issue and the implications of such treatment for social agency governance. When Congress defines national intent loosely to allow diversity, such behavior in a larger sense fits the needs of democratic federalism. At the same time, this *looseness of definition must be purchased with the currency of control*. Congress still can create the appearance of tight control with stringent language that speaks as if the agencies can exert strong direct control, but neither it nor the agencies can circumvent the iron laws of control.

The first law pertaining to the governance of complex social programs is that the maximum ability of the federal government to establish control exists at the point *prior* to the basic congressional decisions on allocation and distribution. For example, if Congress really intends that there be a narrow band of eligibility for public service employment jobs restricted to low-income workers, long-term unemployed persons, or welfare recipients, it must both set out eligibility definitions (e.g., income levels, weeks of unemployment) and specify that funds can benefit *only* the defined groups. As the CETA public employment experience makes so clear, defining eligibility broadly, exhorting hiring the disadvantaged, but leaving choice to local discretion results in employers choosing the most highly qualified workers available.[17]

The second iron law is the more general one looked at earlier that tight control demands clear boundary points and strong sanctions to punish violations. The first requirement, for the kind of unambiguous specificity that makes clear what is to be done and leaves no large es-

---

[16] Our colleague Richard Elmore has pointed out to us that what often appears to be a decentralized system is better described as a sophisticated adaptation of a centralized system to complex environments. That is, boundaries are tightened wherever possible by restrictive means. Such grudging "decentralization" and the loosening of a centralized system are hard to distinguish.

[17] For a good discussion of the public employment experience, see William Mirengoff and Lester Rindler, *CETA: Manpower Programs under Local Control*, National Academy of Sciences, 1978, pp. 158–193, 213–214.

cape clauses, is hard enough. The second requirement, for sanctions that are likely to be applied even in the face of strong pressures by constituents, may be even more difficult to meet.

Providing an appropriate base for the social agencies to exercise tight control places great strains on Congress. Even in those cases (e.g., distributional outcomes) where Congress may be able to establish boundaries and sanctions to support strong hierarchical authority, it has almost always opted not to do so. Congress seldom if ever wants to pay the price of the required specificity and sanctions. It finds strong agency control, even if available, not worth buying.

This set of circumstances, however, has not deterred either Congress from acting as if the tenets of strong hierarchical control could guide action or the agencies from responding in rather perverse ways to create the image of such control. As for Congress, the tendency is to overreach in fixing social agency responsibilities and to charge the agencies with too much. As the case materials make so clear, to meet these unrealistic demands the agencies enshrine compliance—and usually rather narrow administrative compliance—as the highest mark of control. This narrow focus on compliance so often brings harassment and establishes impediments at the local level. The locals respond in kind, trying to counter agency action. Both the feds and the locals exercise their strong suit, which is to block the efforts of each other.

Perhaps the most important case of federal overreaching involves fixing responsibility for the long-run improvements in social conditions—that is, for the final outcomes desired in legislation. The federal government in general and the social agencies in particular have very limited direct influence over these final outcomes. In the first place, exogenous factors may be the major determinants of such outcomes. Even in the areas of the government can affect, the agencies are severely restricted by the kinds of political–bureaucratic limitations already mentioned and specific technical deficiencies. Consider these deficiencies.[18] First, there is a lack of proven programmatic approaches. Second, final outcomes are difficult to define in uncontroversial terms, or the agreed upon definitions may be so broad (in order to get agreement) that they lack the precision needed to support field measurement. Third, measurement itself is difficult and the results usually are subject to challenge. Evaluations of social service delivery programs so often yield controversial information that does little to enhance the direct control of social agencies over desired final outcomes. The results simply do

---

[18] These technical issues are discussed at greater length in the next chapter.

not provide a sufficiently sound empirical base for exercising direct control.[19]

Because of this lack of agency power, it is highly questionable for Congress to charge social agencies with responsibility for final outcomes. In so doing, Congress commits what can be labeled "the final outcome fallacy": Congress desires certain final outcomes for social service delivery programs. Congress itself has *direct* power over social agencies but not over the local jurisdictions that operate programs. Hence, Congress charges the agencies with *direct* responsibility for the desired outcomes.[20]

This outcome fallacy violates the basic management principle of linking responsibility and authority. Nothing is more fundamental to management than the principle that those who are charged with a mission have the commensurate authority and capacity to carry it out. Only under such circumstances does accountability for performance make sense.

Local grantees appear to be the only unit that legitimately could be held accountable for final outcomes in social service delivery programs funded under the shared responsibility model. This is not a philosophical or political judgment that "the locals know best," but recognition that a reasonable level of direct power over final outcomes in the shared power model, *if such a level exists at all*, resides with the local organizations that deliver services.

The stumbling blocks in the administrative and support domain seem sure to continue until the agencies are freed from the charge of direct responsibility for these final outcomes. The retreat from direct social agency responsibility for final outcomes paradoxically may be the only means over time to increase the federal government's impact on such outcomes.

Even without direct responsibility for final outcomes, there are still demanding charges that can be given to a social agency under the mixed funding model for social service delivery programs. Such charges might include increasing (a) the degree of compliance to legislative directives; (b) the commitment and capacity of local organizations to implement and administer programs and projects; and

[19] We are not arguing that final outcome evaluations of social service delivery programs are useless activities. Later discussions will consider how they might be employed.

[20] The nature of the fallacy is captured by the old joke in which a drunk man at night is searching for a lost wallet under a street light. When asked if that is the spot where the wallet was lost, the man replies that it is not but that the street light is the only place with enough light to see.

(c) the capacity of local institutional processes to move programs toward the specified objectives of social legislation.

However, here too, the iron laws of control apply so that decisions about what the social agency's mission ought to be should depend on the real power base of that agency. Unless Congress is able and willing to set specific boundaries and fix sanctions, the social agencies will have deficient "selectors, detectors, and effectors." Under such circumstances, a social agency simply cannot exercise tight control in the field across political jurisdictions.

The tenets of hierarchical control offer a dubious framework for guiding decisions and action in social agency governance. The notions of hierarchical authority and tight organizational control seldom make sense as guides to social agency behavior toward subnational governments in the grants-in-aid era.[21]

POWER ACROSS POLITICAL JURISDICTIONS: THE BARGAINING MODE[22]

Daniel Elazar has written "It may not be too great an exaggeration to suggest that the historical model that most closely resembles the federal government in its domestic role today is the Holy Roman Empire in those periods where the Emperor's domestic powers were contingent on the cooperation of his barons."[23] This shared governance of social service delivery programs seems certain to require a high level of

[21] Let us underscore that at this point we are speaking only of social agencies in the shared responsibilities model, not social organizations in general. In particular, we are not addressing organizational control issues in social service delivery organizations where we would need to explore the complex relationship of technology, structure, and control. For the type of questions that would need to be considered, see Ouchi, "The Relationship between Organizational Structure and Organizational Control," pp. 95–100.

[22] Our discussion of bargaining has drawn upon Graham T. Allison, *Essence of Decision*, Little, Brown, Boston, 1977; Richard F. Elmore, "Organizational Models of Social Program Implementation," *Public Policy*, Spring 1978, pp. 185–228; and Helen Ingram, "Policy Implementation through Bargaining," *Public Policy*, Fall 1977, pp. 499–526. Allison provides a general treatment of bargaining within government. Elmore uses the bargaining framework for one of his organizational models, with the bargaining model operating within the organization rather than between organizations. The ideas, however, apply to the latter context. The Ingram piece is a detailed treatment of bargaining between governments as a factor in the implementation process. All three works provide extensive listings of references of what has now become a mammoth literature on bargaining.

[23] Daniel J. Elazar, "The Problem of Political Distance," *National Civic Review*, July 1978, p. 338.

adaptive behavior on the part of both federal and subnational governments. In the implementation process over time, adaptations need to be worked out that respond both to political differences (say, as to goals) and to substantive difficulties where none of the actors necessarily had answers at the outset of implementation.[24] The notion of a bargain captures the flavor of this adaptive implementation behavior in social service delivery programs. As Elmore observes "[The] bargain is a two-way affair, inherently different from hierarchical control. A contract is not an instrument of coercion."[25]

The rules of the social service delivery performance game fix a formidable task for social agency leadership in the grants-in-aid era. At the bargaining table with local governments, the social agency is at best an equal. There is no trump card of hierarchical authority to play. Rather, the game requires that the social agency possess subtle skill and much knowledge about the roles, the players, and available strategies in the federal–local bargaining situation.

Federal–Local Bargaining

Two bargaining situations need to be distinguished (a) national-level or macro-bargaining in the decision domain to determine overall program allocations and the distribution of those program funds; and (b) local-level or micro-bargaining in the administrative and support domain to determine funding levels and restrictions in individual localities. Although most of our attention will focus on micro-bargaining, macro-bargaining needs to be considered because it materially affects the bargaining advantages at the local level.

NATIONAL–LEVEL BARGAINING

National-level or macro-bargaining can be thought of in terms of two interrelated games. The first is to determine how many dollars will go to a broad funding area such as employment and training programs. In such an area, the best bargaining strategy, generally speaking, is for potential fund recipients to work in a coalition for the highest possible budget figure. There is likely to be cooperation among the different

[24] For interesting discussions of adaptive behavior in implementation, see Paul Berman, *Designing Implementation to Match Policy Situation: A Contingency Analysis of Programmed and Adaptive Implementation,* Rand Corporation, P–6211, Santa Monica, California, October 1978; and Milbrey McLaughlin, "Implementation as Mutual Adaptation: Change in Classroom Organization" in Walter Williams and Richard Elmore (editors), *Social Program Implementation,* Academic Press, New York, 1976, pp. 167–180.

[25] Elmore, *Complexity and Control,* p. 36.

types of subnational governments and their key lobbying groups, often with either up-front or sub-rosa help from the social agency, to get more funds overall.

The most interesting situation comes when the parties turn to dividing up the now fixed amount of available funds. Then the distribution becomes a classic zero sum game—any winnings by one player will be offset exactly by the losings of another. During distribution play, allocation alliances may no longer be appropriate. More accurately, since the process of legislation often mixes together allocation and distribution, there is watchful cooperation in trying to get more funds, lest one of the competitors try to gain advantage in the distribution game.

A number of factors, including the tightness of the federal budget, can make allocation a generally uninteresting issue most of the time. The politics of distribution, however, is the longest running game in town. Here the battleground is broader than the higher reaches of the decision domain. Agency actions are necessary to implement distribution decisions. The classic battles of city and suburb or Sun Belt and Snow Belt can go on every day in the halls of Congress and the agency.

Macro-bargaining is important to an understanding of bargaining at the local level. First, the various alliances that get established at the national level, even though fragile at times because of battles over distribution, do represent a key power base to help local governments in their bargaining with the social agencies. The social agency may well hold back because it knows that any adverse action against a local jurisdiction can trigger efforts by an alliance of Washington-based groups to stir up members of Congress or staff in the executive office. Both city and suburb are concerned generally that the social agency does not beat down a particular local jurisdiction, since success today in one location may be translated into more social agency backbone, including a national guideline to expand the local victory.

In a formula grant, a computer can implement the first distributional decision that says how much funds will go to particular jurisdictions. But beyond this, the distributional decisions concerning target groups and geographic areas require interpretation, checking, and usually specific enforcement actions by the agency. Since these distributional outcomes are likely to be much more the concern of interest groups than are specific programmatic activities, there is likely to be a great deal of pressure on Congress and the agency to develop national guidelines that give desired interpretations and to see that the expected distributional outcomes occur.

Controversies over the implementation and administration of

distributional decisions can be a, perhaps *the*, primary driving force in federal compliance efforts. No pressures on the agency may be as intense as those from external advocates to enforce distributional requirements. And those who suffer from increased federal control efforts may at times be members of coalitions that push for exactly such controls. Indeed, what is interpreted at the local level as a tactic devised within the social agency to win back federal power may really be a harried response by the agency to strong interest group pressures to implement and enforce distributional decisions. Powerful enough outside pressures to enforce distribution decisions can unleash the ultimate weapons of fund cutback and even cutoff.

BARGAINING AT THE LOCAL LEVEL

The bargaining advantages of a specific local community vis-à-vis the social agency will depend upon the general power of its allies, its individual power base, the past funding history and programmatic experience in a particular funding area, and the political, bureaucratic, and technical capabilities of the locality in the specific programmatic area. The first is independent of the locality per se (the clout of local governments or suburbs as a group) but may fluctuate over time depending upon the political climate. For example, suburbs were favored in the Republican administration, with central cities appearing to gain in the Carter administration. This basically is the power that carries over from the macro-bargaining setting, so we need no further discussion. We also need not dwell upon the tremendous power a locality may have because its mayor is a political favorite or its congressional delegation is not one to be crossed, except to observe that while it lasts this unique political clout may be the biggest bargaining advantage of all.

The history of governmental activity in a social service delivery area may be important. The more that local governments have been involved in providing services in the past and the greater the size of the local involvement compared to the amount of federal contribution, the more the social agency may constrain itself. For example, when the Elementary and Secondary Education Act of 1965 was passed, state and local domination in elementary and secondary education was viewed as an almost sacred right. Further, the federal government invested a relatively small amount of funds as compared to the total funds spent by state and local governments. We cannot say conclusively how much this past history explains subsequent events. However, the Office of Education did almost nothing to enforce Title I of this act, especially in its early days.[26] Nor did Congress object, joining the federal agency, one would guess, in fearing the dangers of the sticky grounds of state rights in education. There may be no better example of federal reluctance to enforce a law.[27]

Program experience may enhance political, organizational, and technical skills. We have seen in both CETA and CDBG that significant involvement in past categorical programs such as model cities added to a locality's bargaining advantages. The social agencies appeared more likely to try to push around the relatively inexperienced fund recipients than those that had a track record.

In addition to localities gaining skills through the experience of administering and operating programs, the social agency may also direct its efforts toward building these skills. This presents a dilemma for the agency. Keeping localities relatively weak and dependent upon social agency technical assistance enhances agency strength at the bargaining table. On the other hand, the lack of capability at the local level threatens performance. Although we think that reasonable policies can reconcile this dilemma to some extent, it must be recognized as one of the continuing contradictions that complicates federal policy in the field.

WEIGHTING THE LOCAL BARGAINING ADVANTAGES
IN EMPLOYMENT AND TRAINING AND COMMUNITY
DEVELOPMENT PROGRAMS

To close this section, let us try to put the notions developed in it in perspective by sweeping quickly from the inception of the second social revolution in the early 1960s to the end of the period of our field observation at the close of the Ford administration. In these two periods of the grants-in-aid era (the Johnson and the Nixon–Ford administrations), the federal government provided almost all of the public sector funds in the employment and training and community development areas, whereas prior to the 1960s, there had been almost no government efforts. Further, over time there was a distinct shift to

[26] For two excellent accounts, see Jerome T. Murphy, "The Education Bureaucracies Implement a Novel Policy: The Politics of Title I of ESEA, 1965–72" in Allan T. Sindler (editor), Policy and Politics in America, Little, Brown, Boston, 1973, pp. 160–198; and Milbrey W. McLaughlin, Evaluation and Reform: Elementary and Secondary Education Act of 1965/Title I, Ballinger, Cambridge, Massachusetts, 1975.

[27] Michael Kirst, who has followed Title I since its inception, tells us that efforts to enforce the law are much more extensive, moving unfortunately toward narrow compliance issues in many cases.

general purpose governments from nongovernmental organizations or organizations with strong ties outside of local governments. This brought more cities and counties directly into manpower and community development issues. Also, representative public interest groups, such as the National Association of Counties or the National League of Cities, became more involved in the macro-bargaining for these funds.

By the mid 1960s, subnational governments had gained some general skills in grantsmanship from the first wave of mainly physical investment grants. But the social agencies had early bargaining advantages. First, the philosophy of federal activism was in vogue. Second, federal staffs usually were superior in skills and experience. Third, the grantor generally had its maximum clout at the outset of a grant. As Ingram points out: "The leverage that comes from this potential power [of fund cutoff] is most credible in the early stages of a grant program, before a routine and pattern of expectations has been established."[28]

Time, however, was on the side of the locals. Not only did the locals become relatively favored ideologically, local governments and their national interest groups got on-the-job training in the specifics of particular program areas. Further, both general revenue sharing and block grants have intensified the movement, which had started gaining momentum in the categorical days, toward increased local political power vis-à-vis the federal government.

A *reverse presumption* now appears to operate in situations where continuing funds are both required and expected.[29] At fund renewal time, the burden of proof might be expected to rest with the local entity to show funding should be continued. However, the presumption apparently lies in the opposite direction: Once granted, the funds "belong" to the local government, and without new national level distributional decisions, the agency has to make a strong case to undo continued funding at the same amount or higher.

The earlier bargaining advantages of federal bureaucrats are most unlikely to be restored except in the case of severe political or economic changes. Federal advantages are not going to be reinstated, we are convinced, by going back to categorical grants or providing funds to nongovernmental organizations. The bargaining advantages at the local level are too strong.

---

[28] Ingram, "Policy Implementation through Bargaining," pp. 509–510.

[29] This funding setting contrasts with either one-time grants such as those for a physical investment (e.g., a building renovation), where continuing funding is not needed, or a start-up program, where the yearly operating funds may be needed but are expected to come from nonfederal sources at a later date.

The Bargaining Mode

Good bargaining strategy requires a search for leverage points—
those places where the bargainer's positional advantage is likely to
yield a high return because he has a scarce resource the other party
wants. For example, assume an individual owns a parcel of land that is
critical to a shopping center and one of the last pieces yet unpurchased
by a developer. Even though this key piece of land may equal only 5%
of the total shopping center acreage, the owner may demand 10% or
even 20% of the total payment for the shopping center land. The same
may be true if a city has an urban development package where HUD
money represents a small but critical segment. HUD might bargain for
jobs or amenities for the disadvantaged to be financed through other
(non-HUD) parts of the package.

Leverage points can be found only where other players already
seem likely to move in the desired direction. That is, leveraging makes
sense only when two or more parties see gains from bargaining.
Leveraging becomes particularly important where the brute power
does not exist to force desired behavior. Those who can command an
action be taken and insure its execution with the threat of strong sanctions need not bother with either the hard search for potential leverage
points or the subtle moves to secure the bargain. Those with great
power do not have to scurry about for positional advantage where a
relatively weak push may tip the scale. Such luxury is not possessed by
social agencies in the performance game. As Ingram has pointed out in
her discussion of federal grants-in-aid to states:

> As a result of grant bargaining, federal administrative agencies can facilitate change
> in a willing state. But in the absence of state commitment, the federal agency cannot
> compel state policy change. The federal government is at best a peripheral partici-
> pant in the state political process.[30]

For leverage, the player must not only find a positional advantage
but have flexible resources to put up at the leverage point. Money may
be the most flexible resource; yet technical aid or organizational power
such as granting a rule variation may be more useful. However, all
such resources need to be discretionary. As discussed earlier, the provision of federal funds to nonfederal organizations for continuing activities locks funds in by creating a reverse presumption (the funder
provider must "prove" the case for withdrawal). The agency needs to
be able to come to the bargaining table with uncommitted resources in
its pocket.

[30] Ingram, "Policy Implementation through Bargaining," italics in the original,
p. 521.

Bargaining in the Performance Game

Bargaining can be a trap if it lures players to overemphasize the immediate results of the deal at the bargaining table. Good bargaining in the performance game is more than a virtuoso display of political wits in action.

The critical point is that the two bargainers are not like buyers and sellers who go their separate ways after the transaction but rather are engaged in a continuing relationship where they are also partners, albeit uneasy ones. The bargain is a good one for the federal government if it increases the likelihood that the other partner will move toward better organizational and program performance—that is, only if the local bargainer *can* carry out its commitment. Getting a local organization to overcommit itself in the bargain, even though it fully intends to fulfill that promise, is not a good federal deal. The agency must recognize that a fundamental need is for local organizations to have sufficient competence to administer and operate programs in the field.

There is a hard base to bargaining. The federal bargainer must know the playing field including the social agency's own limits, local limits, local needs, and the kinds of resources likely to address those needs. This demands homework. The agency must search for appropriate leverage points and undertake sufficient analysis to determine how the bargain will affect local performance. There must be analytic capacity to assess the implications of counteroffers once the negotiations begin.

These more technical activities depend upon the agency's capacity to develop useful information. The most useful information will indicate what local operators need to increase their commitment and capacity. Knowledge about what resources the locals need is far more important in indicating how the federal government can help in a joint effort than it is in showing what the federal government can wave before the locals as a bargaining chip. The highest level of federal credibility should come when the locals realize that the social agency staff is sensitive to this situation and its implications in the program performance game. This is what will make the continuing game, with its recurring bargains, productive.

FIXING THE PERFORMANCE GAME

Central to fixing are the complexity and indeterminancy of social service delivery programs funded through grants-in-aid. Underlying uncertainty amid the dynamics of the performance game hampers efforts to do detailed planning and to act.

Consider detailed planning first. The planner can be trapped by the framework of formal planning, misguided by a language that promises far more certainty than can be attained. The critical insight about planning in complex social service program areas is that at any point in time, it must be constrained. Perhaps, no one has captured this notion as well as Levine:

> [T]he contention here is that we need a new sort of planning. Rather than selecting desirable future states and laying out courses over deceptive terrain, both policy-making and policy planning should be directional. That is, policymakers should decide what general sort of future would be better than an alternative, and policy planners should lay out steps that show a probability of moving in that general direction. . . . It means trial-and-error iteration of policies; if a planned step moves in a direction other than the expected one, it can be corrected.[31]

A "fixer" is needed to provide that correction. In *The Implementation Game*, Bardach found a fixer in Assemblyman Frank Lanterman of California. Lanterman's extended efforts over time guided the implementation of the Lanterman–Petris–Short (L–P–S) Act of 1967, termed "the Magna Carta" of the mentally ill. Lanterman's position made him an ideal fixer. First, he was the senior Republican on the powerful Ways and Means Committee. "[M]ental health policy," as Bardach points out, "was Lanterman's territory and . . . no significant changes in that area could be made without his consent or, alternatively, without having him exact a price."[32] Second, Lanterman was near the end of his career. The L–P–S Act was to be the capstone of his work, particularly in his special area of mental health.

Lanterman knew the direction that the act was to go, had the power to intervene, and was willing to take the time to make needed adjustments along the way. He clearly was in a pivotal position. Here was the fixer par excellence with the commitment and the capability to make on-the-spot adjustments in the dynamics of play.

Position alone, however, is not enough. A fixer needs help. As Bardach indicated in discussing Lanterman's role:

> Is all this to say that only "power" counts when it comes to fixing the implementation game? Not at all. Formal authority and formal political resources count for much but not for everything. The fixer must be able to intervene effectively, but he or she must also be able to know where, when, and about what. To know these things, he or she must have access to a great deal of information and have the flow of information summarized, interpreted, and validated so that he or she can make sense of it. . . . Just as money attracts money, information attracts information.

[31] Robert A. Levine, *Public Planning: Failure and Redirection*, Basic Books, New York, 1972, pp. 164–165.

[32] Eugene Bardach, *The Implementation Game*, MIT Press, Cambridge, Massachusetts, 1977, p. 13. See p. 9–35 for the account of Lanterman in action. This and other

Without information about how implementation games were being played "out there" in the field, Lanterman would have been powerless to do any fixing.[33]

A fixer can do without an underlying base of technical and organizational resources. The organization must be capable of generating needed information and analyzing it to yield new strategies and tactics to support the fixer over time.

Generally, we will put bargaining and fixing together as the preferred mode of play in the performance game. Sometimes through negotiating, sometimes through repairs, sometimes through renegotiating after repairs, the agency tries to move local units toward better organizational and program performance. In action, bargaining and fixing blend together.

However, we should be aware that fixing is more difficult to do than bargaining. Making repairs often relies far more heavily upon technical than political judgments, but top-level fixing demands political–bureaucratic manipulation and leadership. This must be done without the power of hierarchical authority or the safety of clear rules. Bardach has captured the essence of fixing when he observed

Game-fixing is quintessentially government by men rather than laws. It is not necessarily, though, irresponsible government. [The real problem] is that too few of the would-be fixers know how to do the right thing, are willing to do it if they do know how, and have the political resources to make their will effective. The most problematic role in the fixer coalition, the one that is hardest to come by, is the intervener at the top, the person or persons with powerful political resources.[34]

INDIRECT CONTROLS: THE SEARCH FOR MARKETLIKE FORCES

One of the most vexing aspects of the federal funding system for social service delivery programs is the lack of pressure points pushing the social agencies and the organizations they fund toward better performance in the field. More and more, the conventional wisdom is that governments are unresponsive to performance concerns. This has brought a growing call for indirect controls that rely on marketlike (competitive) incentives. Some of these are similar to management control measures now used by private industries. These include performance incentives for government employees or organizational incentives, as when the National Academy of Sciences Committee on

---

references to the same article are under copyright © 1977 by the Massachusetts Institute of Technology.

[33] Ibid., pp. 277–278. See pp. 268–284 for a discussion of fixing the implementation game.

[34] Ibid., p. 279.

Evaluation of Employment and Training Programs recommends that the Department of Labor in CETA should "encourage innovation by offering incentive funds [to prime sponsors] or by subsidizing some of the risk."[35] Other approaches include efforts to create pressures among different units within the agency or to stimulate citizen pressures on local government for performance.

The strongest message of indirect controls is to use government less and market forces more. In setting out a number of "postliberal heresies," Bardach puts the case against government most forcefully:

> A second heresy has asserted that even when we know what ought to be done, and can get political leaders to agree to mandate it, government is probably ill suited to do the job. At the very least, it is likely that the bureaucratic and regulatory strategies government has traditionally relied upon are ineffective if not mischievous. Economists, both liberal and conservative, have taken the lead here and have argued persuasively that manipulating the marketplace may often be a better strategy than trying to abolish it or inventing a substitute for it.[36]

The argument is that the unseen hand of Adam Smith, the forces of supply and demand, competition with far less government involvement will make for greater efficiency and effectiveness in government policies. Although indirect, such forces are expected to push toward better performance more effectively than direct means of organizational influence.

The problem with the market model is that it works well only under rather restrictive conditions. As Richard Nelson observes "It must be recognized, however, that the great efficacy alleged from marketlike organization rests on two empirical propositions. One is that the market-failure problems are not very serious in most sectors; second, that the remedies for these problems often are easy to apply and effective."[37] Moreover, the market model is most likely to break down in the complex service areas that we are considering

> The conventional wisdom is that no one knows self-interests better than the person or group affected, but there are serious reasons to doubt that this holds in all cases. . . . Many parents know little about what goes on in the school their children

---

[35] Mirengoff and Rindler, CETA: Manpower Programs under Local Control, p. 254.

[36] Bardach, The Implementation Game, p. 4. The need to rely upon market forces in the public sector has been espoused by a number of individuals—the most useful general treatments being by Charles Schultze and Robert Levine. Schultze has made his argument over a number of years, with the most recent statement being Charles L. Schultze, The Public Use of Private Interest, Brookings Institution, Washington, D.C., 1977. Levine's most extended treatment is presented in Public Planning, cited in footnote 31.

[37] Richard R. Nelson, The Moon and the Ghetto: An Essay on Public Policy Analysis, Norton, New York, 1977, pp. 46–47. Nelson goes on to point out on p. 47: "If

are attending, and have little information and knowledge on which to judge alternatives; clearly, parental choice cannot bear the full weight of the decision mechanism. Indeed, in a large number of our problem sectors there is reason to doubt that consumers or voters have enough knowledge to make good choices. . . .

Nor does reliance on for-profit enterprise seem a general solution to the problem of supply organization. The case for for-profit supply is strong where the good or service in question is easily evaluated by consumers, and where there is considerable competition among suppliers. Where these conditions do not hold, there is good reason to adopt regimes of supply organization that can internalize, to some extent, the demanders interest—governmental or not for-profit forms, or other mechanisms of public control that damp or channel the profit motive.[38]

An example of a market device for social services will show both the potential and the problems. Consider the case of granting purchase vouchers directly to those eligible for training under a program such as CETA. Employment training would be provided by either a teaching institution such as a community college, with the voucher covering tuition and other educational expenses, or an employer, with the payments from vouchers being used as a form of wage subsidy. The voucher by coming directly to the trainee permits that person to search through alternative opportunities rather than being forced to take what CETA offers. The institutions interested in providing either classroom or on-the-job training will compete for clients. Here are the forces of the marketplace with lots of buyers and sellers engaged in the kinds of efforts seen as pushing toward better services, lower prices, or both.

But even under the voucher plan, some level of government would need to determine eligibility for a voucher, probably based on income level and employment status. In addition, there could be efforts to regulate suppliers, although the danger exists that this might be perceived as too much government interference. If eligibility determination is the only additional government activity beyond already existing regulation of suppliers (e.g., existing state and federal laws pertaining to educational institutions), then there should be a reasonable base for the promised efficiencies and benefits of private market forces.

The results, however, may fall short of expected outcomes. Vouchers as such have not been tried on a large scale, but there have been a number of employment programs (the Johnson administration JOBS being, perhaps, the most ambitious) predicated at least in part on

---

political scientists can be accused of seeing the hand of formal government everywhere, and the need for it almost everywhere, the economist can be accused of arguing away the need for government almost anywhere, and advocating the almost universal superiority of the hidden hands of consumer sovereignty and competition among suppliers to meet consumer demand."

[38] Ibid., pp. 48–49.

the assumption that incentives to businesses would induce them to find better means of training for the disadvantaged. Whatever the relative success of these business attempts at training compared to public sector efforts, there is no compelling evidence of huge success.

The efficient and effective training techniques that have eluded people thus far are likely to elude those offering services in the marketplace. The "law of markets" does not guarantee technical breakthroughs or automatically solve the organizational problems that bedevil complex social service delivery programs. The potential benefits of marketlike forces must be cast in realistic terms.

Individual purchase vouchers with their reliance on market forces also raise the basic political question of government's willingness to stop in the face of less-than-desired outcomes. Do politicians and interest groups say philosophically, and perhaps quite realistically, government has done all it can in providing financial support—the basic opportunity—to get needed training? Do they say this even though large numbers of participants do not benefit as they and we hoped, and even though the nation does not gain the increased productive power that also was desired? As Schultze has observed

> Because incentive-oriented approaches to social intervention rely on decentralized reactions to prices, they seem to deprive government of control of case-by-case results. If nothing else, this would make legislators nervous. They would have to forgo the opportunity to provide their programs with all sorts of adjudication procedures drawn up to take care of specific losses. They would also forfeit the opportunity to second-guess administrators and to provide services for constituents through intervention in administrative decisions.[39]

The temptation remains for government to do more, to intervene more forcefully. There is no pat answer that can tell when to accept the outcomes from that process or from vouchers or any other market approach. In short, going the market route does not escape organizational and political issues that are at the heart of social policy. However, Schultze's warning should be heeded "[I]n all cases the comparison should be between an imperfect market and an imperfect [government] regulatory scheme, not some ideal abstraction."[40]

There is another aspect of recommending the use of marketlike forces that needs to be discussed. The call for employing market forces so often is part of a general desire to bypass government generally and government organizations specifically. Organizations are viewed as in-

[39] Schultze, The Public Use of Private Interest, p. 72.
[40] Ibid., p. 38.

hibiting factors, never vehicles for resolving complex public problems. This can be misleading, as Elmore has observed

> [Forcing] a choice between market and nonmarket structures diverts attention from, and trivializes, an important problem: *how to use the structure and process of organizations to elaborate, specify, and define policies.* Most policy analysts, economists or not, are trained to regard complex organizations as *barriers* to the implementation of public policy, not as instruments to be capitalized upon and modified in the pursuit of policy objectives. In fact, organizations can be remarkably effective devices for working out difficult public problems.[41]

Where does this leave us? One obvious problem is not to be trapped by the lure of the market as a panacea. It will not let us off the hook anymore than passing responsibilities to local governments did. That point should be clear before there are any leaps to the free market bandwagon with vouchers or direct payments to industry. At the same time, it does appear desirable to seek marketlike pressures that operate indirectly as goads to better performance as a supplement to direct control or influence measures. They are a potential part of—not a substitute for—an organizational strategy. The difficulty is in finding ones that make technical, bureaucratic, and political sense.

Let us take stock for a moment. The most basic point of the chapter is this: The structure of the performance game (the distribution of power, the rules of play) is such that the bargaining and fixing mode should be the dominant framework determining choices in the performance game. It is critical that social agencies recast their style of play.

To this point, our concern has been primarily with the guiding thought process (e.g., the implications of negotiating rather than demanding) and with the nature of the bargaining, fixing, and indirect controls. The next issue is that of the availability and use of resources. We will be looking at the organizational structure and capacity that form the hard base needed to support bargaining and fixing in efforts to move local organizations toward better organizational and program performance.

---

[41] Richard F. Elmore, "Mapping Backward: Implementation Research and Policy Decisions," *Political Science Quarterly,* Winter 1979–1980, p. 606.

9 AGENCY RESOURCES

Resources are the base of agency power—the assets to be drawn on in current efforts to exert control or influence or to be built on (investment) for future efforts to exercise power. Resources can range from money, equipment, and matériel (the traditional business balance sheet items) to personal skills and established organizational and political ties. In his discussion of the Cuban missile crisis, where the joint chiefs of staff played a prominent role, Allison proferred this list of "bargaining advantages" that are equivalent to our resources:

> [B]argaining advantages include formal authority and responsibility (stemming from positions); actual control over resources necessary to carry out action; expertise and control over information that enables one to define the problem, identify options, and estimate feasibilities; control over information that enables chiefs to determine whether and in what form decisions are being implemented; the ability to affect other players' objectives in other games, including domestic political games; personal persuasiveness with other players (drawn from personal relations, charisma); and access to and persuasiveness with players who have bargaining advantages drawn from the above (based on interpersonal relationships, etc.).[1]

At issue is how a social agency can manage its resources over time to pursue the objectives of social legislation.

This chapter is restricted to a consideration of three general resources—the technical knowledge base or state of technology, infor-

---

[1] Graham T. Allison, *Essence of Decision: Explaining the Cuban Missile Crisis*, Little, Brown, Boston, 1971, p. 169.

211

mation, and technical assistance. The remaining discussion of resources comes in Chapter 10, because it is easier to treat other resources such as money and staff in a discussion of strategy.

The technical knowledge base, information, and technical assistance are interrelated. The knowledge base is built up through acquiring information and may be imparted through the provision of technical assistance, or the existing knowledge base can shape the information development and technical assistance functions. For example, a well-developed but complex technology may call for highly specialized scientific skills for those providing technical assistance to users. Further, for such a technology, information needs may be well defined, with precise quality control and production standards available as guidance.

We need to consider the technical base, information, and technical assistance in terms of limits. What is the state of technology in the social service delivery areas? What are the technical and organizational limits to producing useful decision-making information? What are the organizational and technical difficulties of delivering technical assistance? It might be said that we are searching for "net" resources, determining what real capacity is left after taking account of various limitations.

BASIC KNOWLEDGE DEFICIENCIES

The technological limits in the capacity to deliver social services is the starting place for considering general resources. Fundamental deficiencies in the underlying knowledge base shape much of what follows. In his penetrating essay *The Moon and the Ghetto*, Richard Nelson observed

> "If we land a man on the moon, why can't we solve the problems of the ghetto?" The question stands as a metaphor for a variety of complaints about the uneven performance of the American political economy. In an economy with such vast resources and powerful technologies, why can't we provide medical care at reasonable cost to all who need it, keep the streets, air, and water clean, keep down crime, educate ghetto kids, provide decent and low-cost mass transport, halt the rise in housing and services costs, have reliable television and automobile repair service?[2]

The moon–ghetto metaphor comes from the American faith in the existence of sure technological fixes—a clearly better product that is

[2] Richard R. Nelson, *The Moon and the Ghetto: An Essay on Public Policy Analysis*, Norton, New York, 1977, p. 13.

easier to use than the old one and causes no disruption. But there are seldom if ever such products available for the complex social service delivery areas. Science does not yield a clear technical fix for our social problems. In particular, we never seem to have a nice, simple, straightforward solution that is a surefire winner both producing material improvements at feasible costs and leaving bureaucratic or political waters undisturbed. So those who would proffer expert advice on social programs have to fall back on recommending approaches that may be unproven, demand resources not readily available, have threatening social or organizational consequences, or all of the above. Indeed, there is a fundamental credibility issue for those offering social program advice, since there are no "real experts" in Rourke's terms:

> Two characteristics are especially valuable in enhancing the influence of any body of experts within a bureaucracy. The first is the possession of a highly technical body of knowledge that the layman cannot readily master, and the second is a capacity to produce tangible achievements that the average man can easily recognize. This combination of obscurity in means and clarity of results seems an irresistible formula for success as far as any professional group is concerned.[3]

An even more basic point is that the emphasis in complex social service delivery programs on technology misleads as to the most pressing needs for information and technical assistance. Since there is no single dominating technical fix for all situations, but rather a number of possible approaches that might work if tailored to the particular situation, the central concerns in technical assistance should be on process. As Berman and McLaughlin have observed in the final volume of the major Rand study of educational change projects:

> Technical assistance . . . starts from a correct premise—school districts need help. However, the various federal programs generally have failed to provide relevant assistance or they have given the right assistance in the wrong way. For instance, some aid has been narrowly technical and overly detailed, usually because it tried to replicate success that occurred elsewhere. As a result, local project staff would either dismiss the assistance or find it unworkable. The underlying problem in this approach to technical assistance resembles difficulties encountered in the technocratic approach: The innovation is thought of as a *product* rather than as a *process* requiring adaptation.[4]

The fundamental knowledge deficiencies and the scientific mystique are at the foundation of information and technical assistance

---

[3] Francis E. Rourke, *Bureaucracy, Politics, and Public Policy*, Second Edition, Little, Brown, Boston, 1976, p. 84.

[4] Paul Berman and Milbrey W. McLaughlin, *Federal Programs Supporting Educational Change, Vol. VIII: Implementing and Sustaining Innovation*, Rand Corporation, R-1589/8-HEW, Santa Monica, California, May 1978, p. 38.

problems in the social service delivery areas. The limits of technology mean that there is no established scientific base that delineates firm and clear guidelines for developing information and providing technical assistance. The basic deficiencies cast a severe burden on the information development and assistance functions.

INFORMATION: THE BASIC RAW MATERIAL OF GOVERNANCE

The term *information* as used here has the common dictionary meaning of that which informs. In the agency policy process, all sorts of information having to do with social, economic, political, and bureaucratic phenomena may be useful.

In what follows, the main concern will be with information that might support agency field governance. What qualities does such information need to have if it is going to be useful for field governance? First, it needs to be sound and timely. The notion of soundness can be cast in rather standard statistical terms having to do with how accurate the information is, whether it is a valid indicator of what it purports to show, and the extent to which generalizations can be made from it (that is, whether or not a particular piece of information has general applicability or should be restricted at least by statistical standards to the situation that has been observed). Timeliness is an obvious requirement for useful information. Information is needed before, not after, a decision. However, if data require significant amounts of time for their development, the issue of timeliness—especially when there may be important decision or budget points—can become a critical factor.

The most fundamental requirement for information to be useful is that it aids policymakers in deciding about a number of relevant policy issues. Thus, in the social service delivery areas policymakers need to be able to answer such questions as the following: Who is in need (e.g., what is the target population for employment and training)? How well are current programs and projects serving the target groups in terms of such factors as compliance and performance? What alternatives to or modifications in current service delivery efforts are available to support directives or advice aimed at improving compliance, performance, or capacity? How can these possible changes in service delivery efforts be implemented?

The development of policy information may require highly specialized techniques and skills that establish important boundaries as to what can be done. We must investigate how available technical capabilities limit the supply of information useful for the field governance of social service delivery programs. This will require rather extensive discussion.

Definitions

In this section we consider some definitions needed to discuss information development. First are three definitions classifying organizational and program information. Second are the definitions of field techniques used in information development.

INPUTS, OUTPUTS, AND OUTCOMES

Most of the concern in this section is with organizational and programmatic information deriving from programs and projects in the field. We can classify this field information under three headings: inputs, outputs, and outcomes.

Inputs describe elements (e.g., a particular training manual) or physical arrangements (an intake desk that applicants are to come to before being assigned to a job counselor) in a project or program. Inputs can include personal qualifications that establish quantitative dimensions of specialized training or experience—a teaching certificate, a board-certified practitioner, or 3 years experience in working with handicapped children. Inputs are the static factors or components that characterize an activity and can be verified without extended observation or qualitative judgments.

Outputs are used to describe organizational behavior. They refer to the tasks done by staff members in serving clients and administering the organization as an institution. Outputs have a dynamic quality that must be observed and judged over time. For example, an employee may have certain educational qualifications on paper, but he or she must be observed in action to determine how the various inputs are used in providing services.

Outcomes point to what happened to participants after receiving transfers or services. *Distributional* outcomes indicate whether particular classes of individuals (e.g., black, aged, female, or poor) or geographic areas have received intended transfers or services. *Final* outcomes indicate whether a program or project is yielding benefits that improve the long-run status of the participants, such as a significant positive change in a person's capacity to earn or to learn. *Proximate* outcomes are ones expected to lead toward desired final outcomes. In a training project where the desired final outcome is increased earnings over time, proximate outcomes might be obtaining a job after training, getting a job in a particular training speciality such as welding, or holding a job for 6 consecutive months after training.[5] These proximate outcomes do not show conclusively that a participant has improved his or her long-run earning capability. However, their presence does suggest that individuals are moving in the right direction. Their absence indicates even more strongly that participants are not getting longer-run benefits.

It is helpful to tie these definitions to the critical notions of compliance and performance. Compliance focuses primarily or exclusively on administrative inputs (financial, accounting, and personnel procedures), organizational and programmatic inputs, and distributional outcomes. That is, legislation and guidelines may direct fund recipients (a) to follow particular accounting and personnel practices; (b) to have projects of a certain general type (public employment, residential training), with specific elements such as literacy training, counseling, and on-the-job experience; and (c) to serve particular target groups. Performance addresses what the organization does in action (outputs) and proximate and final outcomes. Organizational performance is measured by how resources are employed—how people in organizations actually use inputs and behave. Program performance is shown by proximate and final outcomes—what benefits (beyond distributional ones) accrue to program or project participants or others affected through the delivery of social services.

EVALUATION RESEARCH, IMPLEMENTATION
ASSESSMENTS, AND MONITORING

The terms used to describe field techniques in both the research community and the social agencies are neither uniform nor consistent. In the research community, evaluation research has been defined as "the application of social science methodologies to the assessment of human resource programs, so that it is possible to determine, empirically and with the confidence that results from employing scientific procedures, whether or not they are useful."[6] The broad definition

---

[5] Distributional outcomes bring classification difficulties. First, these outcomes in social service delivery programs often may be viewed as a particular kind of proximate outcome. Take a training program for disadvantaged persons as an example. That a trainee is disadvantaged is the first proximate outcome. Second, because distributional issues have such great political importance, distributional outcomes may be viewed politically like final outcomes—it is enough if my constituents got their fair share (or more) of funds.

[6] Howard E. Freeman, "The Present Status of Evaluation Research," in Marcia Guttentag and Shalom Saar (editors), *Evaluation Studies: Review Annual 1977*, Sage, Beverly Hills, California, 1977, p. 25.

seems somewhat pretentious in what it promises but does describe the general direction and focus of the social science-based studies. Within this broad category, the single distinction will be made between studies that focus upon outcomes (or "impacts"), referred to as evaluations, and studies that look at inputs and outputs, labeled implementation (organizational) assessments.[7]

In the agencies, monitoring usually describes shorter run efforts to look at inputs and distributional outcomes and to some extent outputs. Evaluations generally speaking define longer run efforts to consider proximate and final outcomes. But these distinctions about outputs and outcomes are not uniform. For example, HEW defines efficiency or management evaluations as those that "focus on ways to reduce costs or streamline procedures within a program or process."[8] Nor is there consistency as to methods employed in terms of either time or technique. Either monitoring or evaluation may be used to describe a brief site visit (the one-day "quick and dirty") or quick perusal of field reports at a desk. In what follows, we restrict the term *evaluations* to science-based studies of outcomes and try to be clear what we mean when we use the term *monitoring*.

Field Techniques Available for Gathering Information

This section will consider the underlying capability of available information techniques to generate sufficiently sound information to support the field governance of social service delivery programs. Most of the discussion focuses on information needed to exercise the approval

---

[7] The distinctions made by various writers within evaluative research create confusion for our purposes. In his review of evaluative research, Freeman distinguishes between evaluations (outcomes), process evaluations (inputs and outputs), and comprehensive evaluations that look at both impacts and process (see ibid., pp. 18–51). In another review of evaluation research, Rossi and Wright generally label all outcome studies as evaluation or evaluation research and then distinguish between process evaluations and implementation studies (see Peter H. Rossi and Sonia R. Wright, "Evaluation Research: An Assessment of Theory, Practice, and Politics," *Evaluation Quarterly*, February 1977, pp. 5–51). The distinctions between the last two are not in terms of what is being studied but rather between the approaches taken in the studies. As we read Rossi and Wright, they seem to be saying the process evaluations in the past have been too ideological and unscientific and that implementation studies have been more rigorous (see ibid., pp. 21–26). In what follows, we will not use the term *process evaluation* but refer to efforts to study inputs and outputs as implementation or organizational assessments and restrict the term *evaluation* only to outcomes distinguishing between distributional, proximate, and final outcomes when appropriate.

[8] Henry Aaron (Assistant Secretary for Planning and Evaluation, HEW), Statement before the Committee on Human Resources, U.S. Senate, 27 October 1977, p. 7.

function and provide compliance technical assistance that in combination are the main elements of control efforts in the field by a fund-granting agency. From this base, however, we can also discuss information needs and capacities for other activities such as advisory technical assistance.

Past efforts to gather field data have bogged down the most at opposite ends of the spectrum. On the one hand, these activities have been overly concerned with the minutiae of compliance, focusing on form more than substance. By concentrating on low-level procedures and practices, federal staff often avoid major questions or hinder the consideration of programmatic and organizational issues. The CETA and CDBG case materials gathered for this study speak clearly to this problem.

At the other extreme, attempts to measure final outcomes—so compelling because these are the bottom line of program performance—are marked by difficulty. In an analysis of evaluation techniques, we will start with these final outcome measures, because the difficulty of doing this kind of measurement is central to information development. First, as already emphasized, difficulty in measurement raises basic issues concerning responsibility and control. Second, it underscores the critical question of what can be done if we cannot get good measures of final outcomes. We need to examine how influence might be exerted through the development of accurate "intermediate" information on inputs, outputs, and distributional and proximate outcomes.

FINAL OUTCOME EVALUATIONS AND THE EXERCISE OF FEDERAL FIELD CONTROL

Final outcome evaluations were to be the hard-nosed, science-based means of developing definitive empirical evidence assessing the effectiveness of social policies.[9] Such studies would provide the hard base of field control—the "detectors" and "selectors," to use the Anthony and Dearden terminology from the last chapter. A host of difficulties, however, have come to limit severely the direct usefulness of the results of final outcome evaluations in exercising field control over local projects by federal administrative and support domain staffs.[10]

---

[9] Two of the most important books reflecting the call for evaluations were Joseph S. Wholey and others, *Federal Evaluation Policy,* Urban Institute, Washington, D.C., 1970; and Alice M. Rivlin, *Systematic Thinking for Social Action,* Brookings Institution, Washington, D.C., 1971.

[10] It should be emphasized that we are not discussing whether or not final outcome evaluation results may be relevant for supporting the high-level decision domain allocation and distribution decisions concerning total program funds or overall shifts in a program. This point will be returned to later.

Certainly, no relatively short discussion can do justice to the complex issue of whether or not evaluation research can provide relevant data of sufficient soundness and timeliness to allow federal staffs to exercise control over locally operated and administered social service delivery projects. However, we can spell out in nontechnical terms some of the difficulties involved in evaluation research.[11]

The main problem in evaluating social service delivery projects stems from the already discussed limits in the knowledge base and the complexity of the social setting. The result is that social goals are vague and available treatment technology is weak, although programs still get packaged in the rhetoric of high accomplishment.

The research problems are legion. The vagueness of both objectives and programs goes to the foundation of evaluation methods, as Rossi and Wright observe "In all cases, the basic assumption of evaluation research is that the program itself, its goals, and the criteria for its success are sufficiently well-defined so as to allow an appropriate research plan to be designed."[12] Further, the weak treatments that are likely to yield only marginal outcomes mean "that the evaluation methodology must be sensitive or powerful enough to detect small effects."[13]

These criticisms pertain to evaluations at all levels. Evaluations of individual projects raise even more problems in terms of exercising control. An evaluation of a specific project that takes a year or two to complete may see the project director, staff, and social service components change dramatically. Whatever the relative merits of the evaluation in technical terms, the present staff director who came after the evaluation started can point—probably quite legitimately—to *past* management failure and *present* project differences that render the evaluation results out of date. As Berryman and Glennan observe "The longer the [evaluation] study takes, the more likely it is that the policy

[11] The most pointed critique of large-scale final outcome evaluations carried out by a federal agency is found in Sue E. Berryman and Thomas K. Glennan, Jr., "An Improved Strategy for Evaluating Federal Programs in Education," A *Rand Note* prepared for the U.S. Department of Health, Education and Welfare, N-1290-HEW, August 1979. Berryman and Glennan spell out in detail both the methodological and the organizational–political difficulties that call into question the usefulness of large-scale final outcome evaluations. The previously cited article by Rossi and Wright, "Evaluation Research: An Assessment of Theory, Practice and Politics," provides a sound, but not highly technical, critique of available methods and recent studies. Rossi and Wright are somewhat more optimistic about likely payoffs from evaluation research than we are, but they too are skeptical on the usefulness of techniques.

[12] Rossi and Wright, "Evaluation Research: An Assessment of Theory, Practice and Politics," p. 7.

[13] Ibid., p. 10.

community will reconceive the problem during the study."[14] We have the seeming paradox in which the more time taken in a final outcome evaluation to develop sound information, the more likely it is that project changes will have negated the relevance of the data for exercising control over ongoing activities.

Evaluation research is almost certain to be subject to challenge. As Williams has observed "[N]o evaluation can be expected to be unassailable in terms of its methodological and field development. And these deficiencies open up the debate so that ideological or political concerns can be pursued in a methodological framework."[15] Limited evaluative techniques can get overwhelmed by internal bureaucratic factors and external realities. Both politicians and bureaucrats may use the technical limitations in final outcome results to avoid making decisions. Difficult political choices can be postponed indefinitely on the basis of need for further, more authoritative (read politically incontestable) information.

These technical, bureaucratic, and political barriers do not imply that final outcome evaluations should be ruled out. In particular, such studies well may have a place in supporting high-level decision domain choices on overall questions of allocation and distribution.[16] What we

---

[14] Berryman and Glennan, "An Improved Strategy for Evaluating Federal Programs in Education," p. 44.

[15] Walter Williams, *Social Policy Research and Analysis*, American Elsevier, New York, 1971, p. 104. There are other more complex problems well beyond the scope of this section. First, the experimental tradition that has dominated large-scale final outcome evaluations often makes for studies that have academic respectability but limited policy usefulness. Such studies may yield either the wrong data for decision making or data that could be useful in the wrong time frame for policy purposes. For an excellent treatment of these issues, see Berryman and Glennan, "An Improved Strategy of Evaluating Federal Programs in Education," pp. 19–29. Second, the effect of social programs may not be measurable in terms of specific participants. Take the employment and training area. Effects may occur only over an extended period of time in terms of broad labor market movements. For example, employees in a geographic area may consider people being trained in projects as inferior workers. These views may come about from racial prejudice or past experience. Only if those attitudes change are trainees likely to show marked benefits from training. So measurement before such changes may be most misleading. While the pursuit of this issue is well beyond the scope of this section, its implications reinforce what is being said about measurement difficulties. For a useful discussion of this issue, see Henry J. Aaron, *Politics and the Professors*, Brookings Institution, Washington, D.C., 1978, pp. 125–138.

[16] Congress, for example, continues to demand that agencies do final outcome evaluations of entire programs to provide data for making allocation and distribution decisions. We simply are not commenting on these kinds of evaluations. See Wholey and others, *Federal Evaluation Policy*, pp. 24–26, for a general treatment of different types of evaluations.

are questioning is the usefulness of final outcome evaluation results to support *direct social agency field control* over projects that are administered and operated by local governments or other nonfederal entities. The ambiguity at this critical point of decision making imposes limits on the degree of field control from above, with profound implications for social agency structure and function.

DISTRIBUTIONAL AND PROXIMATE OUTCOMES
IN FEDERAL FIELD CONTROL

Distributional and proximate outcomes are less subject to methodological controversy over the interpretation of the measure than are final outcomes. In a welding program to train Vietnam veterans, determining that a former trainee was a veteran and is holding a welding job hardly seems subject to debate as a reasonable indication of change in the desired direction, even if causality cannot be determined. Unlike the case of final outcomes, the measure is not a proxy for some immeasurable phenomenon such as higher earning capacity but the result that was desired and that has been observed at a particular time point.

Distributional and proximate outcomes often may be determined through quite straightforward field methods. If the distributional target is easily defined and ascertained (e.g., by race, ethnicity, age, or sex), the demand is for simple head counting. If a poverty group is the target where determining yearly income is difficult, methodological complexity will increase along with the cost of getting information. Much the same can be said about proximate outcomes. Employment, length of employment, wage rates, hours of work per week, and similar factors can be measured with a relatively high degree of accuracy by trained interviewers. Precisely this kind of information is gathered monthly in the Current Population Survey (the instrument used to determine monthly unemployment rates) and other periodic surveys.

Measures of distributional and proximate outcomes are more modest in intent than those of final outcomes in that they are not expected to indicate whether projects are producing lasting benefits for participants. However, these intermediate measures can show the extent to which projects are complying with legislative and agency demands. Moreover, through comparisons along distributional and/or proximate lines, project ratings systems may be developed that yield valuable data on relative performance.[17] In the case of relatively poor project

[17] Project ratings are discussed in ibid., pp. 25–26, 101–103. It may be necessary to group projects together on some dimensions (e.g., area unemployment rates) to permit fairer comparisons.

performance (e.g., trainees get few jobs, lose jobs quickly, or work few hours relative to comparable projects), one can see that projects are unlikely to yield long-term benefits.

There are problems too in using proximate and distributional outcomes. Causality is a critical concern. However accurate a particular measure, the question remains as to how much it tells about movement toward the desired final outcome. For example, to what extent does a verified placement evidence enhanced earnings capability? A 3 July 1978 *Washington Post* article reported

> [A] new study shows that, in one national sample, 58% of those leaving CETA training or job slots were in nonsubsidized jobs within three months. But no one is certain whether this is a result of their CETA experience or whether they would have obtained such jobs anyhow.

Most unemployed people eventually get jobs without government programs. Unless there is a basis of comparison (e.g., a similar group of people who did not have the CETA experience), we do not know if the 58% rate is good or bad. Even if it is a good rate, there is no direct indication of earnings enhancement. We have only ruled out the intermediate outcome of poor placements.

Beyond placement, there is the issue of job quality. Is the position temporary or permanent, full-time or part-time, well paying, or in the trainee's area of training? If there had been a comparison group for the CETA trainees in the study just quoted, those people not having the CETA experience might have looked hard for nonsubsidized jobs and found better ones than the CETA people. The more complex and sensitive the proximate outcome, the more that technical problems emerge with each additional bit of information posing the accuracy issue anew. Even when resolved, one must judge whether or not the pieces add up to valid indicators of movement in the desired direction.

These distinctions may seem obvious. But in the field, how often does accuracy give a measure undue importance? How often do people rely on that which can be easily measured without thought of the measure's meaning? Proximate outcomes can take on a life of their own. Body counts in Vietnam serve as a most notorious example. Placements in the United States Employment Service were once defined as jobs of 3 days or more. A disproportionate placement effort was directed to temporary jobs in order to register a good "placement count." The relative simplicity of these intermediate outcomes can invite a mindless reliance on the availability of hard numbers and, in the process, drive out reasonableness.

IMPLEMENTATION (ORGANIZATIONAL)
ASSESSMENTS

Implementation assessment is the label given to research-oriented efforts to investigate inputs and outputs.[18] These studies, as the name implies, have concentrated upon the critical problem faced by organizations (usually large-scale ones) in moving from a decision to start a new program or modify an existing one to making that innovation operational. As we will try to make clear in what follows, this label has become too restrictive in that the field techniques being developed can be used in the assessment of organizational activities after they are fully operational. Hence, organizational assessment seems a better label, but we will continue to use implementation assessment primarily because of the historical background of the term.

Implementation assessments are of relatively recent origin, with most of them having been undertaken in elementary and secondary school settings.[19] These studies resemble evaluations in that both examine what has happened ex post facto, that is, after a program or project is in the field. They focus on the extent to which project inputs and organizational behavior have changed over time in response to implementation efforts.

The major emphasis in implementation assessments is on organizational behavior, that is, how people act in their organizational status or roles. This behavior is shaped both by the internal resources and structure of the institution and by the external demands of the environment upon that institution. Of importance are four overlapping, but distinct kinds of organizational behavior: (a) what organizational staff members do with nonhuman resources, such as programmatic elements and internal organizational arrangements; (b) how staff members behave with each other; (c) how they behave with staff members of other organizations with which their organization must interact in its external environment; and (d) what they do in treating those who are expected to benefit from their services.

Such behavior is dynamic. For example, we may learn little from knowing that a person receives counseling or from looking at the ar-

---

[18] For a more detailed discussion of the notion of implementation assessment, see Walter Williams, "Implementation Analysis and Assessment," in Walter Williams and Richard F. Elmore (editors), *Social Program Implementation*, Academic Press, New York, 1976, pp. 267–292, especially pp. 282–286.

[19] For a discussion of the origins and development of such studies and a bibliography, see Walter Williams, *The Implementation Perspective*, University of California Press, Berkeley, 1980, pp. 10–12.

rows on a chart that depict how services are to be offered. Until we see a counselor provide his or her services or observe how the process of service delivery actually is carried out, we have little or no indication of what is really happening. Hence, the central concern of implementation assessment is with what staff members do when they interact with each other, with members of other organizations, and with clients.

The study of such behavior often is difficult, because individual behavior is complicated and becomes even more complicated when organizational demands and constraints are added. So implementation assessments may include complex sampling designs, rigorous efforts to determine interviewer (rater) reliability where several observers are used, and sophisticated statistical techniques to examine the extent to which various factors contribute to implementation success. However, even the most complex studies generally employ three standard techniques: direct observation usually over an extended time period; detailed investigations of existing documents; and extensive questioning that often is open ended.

The most important aspect of these studies is that they can provide rich detail about an organization's history and procedures and the behavior of its staff. Careful observation and questioning can yield information on the extent to which there is confusion, lack of clarity, or outright contradictions in terms of desired organizational behavior; how administrative duties are actually carried out; what the staff is doing to deliver services; and what is happening in the decision-making process, including the extent to which clients and other citizens have a real say.

In terms of the approval function, available techniques may yield strong evidence that a project is making no effort to do what is desired or is fouling up that effort. The claim is not that present techniques can distinguish small differences but that clear losers can be spotted.

It is in the areas of technical assistance, particularly advisory technical assistance (discussed in the next section), that implementation assessments may offer the greatest potential for improving agency field governance. Looking in detail at the implementation process should show where adjustments are needed or where organizations appear to be doing the right thing. Even if one may not be able to generalize from the findings in the strict statistical sense, ideas about what works may still be useful in offering advice about changes.[20]

---

[20] Even if a good study design can be developed to support generalization, time factors may rule it out. For example, if a single exemplary training project is found, will decision makers wait years for a testing out of the concept? For a discussion of these issues, see Williams, "Implementation Analysis and Assessment," pp. 283–285.

We must be careful not to oversell what can be done, since there are major problems. First, studies of implementation just as evaluations require measurable criteria if there is to be a judgment about success. Second, the precise measurement of complex organizational behavior using observation and interviews is difficult. Clearly, the results are often subject to challenge. Despite these caveats, we think useful decision-making information can be gathered from observation and interviews indicating in detail the extent to which an organization is trying to do what is desired.

Monitoring is the closest thing in agency procedures to implementation assessment. Unfortunately, monitoring efforts in general have been none too good. As Waller and his colleagues at the Urban Institute have observed "Government offices are full of 'monitoring reports' that have not been read by anyone except their authors. Personnel expected to use such monitoring reports frequently find them useless."[21] Monitoring efforts in the past have been far too much concerned with inputs in a static sense, relatively low-level administrative practices, and issues of financial accountability. That is, monitoring efforts have focused primarily on narrow compliance issues with little done to assess how an organization's staff behave in broader terms.

Better agency monitoring can be performed with available techniques. As Williams has observed

> [P]eople with well-honed bureaucratic sensitivities should be able to assess within tolerable limits how well an activity is going and whether it is beginning to fit into its institutional environment. Surely it ought to be possible to spot the bad cases—but not necessary to know what to do about them, since that step requires ex ante prediction.
>
> The central role of reasoned judgment in assessing implementation should be clearly delineated. A static checklist of all the specified inputs (one teacher, two teacher aides, three talking typewriters, and so on) will not indicate the viability of the project. On the other hand, enough missing pieces may spell trouble. The exercise of judgment or of a composite of judgments of an activity in motion seems the only way to determine viability. At the same time, technique may facilitate judgment. A set of "dynamic" questions (e.g., does the principal support the project?), a common scaling system, or a sampling frame may keep those carrying out the assessment from missing important issues, provide a useful means of comparing judgments, and avoid selectivity biases. Good judgment, however, remains the key element. Methodology simply does not appear to be the big barrier. Nor do I see the need for highly trained social scientists to carry out the various tasks. The biggest

---

[21] John D. Waller and others, *Monitoring for Government Agencies*, Urban Institute Report No. 783–41, February 1976, p. 11. Very little has been done to study government monitoring efforts. The Urban Institute study is a useful exception. It should be noted that the authors use the term *monitoring* broadly to include outcomes.

need is for competent, reasonable people with sound substantive knowledge of programs and of bureaucracy.[22]

TECHNICAL ASSISTANCE

Technical assistance crystallizes the resource issue in the administrative and support domain. Despite the need for highly differentiated technical skills, the case materials of this study indicate that regional and area offices, with some exceptions, have little of the division of labor that has marked modern large-scale organizations. Usually lacking are staff specialists who have the technical skills or extended experiences relevant to the organization, administration, and operation of these programs. Nor did we find that these deficiencies in the field were made up in the headquarters elements of the administrative and support domain.

This primitive, undifferentiated state of the federal portion of the administrative and support domain seems certain to inhibit field governance. Here is where federal managerial and staff resources are needed to make the critical investment required to raise local-level organizational and technical capability. Why then the substantive technical assistance failure?

The starting point for looking at substantive technical assistance problems is the deficiencies in the underlying knowledge base for social issues. These deficiencies explain absolute weaknesses. But as we have emphasized, these difficulties make the need for federal and local staffs to work together even greater. There is more of a burden placed on federal staffs to come up with specific organizational and program advice that fits the specific situation. We then must ask why so few of the needed kinds of people are found in the field. Why does the field get a disproportionately small number of the available high-level managers and outstanding junior staff? Part of the answer is that the power in being close to big action and the excitement in actually serving directly those people who need social services have been located disproportionately in the decision and local operations domains. The pull at the top of an agency often brings good people to government. One can be a junior person and still be on staffs that serve high-level decision makers directly. And these decision makers have first pick in the hiring game. Here too are larger rewards and higher status. At the other end, direct service to social service delivery program participants has another kind of excitement and provides rewards coming from direct involvement. At the local level, one is more

[22] Williams, "Implementation Analysis and Assessment," p. 286.

likely to find deep commitment and a willingness to try something new. The administrative and support domain—that gray, ill-defined area in between where rewards tend to come slowly and often come from internal bureaucratic factors—seems far less appealing to relatively competent staff.

In addition, the field and the lower reaches of headquarters may become a dumping ground for unwanted people. Nathan closed a long statement cited earlier with the observation that "the old liners are the ones typically 'selected-out' for field assignments when changes are sought either within the bureaucracy or from outside."[23]

Also, the agencies have not recognized these problems and have stretched their technical assistance resources too thin. For example, they have often viewed the training to be offered as a requirement for all local units, even though the better local staffs may have far more capability than the trainers. Given both limited federal field resources and a wide distribution of local government capabilities, it surely makes sense to concentrate the effort by matching resources and needs. The "treat-everybody-alike" approach in training has yielded the negatives of both resource misallocation and loss of credibility for federal staffs.

The confused roles of the federal government in the New Federalism—particularly in the early period—well may have exacerbated these problems. In particular, HUD was not sure whether or not it was supposed to provide technical assistance at all. However, these problems go beyond the early confusion of the New Federalism to a basic misunderstanding by the agencies of the need to allocate a reasonable level of resources to the field.

The power rivalries between federal and local units have mitigated against the provision of useful technical assistance. On the one hand, the federal staffs may not have wanted to increase the capability of the local staffs too much because greater capability cuts into their bargaining resources. The local people in turn may have viewed the proffered technical assistance less as help and more as a ploy in the power relationships—an effort either to put them down in gamesmanship terms or else to establish a beachhead of overt control. In this scenario, technical assistance is no longer only the neutral, benign good of our earlier description, it becomes a weapon in the power game.

Not only are the federal and local staffs bargaining-table rivals, they also may distrust each other. A local organization with problems

---

[23] Richard P. Nathan, *The Plot That Failed*, Wiley, 1975, New York, p. 30. This and other references to the same work are under copyright © by John Wiley & Sons, Inc. Reprinted with permission of John Wiley & Sons, Inc.

can view it as risky business to spell out deficiencies to the funding agency in general and particularly to a technical assistance group that is part of the unit that approves funds. In 1968, H. Ralph Taylor, the HUD assistant secretary responsible for the model cities program in the Johnson administration, observed "[W]e are moving to encourage the concept of Independent Technical Assistance—making available to the residents, under their control, resources to provide technical assistance and expertise they trust."[24] Although the emphasis here is upon community residents, the notion of distrust applies also to members of local government staffs.

There is a potential conflict between approval (control) and advice. If the controller and advisor are the same person or else two individuals working together in the program line unit, funded organizations with problems may be reluctant to indicate the full dimensions of problems when seeking advice because of fears either that their confessions will be used against them at funding time or that federal personnel will view any proffered suggestions as directives about what to do rather than as ideas to consider as possible alternatives.

Thus, distrust adds another complication to the technical assistance issue in creating barriers to the free flow of potentially useful information. Fund recipients may (a) hold back from federal staff information about organizational and program problems that would aid the latter in diagnosing those problems, and (b) be reluctant to receive federal technical assistance because they fear it will be construed as a one-way directive from above, not as information to consider and adapt.

If there were increased cooperation, what would it look like in institutional terms? Where the absolute levels of programmatic and organizational knowledge are low, relative capabilities—comparative advantages—become critical to a useful information strategy. Here a distinction needs to be made between generalized and localized knowledge. The former is based on broad sets of experiences and information. Generalized knowledge concerns (a) national needs in social policy areas, including the intent and meaning of legislation and regulations relevant to programs aimed at such needs; (b) the various technical and organizational approaches that might be used in programs; (c) the bureaucratic and political variables that generally impinge on the development and operation of programs in the field; and (d) the var-

---

[24] Remarks by H. Ralph Taylor before the National Association of Housing and Redevelopment Officials, Minneapolis, Minnesota, 27 September 1968, cited in James L. Sundquist, *Making Federalism Work*, Brookings Institution, Washington, D.C., 1969, p. 94. Copyright © 1969 by the Brookings Institution.

ious methods available for analysis and assessment of programs. Localized knowledge includes (a) programmatic needs in a specific community; (b) the past experience in that community in terms of the application of various techniques; and (c) the peculiarities of the local political and bureaucratic structure in which programs operate.

Generalized knowledge increases from a breadth of experiences. For example, information gathered from a number of communities may indicate that approaches such as intensive counseling by a professional or a "buddy system" involving peer trainees work reasonably well under one set of conditions but not under others. Or a problem in a specific community (e.g., placing women trainees, the need for child care services, absenteeism among trainees) may have been treated effectively somewhere else.

Localized knowledge increases from a depth of investigation concerning the specifics of one locality. An approach may make sense in some communities, but another community may not be able to use it until capability is increased or certain bureaucratic or political blockages are overcome.

Cast in these simple and straightforward terms, the division of labor between federal and local governments seems clear. The federal government would seek to develop generalized information, drawing on research and development results and national experience from operating programs. The search would be for information about the process and substance of programs that might have general applicability to large numbers of projects. Local people would develop information both in support of this accumulated general information and also as a means of adjusting those general findings to meet the specific needs of their particular communities.

A lack of proven approaches amenable to straightforward presentation places a real premium on information drawn from extensive organizational and programmatic experience. Here the need is for sufficient depth and breadth of information to support the development of agency policy and of recommendations to field organizations on implementing, administering, and operating programs. Often the only useful information is that of personal experience. Perhaps most of all, people in organizations need advice and help on making marginal adjustments in what they are doing. They seek means of making small changes that do not threaten to disrupt the organization in terms of structure and staffing. In a situation where someone is performing poorly or some project element is causing immediate problems, there is a need for sensible advice on personnel or minor procedural adjustments rather than highly technical advice or elaborate procedures.

The information needed for marginal adjustments and the occasional crisis generally does not emphasize statistical or theoretical knowledge. Rather the demand is for information based on organizational and programmatic experience that can aid in seeing, and sensing, where something is wrong. Such information is likely to come from the competent bureaucratic professional who has lived through past organizational and program difficulties rather than the organizational theorist.

10 | THE AGENCY MANAGEMENT STRATEGY: MAJOR ISSUES

This chapter considers the development of an agency management strategy. The key notion of strategy is drawn from the writings on corporate management where the concept is quite broad. As Andrews has observed

> [C]orporate strategy is the pattern of major objectives, purposes, or goals and essential policies and plans for achieving those goals, stated in such a way as to define what business the company is in or is to be in and the kind of company it is or is to be. . . .
>
> Corporate strategy has two equally important aspects, interrelated in life but separated to the extent practicable here in our study of the concept. The first of these is formulation; the second is implementation. Deciding what strategy should be is, at least ideally, a rational undertaking. Its principle subactivities include identifying opportunities and threats in the company's environment and attaching some estimate of risk to the discernible alternative. Before a choice can be made, the company's strengths and weaknesses must be appraised. Its actual or potential capacity to take advantage of perceived market needs or to cope with attendant risks must be estimated as objectively as possible.[1]

The most basic task of organizational leadership is to determine what are to be the organization's long-term objectives (what the organization

---

[1] Kenneth R. Andrews, *The Concept of Corporate Strategy*, Dow Jones-Irwin, Homewood, Illinois, 1971, pp. 28, 37. What Andrews refers to as corporate strategy is often referred to more generally as *strategic planning* or *strategic long-range planning*. But whatever the name, the important point is that the concept of strategy used here embraces both the broad setting of objectives and the consideration of means of getting to

is or is to be) and how to develop and allocate resources in pursuit of those desired objectives. This guiding strategy needs both sufficient breadth to indicate critical directions that will orient the organization and enough details to shape specific organizational structure and processes.

The call for a strategy is not a call for a detailed planning document that spells out precisely the expected behavior in an uncertain world. At the same time broad objectives alone are not enough. The strategy must address the basic issue of how the organization is to move toward those objectives. There needs to be strategic planning about the allocation of resources, including the nature of the organizational structure and processes that will be commensurate with the strategy. Put differently, the strategy must seek to determine in broad scope the implications of objectives in terms of limits and resources so that there is guidance on moving toward the organizational objectives.

Since the notions of strategy are based mainly on work in the corporate sector, it is well to keep before us the relative difficulties of public management and the differences between public and private management as discussed in earlier chapters. Surely public managers with their short tenure and their lack of service in agencies face a different magnitude of problems from corporate careerists who are likely to be chosen for top leadership from their peers so that the new management knows both the corporation and their subordinates. Nor must a corporate chief executive officer and his management team compete in setting objectives with a legislative body or try to exert control or influence over operating organizations in different political jurisdictions. But with all these difficulties of public management, generally, and of social agency governance, specifically, there still is a need for an agency management strategy. There is a fundamental requirement for agency leaders to direct social agency governance by formulating a guiding strategy. How far social agencies can go in devising such a strategy no one knows, but it is an issue that should not be avoided in considering social agency governance.

---

those objectives. As another major writer in the field, Robert Anthony, observes "[S]trategic planning combines two types of planning that often are viewed as quite distinct from each other: (1) choosing objectives and (2) planning how to achieve these objectives." Robert N. Anthony, *Planning and Control Systems*, Harvard University Press, Cambridge, Massachusetts, 1965, p. 26. See ibid., pp. 24–68 and Andrews, *The Concept of Corporate Strategy*, pp. 26–58, for detailed discussions of the conceptualization of the notion of corporate strategy. For discussion of the need for and difficulties of doing strategic planning in the public sector, see Robert A. Levine, *Public Planning: Failure and Redirection*, Basic Books, New York, 1972, pp. 162–167 and Frederic V. Malek, *Washington's Hidden Tragedy: The Failure to Make Government Work*, Free Press, New York, 1978, pp. 118–140.

What is a reasonable approach to an agency management strategy where the hierarchical control does not apply and variability and mutual dependence predominate? Our argument is that the guiding strategy must reorient the agency toward the field. The commitment of the local organizations that administer and operate projects to better organizational and program performance and the competence of these local staffs should be a central social agency objective. Agency staff should be guided by the agency management strategy in developing means of inducing local organizations to: (a) pursue performance objectives compatible with national intent; (b) strengthen the institutional setting where discretion is exercised; and (c) make institutional investment over time, aimed at increasing organizational responsiveness and technical skills. The overriding need is for the management and staff of social service delivery organizations to have sufficient organizational and technical skills to exercise reasonable discretion at the point of service delivery in providing the particular services that are required and to respond appropriately to future, yet unspecified, implementation demands.

The main focus of the strategic objective of greater local commitment and capacity is on organizational performance, even though the ultimate agency goal is increased program performance. Improved organizational performance is the critical intermediate step toward improved program performance. The policy variables that the agency can manipulate are organizational ones.

The agency objective of strengthening local commitment and capacity has significant implications throughout the agency for resource allocation, information development, mechanisms of control and influence, and organizational structure. Reorienting and reorganizing to shift the agency's main concerns toward the field will be a fundamental agency decision. It is a decision that should be made only after a thorough analysis to determine whether or not the field strategy makes sense in a particular social agency.

A social agency should analyze in depth five key issues to decide whether or not it is feasible to undertake a management strategy that has as a principal guide increasing local commitment to performance and local capacity. The agency needs to determine if it can implement such a strategic objective and, given that implementation seems feasible, how it should go about doing so.

This agency implementation analysis should investigate the extent to which the agency can

1. Make bargaining and fixing primary guides to agency decisions and actions in pursuing organizational and program performance objectives

2. Develop institutional arrangements that reduce the complexity and confusion in the field and increase the credibility of federal administrative and support domain staff
3. Raise competence in the field of federal staff and of grantees
4. Create internal and external pressure points aimed at moving toward better organizational and programmatic performance
5. Develop an information process yielding detailed organizational and programmatic information to support the agency field effort to increase local commitment to performance objectives compatible with national intent and local capacity to deliver social services.

Three general comments are needed about the discussion of each of the issues that follows. First, it cannot be overemphasized that no effort will be made to treat these issues in terms of a specific agency. Such an analysis if carried out without working directly with the staff of a particular agency would be inappropriate because of the lack of details and the need for the organization itself to be heavily involved. Second, each issue will be considered separately without trying to determine potential conflicts between them. This effort too demands the details of a specific case. Finally, it should be stressed that we will be looking at only a single key objective (and one that we, not an agency, have chosen). The agency would need to consider the implications of this objective of strengthening local commitment and capacity along with other objectives. So ours is a partial analysis.

In the remainder of this chapter we will analyze the five issues spelled out above. In the next chapter we will consider how an agency might start such an analysis given that political executives have made a decision to investigate the feasibility of a reorientation toward the field.

A NEW DECISION-MAKING AND ACTION STYLE

Generally, bargaining and fixing together are the preferred style for decision making and action as the social agency tries to raise the performance levels of local organizations funded through grants-in-aid. Bargaining becomes the appropriate strategy where hierarchical authority in traditional terms ends, where the real threat of negative sanctions applying to clear boundary points no longer holds. Even with their own field organizations, top agency managers cannot rely solely on the power of hierarchy to induce lower-level managers to do their bidding, although clearly superior position still has its benefits. But when the social agency comes to the bargaining table with local governments, at best, it is an equal in the negotiations. The trump card of direct hierarchical authority is not there to play. The guide to play needs to be cast in a bargaining mode where power is defined in terms of directional influence, not direct command.

Bargaining is no easy task. At the same time, it needs to be recognized that the bargaining mode uses many of the skills of the organizational health game. "Implementation games," as Bardach observes, "are political games."[2] In political games, action does not depend on command and control or formal planning so much as on an appreciation of political–bureaucratic reality and common sense. Political executives in agencies do not command legislators or White House staff or even middle-level members of the Office of Management and Budget. They bargain.

Bargaining skills at headquarters, however, are not enough. Competence in the field (discussed in detail in a subsequent section) is a necessity if the social agency is to be a sound bargainer. Political executives or top-level headquarters staff may be responsible for and actually engage in some direct bargaining. A bargaining package may be hammered out around a table in Washington, or key headquarters persons may head the federal delegation at a local bargaining meeting. Federal field staffs, however, must have a certain level of competence to do needed homework before these bargaining sessions and to engage themselves in the smaller, less formal bargains that will be struck in the field between field staffs and local officials. Without the significant commitment of resources needed to provide technical support in the field for the bargaining game, political executives and field staff simply may not know what to bargain for.

Fixing presents even more problems, because repairs and adjustments can cut across all domains and range from legislative changes through project repairs. Fixing in broad terms, of course, is being done all the time. What is so problematic is getting a top-level fixer. As Bardach observes of different levels of fixers: "[T]he one that is hardest to come by, is the intervener at the top, the person or persons with powerful political resources."[3]

Bardach's discussion of the top-level fixer indicates that likely can-

[2] Eugene Bardach, The Implementation Game, MIT Press, Cambridge, Massachusetts. 1977, p. 278. This and other references to the same work are under copyright © 1977 by the Massachusetts Institute of Technology.

[3] Ibid., p. 279.

didates are few because of a lack of resources and incentives. He questions political executives on both counts, arguing first that they usually leave office about the time they have finally mastered the implementation game and secondly that the payoffs seem much higher for playing the organizational health game in the decision domain. The same lack of incentives frequently rules out legislators. Both political executives and legislators, if they are drawn to concerns for field performance, find greater rewards by staying in the decision domain discussing new policy approaches. The incentives are for creating, not fixing.

"Top career civil servants," Bardach notes, "may often have the resources, but just as often they are part of the problem rather than part of the solution. That is, they are often heavily committed to certain bureaucratic games that are themselves in need of fixing."[4] Bardach appears to have swept by the likely candidates too quickly, but let us look at this proposed solution before examining potential roles.

Bardach emphasizes that "pessimism is in order."[5] He suggests two possible locations for fixing—one in the legislature, the other in the agency. Consider the agency solution:

> [T]here is the possibility of setting up policy analysis and evaluation groups under the auspices of the department, or even agency-level, budget office. . . . The incentives for analysts to involve themselves in political and bureaucratic action at the necessary level of detail are not insignificant. There is, after all, a specialized but fairly large attentive public in any policy area that will appreciate and credit their good works and that can eventually be tapped for career-enhancing jobs and other emoluments.[6]

These analytic offices at the top of the agency and probably other analytic offices in the headquarters bureaus or in the field may have a major role in the key information gathering and synthesis effort needed to support fixing. But in the same way that the senior analyst in the agency is an adviser to the decision maker and not the decision maker himself, the analyst should not be the fixer. That is, information development and analysis is a *staff* function; fixing is a *line* activity. The policy analyst may serve the decision maker specifically, in executing implementation studies, and generally, in providing information and advice about implementation and the performance game. The actual fixing, however, is going to have to be done by the agency's operating bureaus.

---

[4] Ibid., p. 280.
[5] Ibid.
[6] Ibid., pp. 280–281.

Asking who at the top is to be responsible for fixing the performance game raises the basic question of who is to manage the agency. The latter is a recurrent issue as Seidman has noted "[A Secretary's] principal duties involve matters which are unrelated to the internal administration and management of the institution. . . . Minimal time is [available] for managing the department, even if a Secretary is one of the rare political executives with a taste for administration."[7] Seidman then goes on to observe

> [D]epartment heads remain the weakest link in the chain of Federal Administration. Unless departmental management can be improved, reorganization cannot be counted on to yield more than marginal benefits.
>
> If we are to do something meaningful about the organization and management of the executive branch, we must start first with department and agency [bureau] heads. *New approaches are needed—approaches based on what the political executives' functions really are—not on obsolete concepts of what they should be.*[8]

When the same person is expected to handle political issues having implications both up (organizational health, decision domain) and down (performance, administrative and support domain), the pressures can be overwhelming. Both up and down, or outside and inside, are full-time undertakings, and the crunch becomes most apparent at the top.

In the case of the agency, the standard recommendation for the "secretary's problem" has been that the under secretary should manage the agency as Mr. Inside, while the secretary should operate as Mr. Outside. There are a number of reasons why this sharing of responsibilities has worked so infrequently. First, the number two position in an agency, much like the vice presidency, may be used to meet political needs. For example, the AFL–CIO leadership may demand to clear the under secretary in the Department of Labor, or the housing industry may insist that the number two position be filled by a housing person, if the HUD secretary has not been associated with the housing field. But even if the secretary has complete authority to appoint the under secretary, the new political executive's lack of understanding of large public organizations may keep him from seeing that someone else must be responsible for managing performance. A leadership team is required, with different responsibilities and different skill demands flowing from these responsibilities.

[7] Harold Seidman, *Politics, Position, and Power*, Oxford University Press, New York, 1970, p. 134.
[8] Ibid., p. 135, italics added.

In the ideal situation, both the outside and inside persons will have significant programmatic and political experience and skills. The program experience and skills for the outside person are important in two respects. First, without a grasp of organizational and program performance problems, it will be hard for the outside person to understand the choice that must be made, search for the right individual to take responsibility for fixing, and appreciate the claims that must be made on scarce resources. Second, significant program knowledge by the outside person will permit that individual to "control" his or her time devoted to performance matters. Lacking much knowledge about field performance, the outside person can either be inundated by the homework necessary in that game or else see the unknown aspects of it as too threatening to his game. The top person is likely to be able to devote most of his time to the organizational health game but be able to step in when necessary in the performance game *only* where he knows enough to be comfortable with delegating significant amounts of authority to the top-level fixer.

The basic point is that the agency head needs to say to a top-level subordinate—and mean it—"that's your (performance) game, keep it fixed." This is the first step toward institutionalizing the fixer role. One fixer, of course, is not enough. Fixers are required at key points in the operating bureau with critical fixing responsibilities in the field. Nor is the assignment of responsibility enough. There remains the commitment of significant amounts of agency resources to support bargaining and fixing in the performance game. But clearly, the establishment of the top-level responsibility for bargaining and fixing is the first critical agency commitment.

CONSTRAINT, CREDIBILITY, AND DEFERENCE

Social agency political executives face a dilemma coming from the intrinsic nature of complex social service delivery programs and of political–bureaucratic reality. The situation from the perspective of these managers seems to call for both centralization *and* decentralization in the agency. Since social agency political executives operate with extremely weak controls, it is small wonder that they seem so driven toward tightening up, toward trying to center authority in assistant secretaries or bureau heads, and toward spewing forth guideline after guideline. At the same time, the field setting is highly unpredictable so that no future plan can spell out reasonable responses in advance, yet the cost of delay will be high, and proven field tactics are not available. The need is for decentralization where competent people on the spot have authority to exercise judgment in developing viable tactics.

It is a fundamental dilemma, with these two needs often being in direct conflict. But given the weak control points, and the indeterminancy in the field, what headquarters can do to compel (as opposed to influence) positive behavior is limited. And unfortunately, as we have seen so vividly in the case materials, the power to increase complexity and confusion and to harass is likely to exceed the power to order or to influence.

In the CETA and CDBG case studies, the complexity, confusion, and harassment flowing from agency structure and action came from several sources. One was the basic structural arrangements establishing lines of authority and communication. The case material on HUD illustrated so vividly how unclear lines and garbled or contradictory communications could create complexity and confusion. An organizational structure such as that at HUD during the New Federalism period, with organizational boxes and lines causing people to thrash about without knowing who is to do what, can reduce the organization to a point of being unable to communicate. The DOL case materials, however, indicate that better lines of authority and communication are only a start toward less complexity and confusion, without making basic changes in the agency's orientation toward the field. Indeed, if the agency management strategy is sufficiently misguided, structural confusion may inhibit agency harassment.

An important factor in the field creating complexity and confusion has been the regulatory mentality of the social agencies where control is equated with compliance. As the case materials make clear, compliance in narrow terms—particularly on procedural issues—can become an end in itself. Here can be the arena where agency staff takes out its frustrations on grantees, demanding the strictest adherence to agency directives. The response of finding loopholes brings more directives. Compliance becomes a game of wits in which those providing and those receiving grants become opponents.

It would be wrong to think that this regulatory or compliance mentality flows merely from structure and hence can be changed simply by altering structure. Congressional, organizational, and bureaucratic pressures foster rules and regulations. The regulatory mentality is the natural bureaucratic response fitting both bureaucratic drives for order and bureaucratic needs to show that "control" is being exerted and that legislative intent is being carried out.[9]

To this point, we have cast compliance as an evil, even if a necessary one; but it remains true that compliance can support the clarifying of national intent over time. Local choices are *not* good by definition. Overt attempts to defy national intent, particularly distributional outcomes, may well need to be met by firm responses. But to recognize a need for compliance is not to argue against agency structural constraints aimed at limiting the deleterious consequences of compliance that increase complexity and confusion. It is the tendency of compliance efforts to be unrestrained and often unrelated to important national concerns that are at issue.

Another basic source of field complexity and confusion is the incongruity in the agency between responsibility and authority. The problem may start with Congress making unrealistic or vague charges that seem to give the agency all field responsibility. The agency then overcompensates for initial uncertainty of mission by drawing up pervasive statements overstating the responsibilities of those below. It is the agency's own version of Congress' predilection toward the "secretary shall" and the outcome fallacy.

The assignment of unrealistic responsibilities can force federal staffs to overact. The likely response to responsibility overreach is a flow of rules that elaborate on or counteract existing rules. In this confusion, federal staffs lose credibility. Chasing after unrealistic controls, the agency jeopardizes belief by local organizations that the agency knows what it is doing and can set reasonable tasks. To avoid confusion and loss of credibility, the agency must keep responsibilities in line with authority. Headquarters constraint becomes the operational guide word.

Responsibility in the broadest sense is a political choice in the decision domain, and Congress usually sets these responsibilities for the agencies without necessarily giving much thought to whether or not the agency can really do what is specified. However, the agency has a great deal of flexibility in defining these responsibilities and over time can negotiate with the Congress to determine more realistic ones. Further, most of the responsibilities that the agency assumes are not set out explicitly in the legislation or in congressional intent. Agencies, themselves, appear the main culprits in overpromising.

[9] For an excellent discussion of legislative relationships, see Richard F. Elmore, *Complexity and Control: What Legislators and Administrators Can Do about Implementation*, Institute of Governmental Research, University of Washington, Public Policy Paper No. 11, Seattle, April 1979.

An integral element of governance must be to probe for the real limits of what can be done so as to allow a more realistic alignment of agency responsibilities and authority. As the issue of responsibility moves toward the field, pragmatic kinds of questions should prevail. When the agency comes to the details of setting management responsibilities for units concerned with administering the delivery of services, the reasonable question is not the abstract one, without time dimension, of what the unit ought to be doing but the practical one of what it can do *now* given existing limits and available resources.

Perhaps the most destructive case is when headquarters tells agency field staff and local organizations that the former are accountable for performing at a competence level that is well beyond what they can come even close to doing. Local organizations with any understanding of the gap between responsibility and capacity will question headquarters' motives or competence. If the federal field staffs overact, they also may become suspect. Federal field staffs may work out some kind of accommodation with local organizations that may circumvent federal specifications. But this action itself erodes the local sense of agency believability.

Constraint can be seen as part of the headquarters search for a credible position in the eyes of federal and local field people. Credibility may necessitate a tactical retreat to stronger ground that reflects the realities of the field. The aim is to restrict action to what the agency can do well. And in so doing, the social agency is likely to develop greater influence over organizational behavior and outcomes, not less. What is sought is a strategy of the type Sundquist labeled "deference":

There are many examples, within the federal government, of a policy of deference—but not all are models for emulation. In the case of many programs where funds are distributed among states by formula, deference has meant a virtual abdication of any federal influence at all—a quiet glossing over of inadequate state and local performance. Much is lost, obviously, if the federal government fails to exert leadership. The federal government can assemble expertise that individual communities cannot hope to match. It can collect and evaluate data from many communities. The information and insight of the federal experts must be brought to bear upon the community plans, and the advice growing out of evaluation must be made available. These purposes require an aggressive federal approach but an aggressive attitude is consistent with a policy of deference if the federal influence is achieved primarily through consultative relationships while the plans are being formed, rather than through review and modification or disapproval of the community's proposals afterwards. The one approach is calculated to stimulate local initiative; the other tends to stultify it.[10]

[10] James L. Sundquist, *Making Federalism Work*, Brookings Institution, Washington, D.C., 1969, pp. 251–252.

The notions of agency constraint or deference or credibility all point toward the basic issue of a viable working relationship between the federal and local partners. Can there be a partnership that emphasizes increasing the commitment and capacity of local organizations? The agency must choose between a stress on compliance and a stress on commitment and capacity as the central guide to its organizational structure and behavior. In the natural complexity and confusion of social service delivery programs, it is easy to lose direction. The situation often seems like that of a vessel tossed about to such an extent its crew is unsure whether the ship is generally on course and finds a guiding point on land to orient it. Commitment and capacity provide the fundamental guide. This orientation asks whether agency structural choices increase or decrease complexity and confusion in the field, local adaptability and capacity building, agency credibility, and the exercise of reasonable field discretion.

FIELD COMPETENCE

No issue looms larger in reorienting the agency toward the field than that of the allocation of staff resources between headquarters and the field. All the evidence indicates the difficulties of exerting direct control and influence from headquarters by keeping most of the top-level managers, the highly trained specialists, and the brighter generalists in Washington.

Distance is a tremendous barrier in social service delivery programs. Detailed planning in Washington does not help much; headquarters rules and second-guessing are likely to be confusing, wrongheaded, or both; and control points are difficult to develop and hard to enforce. The need is for more federal resources to support local management and staff in building the capacity of the social service delivery organizations. A basic requirement is federal technical assistance to help local institutions develop the overall managerial and technical capabilities needed to plan for and cope with future problems. Federal staff on the spot must have the capability to exercise the discretion demanded by the complex, highly varied local settings.

The Coopers & Lybrand report points out: "With only 25% of the total staff, HUD Headquarters has two-thirds of all grades GS–15 and higher, whereas the field has most of the responsibility for operating the programs."[11] Coopers & Lybrand recommend that more of the high

[11] Coopers & Lybrand, *Recommendations for HUD Organizational Structure,* Department of Housing and Urban Development, Washington, D.C., March 1976, p. 10.

grades be distributed to the field. Perhaps even more important are less tangible factors. After all, there are some super grades (GS–16 and above) and a number of GS–15s in the field. But as long as implementation and field administration remain inferior positions in the agency, the people attracted to them are unlikely to be first-rate. There must be recognition in terms of status and responsibility as well as money.

Field staff can become the key people making important discretionary decisions intended to influence organizational and program performance. Those in the agency with high career aspirations must see field service both as challenging and as a major route of personal advancement. Only with rewards and status and challenging jobs increasingly in the field can this crucial element be put in place over time. All we know about organizational structure tells us that better staff must want to be in the field. The first need is for competent managers who can direct the use of field resources. Then the special skills, made so prominent by their absence, can be well used.

The biggest specific need is for substantive technical assistance. As Ginsberg and Solow observe: "[T]he sorry fact is that most state and local governments—with some notable exceptions—are poorly structured and poorly staffed to carry out new and innovative tasks. They have a hard time even meeting their routine commitments."[12] Even for the subnational governments that have gained a goodly amount of experience and competence, the need remains for substantive technical help that addresses both specific organizational problems and the general capacity to deliver social services.

A major Rand study of the implementation of education programs found the lack of local staff capability a crucial barrier to improvement and an excellent place for federal activities. As Berman and McLaughlin observed "A major opportunity for federal policy to improve the institutional capability of school districts lies in the largely ignored area of local staff development. . . . [T]he success of any practice depends less on the inherent merit of the technology than it does on the *skills and commitment of the user*."[13] One of the major recommendations made by the Rand research group is to establish "a separate categorical effort [which] would provide a clear signal to state and local personnel about federal priorities; it would imply that the federal

---

[12] Eli Ginsberg and Robert M. Solow, "Some Lessons of the 1960's," *The Public Interest*, Winter 1974, p. 217.

[13] Paul Berman and Milbrey W. McLaughlin, *Federal Programs Supporting Educational Change, Vol. VIII: Implementing and Sustaining Innovations*, Rand Corporation, R–1589/8–HEW, Santá Monica, California, May 1978, p. 42, italics added.

government considers local capacity building to be a fundamental need."[14]

A basic question that the agency must decide is whether or not its own staff can be the major source of substantive technical assistance and capacity building. Potential bureaucratic conflicts, the lack of staff competence, or shortages of personnel may point to the provision of technical assistance mainly by outside sources.[15] Nonfederal sources including peer assistance may be the only realistic option.

If such is the case, a strategy for such purchases and for the management of the procured technical assistance becomes critical. One of the reasons that government has purchased inadequate technical assistance from the outside is that people in the program line see a problem that they cannot handle, decide some technical assistance is required, and then hastily seek to procure the help needed. The purchasing staff may be competent as to procurement procedures, but the badly needed technical skills to address programmatic and organizational questions are not there. Further, once purchased, there is unlikely to be a serious staff commitment made to the demanding task of managing the provision of substantive technical assistance.

The key point is that internal staff competence must exist if there is to be a reasonable likelihood of developing and maintaining external quality. There must be at least a reasonable cadre of people sufficiently knowledgeable about substantive technical assistance to buy and administer help from the outside. High-quality technical assistance is not a commodity picked up off the shelf by executing a requisition. Competence is needed to beget competence.

The development and management of substantive technical assistance has a clear analogue in policy research activities, in part because many outside organizations provide both commodities. The experience in the research area yields evidence that makes the case for a strong internal staff compelling. As Williams has observed

> Developing a high quality staff may require an office sufficiently large to form a kind of *critical mass* that permits both extensive internal staff interaction and time for individual staff members to develop and monitor in detail, when necessary, ma-

---

[14] Ibid., p. 43.

[15] As to the latter, agencies often can find funds to purchase services from the outside but not obtain resources for hiring additional staff. A 18 July 1978 *Washington Post* article stated: "The extent of these outside programs was underlined recently when . . . Secretary Joseph A. Califano, Jr., reported to the Senate Appropriations Committee that in addition to the 144, 256 regular HEW employees the department is paying the salaries of 980, 217 people who work for private 'think tanks,' universities, state and local government agencies and the like."

jor research projects. Surely, an important question is whether or not outside researchers and organizations can gain sufficient knowledge about policy needs that the requirement for internal research development and monitoring is reduced. At the same time it is unlikely that policy offices will buy good research unless they have some qualified people to function as intelligent consumers. . . . Moreover, it is worth noting that *all* of the exemplary cases [of policy research development and management] in the social agencies have been offices with large staffs (a critical mass).[16]

In short, the social agencies are unlikely to be able to delegate the basic responsibility for the development and consumption of a highly specialized product such as substantive technical assistance to some outside organization. The government will be an intelligent consumer only if it is willing to commit a reasonable level of their better staff to that activity.

If technical assistance is to be a major staff activity requiring the significant upgrading of field office management and technical personnel, it presents a number of structural problems. The first is that reallocating higher quality staff to the field can threaten headquarters' capability to respond to issues arising directly in the decision domain. Moreover, even if the initial staff changes are made, there will be continuing pressures pulling this reallocated staff away from substantive technical assistance concerns. Such pulls may be from headquarters itself to handle hot issues or from field managers to treat immediate control problems or crises that threaten organizational health. Since these crises are not going to wither away, high-level headquarters and field managers will be tempted to draw these relatively competent staff members into their immediate problems. Indeed, headquarters over time may start shifting people back so as to return to the old quality balance between headquarters and the field.

No structural arrangement alone is going to keep higher quality staff working primarily or exclusively on substantive technical assistance if agency management decides they should be doing something else. It is possible, however, to structure technical assistance so that the choice to move away from a commitment will have to be made explicitly by undoing a specific organizational arrangement.

The most visible commitment to substantive technical assistance would be to establish separate field technical assistance units headed by individuals of relatively high status and staffed with a reasonable complement of higher grades. After all, the acid test of commitment is status and staff allocation.

[16] Walter Williams, "The Role of Social Scientists outside of the Government in Social Policy," Public Policy Paper No. 7, Institute of Governmental Research, University of Washington, Seattle, August 1974, p. 12, italics in the original.

The cleanest structural arrangement would separate the technical assistance units from the unit or units responsible for approval and compliance. The separation gets at the problem of federal–local distrust discussed earlier where local organizations question whether advisory technical assistance given by those with compliance responsibilities is really only advisory.[17] Such a separation does not imply that the technical assistance resources could not be drawn on by the program line units to help correct problems uncovered in approval and compliance activities. However, it would make sense in light of some of the potential problems of distrust to have the separate technical assistance unit be client oriented, with primary responsibility for advising—rather than directing—outside organizations and groups. Separate technical assistance units would stand ready to answer demands both from within the agency and from outside sources. However, its professional commitment would be to advisory efforts, not control.

Separate technical units offer an opportunity for creating the kinds of marketlike pressures discussed in Chapter 8. Such units without explicit ties to approval would have no overt power to force their product on local organizations. They would be "demand responsive" in that their continued lives would depend upon their services being wanted by people in the field. Making the technical assistance units demand responsive could move them toward a concentrated search for staff who can offer useful advice about organizational and programmatic techniques. If there is deficient demand, a good technical assistance unit director ought to be begging for funds to supplement his own staff and also figuring out how to get rid of some of the losers from that staff.

Separate technical assistance units may present a number of field problems. Even though technical assistance may have been provided poorly in the past by line units, these units will still see a need for assistance in executing their basic responsibilities. That is, when the line unit finds a problem in the field, it may want to direct that change be made. Local units may not want help but rather take technical assistance from the programmatic line unit or suffer the consequences at grant approval time. Since the line units and the independent technical assistance staffs will be offering the same product, the two are likely to be rivals competing for power and worrying about turf.

---

[17] It would be misleading to create the impression that distrust has been established as a major barrier to the delivery of technical assistance. In the field interviews from the New Federalism case materials, the main reasons given for not taking organizational and programmatic problems to agency staff was agency staff weaknesses and lack of information. These, not fear, thus far appear to be the principal inhibitors of demand from the field.

Here we can end up with classic within-organization bureaucratic battles. For example, the head of the technical assistance unit may try to grab power by making the program staff look bad. There is a thin line between efforts to help clients and ones to subvert the field staff.

The basic assumption of demand responsiveness is that units will strive to be useful (like offering a better product in the marketplace) and if they do not succeed will be punished by Congress or the agencies for poor performance. But will this desirable result really come about? Once the separate technical assistance units are planned and staff is in place, they may exist primarily from bureaucratic inertia. It could be that potential users will not understand that the units have no ties to the programmatic line so that a call from one of the technical assistance staff to a funding agency may appear to be a fund-related (supply side) request. Further, units can appear to be busy by undertaking low-level activities that they describe in the dull, bland, but reassuring terms of bureaucratese—an average of 36.3 contacts per month with local officials by each staff member, without, of course, defining contact (a phone call?).

The biggest organizational issue, however, is likely to be moving people between headquarters and the field. In increasing competence in the field, it is not obvious that the actual numbers of people located at headquarters and in the regions would change materially. But the relative number of higher level staff, technical specialists, and good generalists in the field would increase significantly. Can such a shift be done quickly without the shattering effects on morale we saw in HUD? We doubt it. But how is the agency to get started and then to sustain a slow movement in that direction?

The basic clash between the short life span of political executives and the fragileness of the agency organizational structure to rapid change is an inherent problem. As analysts press and poke in the area of organizational restructuring, they will keep coming up against the Catch-22 of a relatively slow, orderly change. The first hurdle is to sell short-term political executives on starting down a path, the completion of which seems far beyond their tenure. Given their acceptance, the next problem is to convince career civil servants to take a direction that could leave them exposed if the next set of political executives they know is coming moves quickly to tear down the framework of the new structure when all their experience tells them that is a highly likely event.

One final point about competence needs to be made. Getting more competent people to deliver substantive technical assistance is not necessarily going to make great knowledge breakthroughs—to uncover great amounts of information that can be generalized. Rather, raising the competence of those providing and receiving technical assistance is intended to facilitate the development of particular organizational and programmatic decisions. There must be more capacity for flexibility—a better "human resource base" for the positive exercise of discretion at the delivery level.

THE REGIONAL OFFICE: BAROMETER OF THE AGENCY MANAGEMENT STRATEGY

The strategic issues of the agency decision-making and action framework, complexity and confusion, and the allocation of staff resources came together in the question of the role and responsibilities of the federal regional offices. The case materials showed how headquarters ambiguity and volatility over the regional offices' status so often was a confusing, debilitating factor in the field. Are regional staffs to act primarily as headquarters outposts, the main responsibilities of which are to provide early warnings of threats to organizational health and to check up on the grantees who might not be following all of headquarters regulations—mainly compliance clerks? Or are the regional offices to be given significant discretion to aid local grantees with specific problems and to provide managerial, organizational, and technical assistance aimed at raising local organizations' implementation and administrative capacity over time?

We have the dilemma of discretion. On the one hand, headquarters' desire for clear lines of authority and communication and for unambiguous accountability pushes toward little or no field staff discretion. The temptation is to reduce field staff to the interpretation of routine questions. The danger exists that the message will be changed, time will be lost, and responsibility lines will be blurred when a directive from Washington must be passed through the various layers of the regional office hierarchy before it is handed down to the field representative or the area office. A tight structure that eliminates all field staff except to provide routine services or develop information needed by headquarters holds out the promise of reducing the confusion and ambiguity in the field that so plagued CETA and CDBG. There is the lure of putting headquarters managers clearly in charge of what the agency staff does—at least capturing within-agency control.

On the other hand, given the complexity and diversity in operating social service delivery programs in the field, a knowledgeable person from the agency who is on the spot to exercise discretion seems highly desirable. Since the tendency of headquarters is to push for uniformity in interpretation, it is important for field staffs to have the authority to allow variation aimed at improving organizational and program performance. Holding too tight a rein increases the turnaround time in the field and decreases the stature of the field staffs. Local people will see little value in discussing anything with field staff when it is necessary to go to headquarters to get a final answer.

The issue of regional office role and responsibility in part is a question of structure—one of organizational boxes and specified authority and functions. But it goes beyond structure to a central issue of the agency's management strategy. The decision about the role and responsibility of regional offices forces the agency political executives to make fundamental choices about the style and orientation of agency governance.

The regional offices are the barometer of whether the agency is serious about implementing a field-oriented strategy. *It is in the regional offices that we are most likely to determine whether or not headquarters has accepted the primacy of the field in the performance game by shifting better qualified staff, by exercising constraint and reducing field confusion, and by stressing advice and capacity over control and compliance.*

PERFORMANCE PRESSURES

The overwhelming view of students of government, including the authors, is that more performance pressure points are needed in social service delivery programs. Whether to shift to vouchers or some other marketlike device allowing social service clients to purchase such services directly from providers of their choice is a basic decision by the Congress and the White House outside of the range of agency management. At question now is whether the agency itself can find pressure devices to supplement its direct control and influence efforts.

The problem is that pressure devices that make technical, bureaucratic, and political sense within the existing structure of the shared power model are difficult to find. As possible examples, we will look at two devices—furnishing information to citizens and making the head of the regional office an advocate within the agency for better field performance.[18]

---

[18] We have already discussed another possible vehicle—the demand-responsive independent technical assistance office—in an earlier section.

Information for Citizens

Outside pressures brought by citizens offer a potential to the agency for indirect influence. Citizens may be able to leap political barriers insurmountable by the agency. But how do we get responsible citizen participation? How do we avoid either sham participation or disruptive, destructive involvement that only blunders or blocks? Participatory democracy is not an easy road.

Since the controversial "maximum feasible participation" of the original Economic Opportunity Act of 1964, the issue of citizen involvement in decisions concerning social service delivery programs has been a prominent one.[19] Both CETA and CDBG stress citizen involvement in the rhetoric of legislation. However, both pieces of legislation concentrated power in local elected officials at the expense of citizen groups. The philosophical argument for recentralizing power in "city hall" was that these elected officials represent all of the citizens of a geographic area. They are the only people who answer to citizens at election time. Such a process assumes power through the vote will move elected officials toward adequate performance.

However, there are two problems in relying only on voting to influence social service delivery programs. First, critical decisions on social projects get made all the time, whereas elections occur every 2 or 4 years. Second, and relatedly, these elections become plebiscites on CETA or CDBG or any other specific program only on rare occasions such as gross mismanagement or illegal acts that flare into newsworthy controversy.

These problems, of course, are endemic ones in a large-scale democracy when candidates stand for general election. Still the issue remains of how citizens are to act meaningfully and responsibly in affecting local policies in areas such as employment and training and community development. How are local citizens to gain information about programs *prior* to the making of decisions? How are they to get the specialized knowledge to formulate questions about performance and to pressure local authorities to provide these answers in understandable language?

The social agency could become a key source of information and

---

[19] For a balanced treatment of this much discussed provision, see Sundquist, *Making Federalism Work*, pp. 35–40, 70–74. For a more general treatment of citizen participation, see William H. Stewart, Jr., *Citizen Participation in Public Administration*, Bureau of Public Administration, University of Alabama, Tuscaloosa, 1976; and Stuart Langton, "American Citizen Participation: A Deep Rooted Tradition," *National Civic Review*, September 1979, pp. 403–410, 422.

expertise. Let us consider the issue by asking how citizens might obtain and use outcome data to help them make more reasoned judgments about program performance in social service delivery programs. Congress could specify that grantees perform evaluations and make that data available to the public. Congress has placed such requirements on the social agencies for years, beginning in the mid-1960s with OEO, but there has been little real impact. This probably has more to do with congressional will than anything else.

There are some strategies that might get us farther than we are now. One possibility would have social agencies themselves doing final outcome evaluations and providing the results to the public. The agencies in this case could have a relatively independent status if they themselves are not held responsible for final outcomes—that is, if Congress has not committed the final outcome fallacy. It is surely moot as to whether Congress would permit agency evaluations in support of citizen decision making. Even if it is done, local citizens still need technical help in using the data.

If, as is more likely, evaluations are left to local governments, even more technical help may be needed by citizens in getting local governments to execute meaningful assessments and to interpret results. The argument becomes even stronger for the provision of technical assistance to raise the capabilities of citizens to make informed substantive comments about social service delivery programs. Here we are back again to basic questions of federal field competence generally and of the specific agency capacity to organize and staff a strong substantive technical assistance mechanism.

Citizens need both sound, relevant, timely information and the technical knowledge to employ it effectively in the local policy process. That process is a political one, so we neither should overvalue information nor underestimate the importance of pure political power and pressure. Rather, the point is that citizens who want to engage in substantive criticism so often are at a disadvantage and need more resources in the political arena. The agency may well see the benefit of supplying such information and aiding local people in interpreting it or in obtaining information themselves.

The Regional Head as Inside Advocate

Inside advocacy requires that the regional head have an organizational position outside of the direct programmatic line from which to exert pressures aimed at straightening out agency rules and practices that impinge on local efforts. Government policy, procedures, regulations, or guidelines are developed with a standard approach, not allowing for unusual circumstances in individual field settings. In addition, particular federal staff in a region may be performing some task poorly, or regional office organizational arrangements may be ineffective.

Regional differences that require advocacy may appear mundane. A problem arises because of a particular city ordinance, a personality clash, historical political considerations, or a weak or arbitrary regional office staff member. Standardized regulations cannot take into account the differences between Boston and Seattle, between Alaska and any other part of the country. Generally sensible provisions can foul up projects, even after sufficient funds have been allocated. In a period of hair-trigger litigation, there is some basis for agency fears that exceptions will beget exceptions. On the whole, however, headquarters appears not to appreciate obvious regional differences or recognize their importance. Advocacy is needed at the local level to make the case to headquarters for variation.

The problem of weak or arbitrary performance by federal staff either in the field or in a headquarters unit with field responsibility can create continuing regional difficulties. The typical case is not the major catastrophe demanding attention but the run-of-the-mill problem that creates distrust, makes unnecessary work, or undercuts initiative.

The issue is not whether advocacy is needed but the extent to which it is an appropriate agency activity. The case for an outside source is strong. Local officials often can bring powerful pressures through their congressional delegation, political party connections, or personal contacts. On major issues, outside forces may be far more effective than a federal functionary.

Limitations on this particular kind of advocacy must be recognized, however. The big victories are largely political in nature. A powerful senator may intervene once or twice, especially on highly visible problems, but there are no guarantees. No court ruling has established a precedent. Headquarters bureaucrats have staying power. They can reverse a ruling the next time it is questioned. Communities cannot depend exclusively on sporadic political pressure as its source of advocacy.

The case for advocacy from within lies with the smaller, less glamorous issues. In the day-to-day arena where field staff are having to wrestle with minor, yet handicapping rules, there may be the need for persistent in-house advocacy. The case mentioned earlier of DOL's $205 error in a prime sponsor's grant modification points up sharply the blockage that can result when unchangeable local regulations run up against unmoveable federal regulations. Weisband and Franck argue that "the requisite for changing policy is *inside* information."[20] Information is most valuable when it is based on specialized technical knowledge and an understanding both of the background in which the information was derived and of the context in which it is being used. The insider has the advantage of institutional access. He or she knows where the bodies are, knows the players in the process and how they operate, and knows the institutional terrain where decisions are made. Again the issue of competence arises.

The desirable dimensions of the advocacy role are high status, relatively small staff size, and the staff capability to develop and analyze information on performance. Being the senior agency official in the field provides the advocate with sufficient status to negotiate both within the agency and with important external constituencies. A limited staff is the strongest bureaucratic barrier to the temptation to meddle too much in line activities. At the same time, if the advocate is not simply to be a political negotiator or a high-level public relations type, but is to influence performance, expert skills are needed that can be focused on the analysis of information relevant to organizational and program performance and policy.

The emerging regional office structure can provide a base for advocacy. We saw that the 1977 HUD reorganization to some extent separated the regional heads from programmatic line responsibilities and reduced their staffs. In HEW, where the regional directors historically had had limited line responsibility, a 1977 reorganization attempted to remove the region heads—redesignated principal regional officials (PROs)—from all program operations responsibilities. A Califano memorandum observed "[PROs will] represent my office, and perform those tasks for which my office must be directly responsible in the field. However, these tasks do *not* include direction of *any* of our programs since that responsibility is *fully* assigned to [program] Heads."[21] In both HUD and HEW, the regional head, in being designed a secretary-in-the-field but severely restricted as to program responsibilities in keeping with the Carter administration efforts to recentralize, became a candidate for an advocacy role.

While the advocate role has potential for increased performance pressures, there are a number of organizational problems. Most of all,

[20] Edward Weisband and Thomas M. Franck, *Resignation and Protest: Political and Ethical Choices between Loyalty to Team and Loyalty to Conscience in American Public Life,* Grossman, New York, 1975, p. 168, italics added.

[21] Memorandum from Joseph A. Califano, Jr., Subject: "Clarification and Revision of Regional Office Responsibilities and Organization," 19 July 1977, p. 1, italics added.

it is a demanding position in terms of personal skill as well as one that organizations may be uncomfortable with. In light of fears that the regional head will usurp responsibilities and in light of bureaucratic sensitivity to any criticism, especially from an insider, about whom it is so hard to claim lack of knowledge, a basic question is whether or not the line units will tolerate pressures from within by a high-status official. It is more likely that the regional head will take secretary-in-the-field as the main or exclusive role by being a political operator, not a performance prodder. Again, it would be a victory for organizational health over field performance.

A FIELD INFORMATION STRATEGY

Berryman and Glennan's paper entitled "An Improved Strategy for Evaluating Federal Programs in Education," which addresses information problems in the United States Office of Education, provides an excellent basis for discussing the main issues of an information strategy.[22] The authors use the term *evaluation* broadly so that both evaluations and implementation assessments as well as studies to determine programmatic needs are included in their strategy. However, the paper is concerned primarily with a headquarters-oriented (decision domain) strategy focusing on a top-level evaluation staff (Office of Evaluation and Dissemination) so that the authors are thinking primarily in terms of relatively large-scale research studies—especially final outcome evaluations—rather than some of the techniques that we might be concerned with for a field strategy. Hence, we will need to look briefly at some questions pertaining mainly to a field strategy.

The Berryman and Glennan Information Strategy

Berryman and Glennan define an evaluation strategy as "a set of prescriptive statements about: what can be known and what it is important to know (*substance*); when it should be known (*timing*); and how it should be learned (*procedure*)."[23] They consider a new evaluation strategy for major federal education programs by treating the three issues of substance, timing, and procedures.

[22] Sue E. Berryman and Thomas K. Glennan, Jr., "An Improved Strategy for Evaluating Federal Programs in Education," *A Rand Note* prepared for the U.S. Department of Health, Education and Welfare, N–1290–HEW, August 1979. This paper was prepared just prior to the establishment of the Department of Education.

[23] Ibid., p. 14, italics in the original.

SUBSTANCE

The authors' propose four criteria for selecting evaluation studies. The first criterion states *"the information that policymakers need should govern the studies selected."*[24] Berryman and Glennan feel strongly the narrow, large-scale outcome evaluations that have dominated the Office of Evaluation and Dissemination provide far less information than headquarters policymakers need in making decision domain judgments about federally funded education programs. Even at the decision domain level, Berryman and Glennan believe that policymakers require organizational and process information of the type obtained in implementation assessments.

The second criterion states that *"studies should assess the reasonableness of major assumptions underlying the program legislation."*[25] Here Berryman and Glennan recognize that the exigencies of policy formulation, particularly at the legislative level, so often forces the use of poor data or the making of policy without information. As we have discussed repeatedly, the legislative style of exact language may cover over how little is known about programs or intent or how much disagreement there is over intent. Berryman and Glennan make this critical point:

> [L]egislation is usually based on inadequate knowledge. The enactment of legislation tends to start, not culminate, public learning about programs and solutions. . . .
>
> The fact that we know so little at the start of most programs argues for some studies that explicitly treat program assumptions as hypotheses to be tested, not as facts. For example, before asking whether a program is achieving Congressional intent, we can reasonably ask whether the intent is feasible.[26]

The third criterion argues that *"the studies should produce an increasing amount of interpretive information about how parts of the program (funding and service delivery systems, intended beneficiaries) interact to produce observed outcomes."*[27] Berryman and Glennan indicate that they use the terms *interpretative information* or *interpretive framework* rather than the more formal terms *model* or *theory* because our present tools, as we have discussed in the previous chapter, are unlikely to yield causal models that specify how inputs and outputs are combined so as to yield desired outcomes. That is, definitive evidence is not likely to be available showing either how different elements of a

---

[24] Ibid., p. 34, italics in the original.
[25] Ibid., p. 35, italics in the original.
[26] Ibid., pp. 35–36.
[27] Ibid., p. 36, italics in the original.

program package can be changed to produce a particular outcome or how to implement such changes. Rather with studies that probe broadly about programs and projects, we may find some useful organizational and process information that suggests how to go about improving programs and projects, including how to implement the possible changes.

The final criterion states that *"studies should establish how diverse the program is."*[28] Legislation and the large-scale final outcome evaluations performed to provide information for policymakers concerned with that legislation do not take account of the great diversity of projects and hence the likely differences in expected outcomes because of that diversity. As the authors observe

> Evaluators should document the nature and extent of service diversity for at least two reasons. First, such studies portray the reality of the program. The Congress can then decide whether the variation permitted by the program legislation fits Congressional intent. Second, evaluators cannot plan intelligent studies of effects without knowing about the variation in services delivered. If a program is supposed to deliver uniform services, using the same measures of outcome across sites is logically valid and defensible. However, if outcome measures presume uniform services and those delivered are diverse *and* responsive to the intent of the program legislation, the program effects will be underestimated.[29]

TIMING

Berryman and Glennan stress the importance of recognizing the life cycle of programs so that information efforts focus on the different stages of a program and are sensitive to variations in the time taken to implement a program depending both on technical issues and on controversy within the program. The evaluation strategy should recognize that programs with a long administrative chain or ones with complex, vague regulations or ones that demand significant organizational changes at different levels of government are going to have long implementation periods that need to be assessed before trying to focus on outcomes. Moreover, if the implementation period is expected to be complex and difficult, it is organizational and process information that is so badly needed for immediate improvement.

PROCEDURE

Most of the discussion in this extended section of the Berryman and Glennan paper focuses on the specifics of headquarters-oriented studies, but two points made are directly relevant to a field strategy.

[28] Ibid., p. 37, italics in the original.
[29] Ibid., pp. 37–38, italics in the original.

Even for the top level of the agency, Berryman and Glennan have grave doubts about the usefulness of large-scale final outcome evaluations, preferring instead numerous more limited studies with much shorter time frames. The huge evaluation studies the Office of Evaluation and Dissemination has conducted in the past take too long and provide far too little information for headquarters policymaking. Berryman and Glennan do not reject outcome data completely but rather recognize the severe limits of its usefulness, particularly if organizational and process data are not available to help in interpreting the outcome results.

The other critical point that Berryman and Glennan make is that the proposed evaluation strategy should be negotiated between the Office of Education (now the new Department of Education) and the Congress. While they are focusing on the highest levels of government, the notion for realistic bargaining to establish an understanding between the executive and legislative branches certainly holds as we move down the information process into the field.

The Berryman and Glennan evaluation strategy for headquarters in comparison to the Office of Education evaluation practices they were critiquing is much more field oriented, much more oriented toward organization and process information, much more oriented toward small-scale studies that obtain a variety of data rather than large-scale outcome evaluations, and much more focused on realistic efforts to negotiate what policymakers want in terms of information. Clearly, these broad notions devised for a headquarters information strategy can also guide the desired field information strategy. However, for the field strategy, we do need to elaborate on a few points that take account of different needs and the power relationships for a quite different set of actors in the administrative and support domain generally and the field in particular.

A Field Information Strategy

The basic question of the agency field information strategy is whether or not information will help federal staffs concerned with individual projects and grants exercise positive influence over the local-level commitment to performance and capacity to carry out that local commitment. The big field need is for specific information on organizational factors or on the institutional process that can aid field staffs in improving local compliance or in raising future performance capacity.

In particular, it would be useful to have field information that tied project means to desired outcomes—that is, to have evidence indicating the transformation process by which inputs and outputs yield better outcomes and the means of getting that needed new process in place. The "ideal" field information would indicate for specific projects both the means of achieving desired outcomes and how to implement those required means. But such a causal model is almost never available. Rather, we may have an interpretive framework that suggests inputs and outputs that may improve outcomes. Moreover, even when there are good indications of relationships generally, there still is the need to tailor information to fit the specific organizational and political setting in which the individual project operates.

The critical point is that improvements in outcomes can come about only through changes at the local level in technique, staff behavior, or both.[30] In particular, where no technical product (e.g., a machine that raises production even though the worker does nothing different) is available, the critical need is to find ways of changing what staff does—to find organizational or process factors that induce different organizational behavior, including, when necessary, providing a better base (more capacity) for that behavior.

This means that outcome data *alone* may be even less useful in the field than at headquarters. This is not to say outcome data cannot be employed either to pinpoint projects or grantees that need improving or to induce improvement by linking rewards to outcomes. But unless there is information about programmatic or organizational problems that suggest why outcome performance is poor, what can federal staff do? How often can outcome data alone be used to force staff or process changes? Even if the federal staff has some ideas about program or organizational changes, how often do they have a reasonable approach to implementing the changes? For those who must exercise control over or provide advice to individual projects, the need is information indicating what is to be done. "It is not working" needs to be accompanied by ideas about how to make it work. As Wildavsky observes of studies showing only that program or project objectives have not been met.

> So what? Such evaluations do not help program managers who need to know which resources under their control they can manipulate to do better. Programs can only be countered by other programs. If a bad program is the best available, it may still be

---

[30] For a more extended discussion of the point, see William G. Ouchi, "The Relationship between Organizational Structure and Organizational Control," *Administrative Science Quarterly*, March 1977, pp. 96–99. As Ouchi observes on p. 97: "[R]eal control comes about only through changing the worker's behavior."

good compared to the alternatives. Bad, however, is not yet beautiful. Constraints need to be overcome.[31]

So often the field demand will be for softer, richer information about organizational outputs and the process of implementing, managing, and operating projects in their complex institutional environment. This is the basic ingredient needed for federal field governance.

Also of great importance in devising a field information strategy is the distinction in social service delivery programs funded under the mixed model between the information demands for exercising control and the information needed for the offering of advice in the field. Field control as exercised through approval and compliance technical assistance demands evidence sufficiently specific and precise to support the claim by agency staff of wrongdoing or the failure to comply or perform by a funded organization. The underlying empirical base of field control will be improved if particular inputs, outputs, and outcomes can be defined in measurable terms that are not subject to significant controversy and can be measured with a relatively high degree of accuracy. That is, as discussed in Chapter 8, a control system requires a strong "detector," to use Anthony and Dearden's term. Conversely, the more a particular measure is subject to disagreement concerning whether it represents the desired result (i.e., are wages immediately after training a good proxy for long-term earnings changes?) or is challengeable on statistical grounds, the weaker is the empirical base for the exercise of control over field organizations.

Advisory technical assistance is more likely to benefit from a broader spectrum of information, including some that may be rather imprecise or loose by statistical criteria. The point is not that advice would not benefit from precise, specific information. It is that those providing advice may be able to proceed without information meeting the statistical standards required for control. In particular, softer, richer information that speaks to how organizational processes and procedures are used in the political/bureaucratic environment in the provision of social services may be extremely useful. One may have to present a strong case pinpointing the validity, accuracy, and generality of results to *force* a change on a grantee but be able to rely on a few good, but untested examples to *offer* alternatives for consideration by that grantee on how to attack a perceived problem. A critical distinction in deriving a reasonable information strategy is determining the intended uses of information.

[31] Aaron Wildavsky, *The Politics of the Budgetary Process*, Third Edition, Little, Brown, Boston, 1979, pp. 182–183.

An information strategy provides a strong indication of the orientation of organizations in terms of objectives and means. An organization may claim it wants to reach some objective or proceed in a particular way, but does the flow of information allow it to assess its progress? In the case of the social agency does its field information strategy indicate a sensitivity to the variability of projects, to the demands of bargaining and fixing, to the requirements of field staff for addressing specific organizational and procedural problems that lessen local commitment and capacity? Or does the strategy produce narrow compliance-oriented information, or simplistic outcomes, that supports a regulatory mentality but offers little on which to base performance-oriented directives or recommendations?

Asking the right information questions does not insure sound field governance, but it is hard to see improved field governance without a better flow of information. At issue is whether or not the agency has the technical and organizational capacity to obtain the field information required to support field governance aimed at increasing local commitment and capacity.

11 THE AGENCY MANAGEMENT STRATEGY: IMPLEMENTATION AND BEYOND

From the last chapter we can draw two general prescriptions. First, federal agencies should be devising management strategies that will guide organizational behavior. That is, agency leadership, within the broad boundaries set by Congress or the president, should be determining what the agency is or is to be. Second, the management strategies of social agencies charged with the governance of social service delivery programs should have as a central objective increasing local commitment to performance compatible with national intent and the capacity of local service deliverers. This central objective, as must be clear from Chapter 10, would demand a basic reorientation and restructuring of a social agency if it is to be well implemented. Here we see vividly the crucial organizational point made in Chapter 5 that strategy dominates organizational structure and processes.

We are not recommending that all social agencies immediately adopt an agency management strategy that has improving local commitment and capacity as a central objective, but rather that specific agencies analyze the feasibility of adopting such a strategy. In this chapter we start by considering the needed implementation analysis that should be carried out to see if the agency management strategy makes sense for particular agencies. Then, in a final section, we try to put the proposed agency management strategy in perspective, asking about its broader implications for the governance of federal social program grants-in-aid.

THE IMPLEMENTATION ANALYSIS OF THE
AGENCY MANAGEMENT STRATEGY

No matter how great the general appeal of a field-oriented decision and action framework, its appropriateness and feasibility for the individual agency must be analyzed. At issue is whether the agency can be reoriented and reorganized to shift more toward field performance and whether a strategy that has increasing local commitment and capacity as a central objective can provide a decision and action framework that fits the agency's particular situation. Can such a management strategy be worked out consonant with critical issues, not only separately as we have treated them in the last chapter, but in terms of their possible interrelationships? Can the central objective of local commitment and capacity be reconciled with other agency objectives? In short, what is the likelihood that the agency can implement such an agency management strategy?

Recent attempts to implement new decision-making approaches point clearly to the need for a thorough implementation analysis. In looking at the experiences with the Planning–Programming–Budgeting System (PPBS), Management by Objectives (MBO), and Zero Based Budgeting (ZBB), it becomes clear that a real commitment within the agency is a necessary ingredient to put a new decision-making approach in place. PPBS, probably the most ambitious of the three and the most widely written about, provides overwhelming evidence of the difficulties of imposing such a system government wide, with the central budget authority having the primary responsibility for implementation of a new way of thinking.[1]

Strong support of both the secretary and other political executives are necessary for changing the decision-making process. Further, the people in the agency who are going to implement the new approach must accept its rationale and its implications. Unlike the earlier decision-making approaches, which were concerned primarily with how issues were conceptualized in the decision domain, the proposed agency management strategy carries major implications for the field. In addition to casting issues in new terms and getting different kinds of information, basic structural changes that shift resources to the field must be made. The people affected must be convinced that the changes make sense and are in their interests. A thorough implementation

---

[1] For a discussion both of the problems in implementing PPBS government-wide and in the individual agencies and of agency analytic offices considered next, see Walter Williams, *Social Policy Research and Analysis*, American Elsevier, New York, 1971, pp. 17–35, 169–188.

analysis of the agency management strategy is necessary, even if political executives are generally convinced of the strategy's usefulness, so that they have the facts to sell it to everyone concerned.

A primary candidate for executing the extended analysis are the social agency analytic offices. Generally, these offices (a) have principal responsibility within the agency for executing analyses in general; (b) occupy a pivotal position in reporting directly to the secretary that will give the undertaking both visibility and clout; and (c) have more concentrated staff capability to execute such an analysis than any other part of the agency.

These offices can be pivotal at start-up and also emerge as a major continuing staff influence operating at the highest level to institutionalize a field-oriented perspective. Analytic offices are located at the critical point where information and decision making intersect so that they can serve as advocates at the top and also keep the agency focused on implementation through demands for information and continuing analyses. Moreover, these offices have begun to represent the institutional memory of the agency so that a commitment to the agency management strategy, even if it wanes at times, will have a basis for restoration.

There also are clear problems with this choice. First, the agency senior analyst in particular and the analytic office generally have focused mainly on the decision domain. The offices have built up skills more in line with demands in headquarters and the broad political arena occupied by the agency, presidential staff, and the Congress. Like other key actors in the decision domain, the concern for organizational and program performance more often than not gets cast in terms of new policies. And the hard truth is that "creating policy" at the top where success is measured by selling it to other decision makers requires different skills than fixing policy once made. In writing about analytic offices at the close of the Johnson administration, one of the authors posed this question that still remains unanswered:

> Is it reasonable to ask the economist/analyst type of person that headed the OEO and HEW analytical offices to have staff responsibility for the problem of implementation? The question of the capability to implement raises very complex organization/administrative/social psychological issues that are not necessarily an area in which one would expect an economist to have a comparative advantage.[2]

Second, the analytic office, however great its status and clout, is a staff not a line function. Yet, the analytic office must think through the

[2] Ibid., p. 185.

implications of the social agency management strategy for the operating bureaus, which are responsible both for making the needed structural changes and for following the strategy on a daily basis. A concerted effort will be required to make the operating bureaus a significant element in the analytic effort. Lynn and Seidel warn that the analytic office can take the lead in such an effort, but that "it does not own the planning process," and further, that there must be "representatives of divergent views so that underlying issues can surface and be discussed."[3] If the analytic office can draw in the operating bureaus, which is necessary under any conditions, the capability for an extended implementation analysis of the management strategy can be found in the social agency.

There is another aspect of the analysis not to be overlooked. The paradox of the performance game provides a reasonable climate for an extended undertaking. There simply is none of the urgency either of crisis or of the potential of selling a new program that so often has made for hasty analyses where great knowledge gaps have been filled by simplifying assumptions. The analytic office has the opportunity to develop a work team of its own staff and key people from the operating bureaus and to take the time for a hard look at the degree to which an agency management strategy that has local commitment and capacity as a central objective really makes sense. Most of all the working group—and especially the analytic staff—can get into the field to see what the real world (as opposed to decision domain) looks like.

Putting an agency management strategy in place will be a long, involved process. The first step must be a commitment on the part of political executives to expend the resources needed for an extended analysis of the feasibility of the strategy for the particular agency.

Initial and continuing analyses are likely to show all of the limits and weaknesses discussed earlier but also some room for maneuverability. Analysis over time is likely to indicate where organizational change is least threatening and where agency resources have potential for a visible impact. The general expectation is that there are opportunities within the social agencies for getting the proposed agency management strategy started and for building an institutional base that will support it.

Analytic staff work, or any other staff work, is not going to implement the agency management strategy. The ultimate agency problems are those on the line. There is no escaping that reasonable progress

---

[3] Laurence E. Lynn, Jr., and John M. Seidl, " 'Bottom-line' Management for Public Agencies," *Harvard Business Review*, January–February 1977, p. 152.

over time demands commitment and competence both at the top and in the key managerial positions at lower levels of the agency as well as more skilled field staff.

We have only gone so far as to prescribe that the social agencies test the water through an analysis of the feasibility of an agency management strategy that has local commitment and capacity as a central objective and to offer a framework for such analyses. Lest there be some misunderstanding, let us be clear about our argument. We favor the use of the proposed agency management strategy for *all* social agencies sharing the governance of social service delivery programs. At the same time, the available evidence indicates both that new decision-making systems cannot be imposed effectively from above the agency and that internal organization changes of which the shift to an agency management strategy will be a major one cannot be put in place successfully without careful analysis and the involvement of key organizational units in the change. At this point, the only sensible suggestion is to do the analysis.

Still, there is guarded optimism that the social agencies can begin to reorient and reorganize to focus more resources on field performance. Realism drawn from nearly 2 decades of intense social policy effort dictates a cautious outlook and the expectation of slow change. But we do feel the social agencies have a reasonable chance for greater success in using their resources to foster a higher commitment in the field to performance objectives and to provide the needed support to facilitate the exercise of field discretion by those who ultimately determine social policy.

THE AGENCY MANAGEMENT STRATEGY IN BROADER PERSPECTIVE

The grants-in-aid era dating from the 1950s has changed the face of American federalism. As the perceptive David Walker has observed

[T]here has been the steady erosion of any real distinctions between what is a state and local issue and what is a federal concern. The last genuine efforts to debate and define national purposes and aid programs in a constitutional context took place in the 1950s and early 1960s. The need to defend or rationalize new federal assistance efforts vanished in the mid 1960s with enactment of a wide range of aid programs (over 240) by the 89th and 90th Congresses, several of which involved wholly new departures for the national government and some of which were novel to any government. While many of these were limited in their scope and appropriations, the "legitimacy barrier" had fallen. Hence, subsequent actions in these program areas, while frequently more expensive, intrusive, and specialized, were not viewed as major departures from the largely collaborative and simple purposes of the initial legislation. Instead, they were treated largely as mere extensions of the original enactments.

In the 1970s, the federal influence spread still further through involvement in more and more subfunctional areas, new regulatory thrusts, sustained stimulation of greater state and local program and personnel endeavors, and greater efforts to achieve more supervisory authority. As a result of this increased federal activity, the bounds of the national government's current domestic agenda span issues of concern to neighborhood, municipal, or county councils, state legislatures, and the U.N. General Assembly—with concerns of a national legislative body occasionally sandwiched in.[4]

The agency management strategy that has local commitment and capacity as a central objective continues to cast a social agency in an active role as the central federal actor responsible for the governance of social service delivery programs. The approach, then, is well within the bounds of the shared responsibilities funding model. As pointed out in Chapter 1, we can justify this choice purely on our strongly held belief that Congress is not going to abandon its prerogatives under this model by providing the funds to local governments or to citizens without federal strings.

We would go a step further, however. We do not believe that other alternatives necessarily hold more promise for moving social service delivery programs toward desired objectives than the agency management strategy that has commitment and capacity as a central objective. There are two main reasons. The first is that none of the alternatives permits escape from the inherent difficulties of social service delivery programs. The second is that the proposed agency management strategy that envisions an active agency role more than other alternatives seems consonant with American federalism as it has emerged over the last quarter century with the growth of federal grants-in-aid.

We can treat the first point briefly. If the federal government runs social programs directly or turns the funds over to subnational governments without strings attached, top-level managers would face similar difficulties and need to devise management strategies of the type discussed here. With pure revenue sharing, of course, the federal government would simply have transferred these problems to another group of political executives. Nor does the evidence indicate that removing all government from social programs except as fiscal agent and operating through vouchers to be used by recipients in the private

---

[4] David B. Walker, "The Balanced Budget Movement: A Political Perspective," *Intergovernmental Perspective*, Spring 1979, p. 17.

market would avoid the inherent difficulties of these complex social service delivery areas. Even though we consider it important to increase marketlike pressures, we do not see these market mechanisms replacing federal involvement. Neither direct federal agency operation, citizen sovereignty as expressed through local government management, nor consumer sovereignty as expressed in the marketplace at this point dominate the proposed agency management strategy.

The great strengths of the proposed agency management strategy are its consonance with federalism and its breadth in being able to incorporate competing alternatives such as incentives. One of the strongest needs is to develop policy objectives and approaches that reconcile national and local perspectives. A critical implication of shared governance is that the reconciliation of legitimate differences between federal and local needs and interests has to evolve in the interplay among major actors. So at the heart of federal governance is the extended set of relationships where (a) realistic boundaries of national intent are to be set (and the expectation is of rather wide boundaries reflecting local variability); and (b) the local commitment to national intent is negotiated within these boundaries. The federal government needs to have an organization in the pivotal spot of linkage between federal and local governments with the resources required for continuing involvement in the field to induce locals to make a commitment to pursue national objectives and to aid them in that pursuit.

The management strategy that has commitment and capacity as a central objective requires that the social agency change its way of thinking, its focus, and its style of behavior. But once the shift is made, such an agency management strategy is quite eclectic. If marketlike forces, technical assistance and better information provided citizens, the agency working directly with local organizations to build capacity, or some other approaches increase commitment and competence at the local level, these are all acceptable in the agency management strategy.

Agency competence and credibility appear to be the two critical factors if local organizations are to be influenced over time. More relevant information, more skilled agency field staff, and better agency management in the field are fundamental to the proposed agency management strategy. Agency staff competence is what can distinguish fixing from meddling or helping from harassing. Credibility, which in good part depends on competence, will come about when the local actors perceive that the social agency knows what it is doing, what the local problems are, and sets doable tasks.

Social agency personnel need to exhibit much greater discipline (constraint) and more reasoned judgment, particularly in the field, than has been exhibited in the past. Most of all, local partners cannot be viewed as the enemy. Casting them in that role is not only unfair in so many cases, it is unproductive. The local organizations that administer social service delivery programs and actually deliver services are going to make the discretionary judgments that determine policy and need all the help they can get in making these choices. Avoiding confusion, offering sound advice on process, building up local competence are the kinds of activities likely to solidify the commitment of nonfederal organizations to performance objectives and to help them in pursuit of these objectives.

That the social agencies can reorient and restructure so as to center on local-level commitment and capacity is far from clear. To call for leadership and greater management capability is not necessarily to get them. The agency management strategy that makes commitment and capacity a central objective demands a significantly higher level of agency effort and far more subtlety and finesse than exhibited in the past. Yet the many pulls away from field performance toward organizational health will remain. Even if the social agencies make a concerted effort to adopt the agency management strategy, the restructuring may run aground, brought down by all the institutional problems we have considered and some we no doubt have overlooked. We need to be explicit about the dangers and difficulties.

First, the reorganization effort itself can do harm, weakening the agency further by lowering morale and increasing confusion. Nothing guarantees that those at the top of the agency will bring those affected by the reorganization into the early discussion or adopt a reasonable time frame for working out the new organizational structure. This, as it has been pointed out over and over, is not the style of political executives.

Second, the agency management strategy poses an opposite danger. It can strengthen the social agency, and thus make it more able to interfere in local matters, without bringing to various agency levels— especially the administrative and support domain—either a real commitment to operate with deference or a recognition of mutual dependency and of the need to aid the local partner so it can better deliver social services. Increased agency organizational strength might be used to gain organizational health and security—to enforce compliance so as to satisfy bureaucratic drives or perceived congressional demands or to insulate bureaucratic power. A clear and present danger is greater government intrusion, greater agency ability to coerce, not a more viable partnership.

Third, a successful agency reorientation and restructuring can still run aground at the local level. A social agency policy of increasing institutional investment at the local level can be both dangerous and frustrating. Much can go wrong. One of the most frustrating paradoxes of building local organizational capacity is that the increasing strength of either administrative or service delivery organizations can well lead to bureaucratic rigidity. As these organizations grow stronger, their staffs have more to lose and hence more to protect. On the road to institutional viability, organizational health can replace performance as the orienting guide for the local organizations, too. No organizational problem looms larger than that of retaining or renewing responsiveness in organizations as they gain institutional strength.

Fourth, there may be unexplainable benefits from the seeming disarray and confusion that keep federalism afloat. As Daniel Elazar, a perceptive long-time student of American federalism, observed at a conference on federalism:

> Running through all the points made today is a theme that leads me to raise the question as to whether it cannot be said that for federalism, in confusion there is strength. That is to say, the worst possible thing for the federal system, given the current attitudes and perspectives, would be to eliminate the confusion and make things neater. If we eliminate that confusion, we would destroy many operationl possibilities. Having just spent several days in Washington talking to people about urban policy, I have my usual shuddering about those who wish to clean things up and make them neat and to "strengthen" the state and local roles. I don't think it would work that way at all.[5]

The genius of American federalism may be a Rube Goldberg setting where confusion and misdirection keeps the various parties from doing great harm and still allows them enough freedom to bring changes.

Finally, there is an obverse, more bleak side of the last notion: American federalism may be breaking down, its limited discipline shattered by pressure groups and a Congress that responds to diverse and often competing objectives, with more and more money and programs, but without any attempt to resolve conflict. Federal grants-in-aid now exceed $80 billion with so many different laws that no one appears able to comprehend or to control them. For example, a host of crosscutting requirements, such as equal employment opportunities, apply to most grants-in-aid. Those who must manage and operate substantive programs could be so entrapped by all these competing demands that

[5] Ellis Katz and Benjamin R. Schuster (editors), *The Practice of American Federalism*, A Roundtable Discussion on Recent Developments in American Federalism and Intergovernmental Relations, Center for the Study of Federalism, Temple University, Philadelphia, 28 February 1978, p. 40.

compliance, not substance, is all they can really strive for. Strengthening agency management and local capacity may do little good until some discipline is exerted over the whole array of federal grants-in-aid. It is not that particular elements of the federal government or the federal government in general or the local governments are too powerful, but that federal grants-in-aid and the other legislation that impinges on them *in total* are overwhelming the agencies and the subnational governments. Here is the powerlessness theme of Chapter 7 writ large to explain the disarray of American federalism.[6]

There is no sure path to improving social program grants-in-aid. At the end of his Harvard Godkin Lecture, after presenting an eloquent argument for the greater use of market forces in domestic programs, Schultze captured succinctly where we are, in observing "I must end rather lamely. There is no instrumental solution. . . . The only available course is a steady maturing of both the electorate and political leaders."[7]

No institutional prescription will bring this maturing. It is the other way around. At the same time, there also must be a maturing of our institutions. At the agency level, which combines political and bureaucratic leadership, that broader maturing must translate into a greater capacity of the agencies and other organizations to provide social services. In asking whether that institutional maturing is possible, a historical perspective is critical. It is only a decade and a half from the marker point of the passage of the Economic Opportunity Act of 1964 that symbolized the beginning of the War on Poverty and the apex of post-World War II confidence. From that high point in American confidence, the nation began a double odyssey. The first was through Vietnam; racial unrest; Watergate; racial, ethnic, and feminist revolutions; international turmoil; and other difficulties and changes. The second voyage in the last decade and a half was through the murky sea of intergovernmental relationships. The latter was marked by rapid shifts in the federal philosophy from centralization to decentralization and back toward centralization. We stand now with general revenue shar-

---

[6] For a perceptive exposition of this thesis, see Neal R. Pierce, "The State of American Federalism," *National Civic Review*, January 1980, pp. 5–9, and Katz and Schuster (editors), *The Practice of American Federalism*, especially the paper and remarks by David Walker.

[7] Charles L. Schultze, *The Public Use of Private Interest*, Brookings Institution, Washington, D.C., 1977, p. 90.

ing in trouble and a movement toward categorical programs for any new dollars and tighter standards for existing block grants.[8]

This decade and a half of social and political shifts was hardly a propitious time for making basic organizational investments to meet the demands of shared governance in the field. It surely is naive to think that this transformation of federalism with all its governmental and organizational complexities carried out so rapidly and in a period of such great social and political turmoil would be smooth or that highly responsive institutional adjustments would occur. The disquiet about performance in part is a vestige of that mood of the 1960s in which people seemingly expected rapid success and remained chagrined with only partial progress. In these terms, the perceived implementation failure—at best, the half-filled cup—that discourages so many students of social programs and pushes them to embrace the market mechanism can be interpreted as a predictable point. Looked at in this way, the past may not give us great hope, but it should not yet lead us to abandon our search for institutions consonant with shared governance. There is too little evidence to bring us to recommend changing the basic shared power arrangement.

The call of our times is to lower expectations. That has been a primary message of the book in claiming that the real limits of governance place severe restrictions on what can be done not only in the federal government but in all governments. The nation is doomed to frustration if it expects solutions that yield rapid progress. Nowhere does this seem more clear than for the social agencies operated under the shared responsibility model. Furthermore, no one knows whether or not the social agencies have made reasonable progress thus far, in the face of all the difficulties. What we do know is that working through the dynamics of federalism takes a great deal of hard effort and time. That our social institutions, including the social agencies, would have adjusted to the new reality of the grants-in-aid era so quickly is unrealistic; that they can do so over time is not.

Yet the excuse of time can only hold for so long. It is not our view, even in the face of Proposition 13 and the cry for balanced budgets, that the nation is abandoning social goals. But there clearly is a tension

---

[8] For an interesting discussion of the negative congressional mood on general revenue sharing that in part explains the propensity for categorical programs, see Will Myers and John Shannon, "Revenue Sharing for States: An Endangered Species," *Intergovernmental Perspective*, Summer 1979, pp. 10–18.

that demands more responsiveness by the social agencies as the primary vehicle of federal governance. There is a legitimate call for better governance of our social policies. The current pause in the growth of social service programs makes the need for better management of the available resources even more stark. The Proposition 13 mood sends many messages, but certainly none more clear than that the agencies must start showing more signs of progress.

A failure to improve field governance raises basic questions about the social agencies' ability to make work the uneasy partnership that has emerged in the grants-in-aid era. At basic issue is whether or not the heavy reliance on federal management makes sense. Let us be clear; this translates into a test of whether or not the social agencies make sense other than as check writers in the social service delivery programs. And the answers in this test must come from the field where social service delivery organizations provide service to local beneficiaries.

APPENDIX
FIELD STUDY INTERVIEWS

Interviews were conducted in Regions X, IX, and I and in Washington, D.C. Neither places nor people were chosen randomly. The most extensive interview activity was in Region X headquarted in Seattle, where our study effort was based. Because we were exploring to find out how deeply into the regional and area office organizations we needed to go, we talked with large numbers of people in Region X. In hindsight, it was more than was necessary. The Regions I and IX interview schedules were more efficient. We started with key positions and picked up additional interviewees based on information from the initially chosen interviews.

In both Regions IX and X, interviews and follow-ups were conducted over a 2½ year period, while only one visit was made to Region I. Interviews were conducted in Washington, D.C., on several occasions. Although there were some follow-up interviews there, we often were tracing a relationship or a specific point considered in the regional interviews. Those interviewed during an initial visit and two follow-ups to Region IX are listed at the end of the Appendix, by the position of the person interviewed.

The typical setting for interviews was the office of the person being interviewed. The sessions in almost all cases were conducted by two persons from our staff, with one taking the lead in posing questions and the other primarily responsible for taking notes and making sure that

273

all intended issues were covered.[1] Interviews ranged from a few minutes to several hours, with the usual session running 1–1½ hours.

Interviews were structured around a set of issues depending upon the stage of the investigation and the position of the person being interviewed. Written questionnaires were not used. Nor did the interview team at each session have a list of specifically worded questions, although the same kind of factual information often was sought from each interviewee.

Mainly the interviews were open ended. Interviewers had freedom to pursue additional factual information, to explore unexpected comments from the interviewee, and to seek the perceptions of the individual in relation to his past experiences and his position in the organization.

To indicate the kind of issues discussed in our interviews, we present a "composite" set of issues discussed during an initial interview, follow-up interviews, or both, with a regional employment and training administrator (RETA). The briefest account of the regional structure is needed to make the issue presentation clear. The Employment and Training Administration (ETA) field office during the New Federalism period was part of a DOL regional office headed by a regional director. However, the regional director had no authority over the RETA. Our concern has been solely with the ETA office.[2] That office has two main components—the ETA regional office staff, composed of the RETA and specialist staff (labeled hereafter simply "the regional office"), and the area office, which has direct contracts with fund recipients. Basically, the regional office has staff responsibilities and the area office has line responsibilities. The local governments that receive CETA funds are called prime sponsors. They may operate projects directly but usually contract with local organizations (e.g., Bay Area Urban League of San Francisco) to run individual manpower projects. The federal staff person dealing directly with prime sponsor staff is called a field representative and is located in the area office. When a prime sponsor is found to be out of compliance, it is asked to prepare a corrective action plan that is supposed to tell how the project will be put into compliance.

The RETA is the senior field officer in the ETA, which is the bureau responsible for all DOL manpower delivery service programs. As one would expect, the interview with the senior DOL official respon-

---

[1] The main exception was the Washington, D.C. interviews conducted by the senior author, who generally was not a member of the two-person interview teams.

[2] In a Carter administration reorganization, the regional director was eliminated, but the ETA office did not undergo basic organizational change, so we will shift to the present tense in this discussion.

sible for CETA administration in the field would be broader, generally speaking, than those for specialists on that person's staff:

1. We sought to explore in depth the relationships between the RETA and headquarters staff. To whom does the RETA report? How frequent is the contact between the RETA and the secretary, the assistant secretary for employment and training, and other staff in ETA's Office of Field Operations? What contacts do other members of the RETA's staff have with headquarters? (Note: We asked the same question of particular staff members.) How much authority does the RETA believe has been delegated to him or her by the secretary?

2. We sought to determine how the RETA perceived headquarters responsiveness as to (a) requests for information and assistance from the regions; (b) requests for modifications of regulations in light of regional variation; and (c) general regional comments concerning headquarters policy and regulation formulation. We sought to elicit specific examples of responsiveness or lack of it.

3. How does the RETA perceive various activities carried out by the regional office, particularly monitoring, evaluation, and technical assistance? What kind of authority do the various regional staff offices have? For instance, are the activities of the evaluation unit restricted to work on and review of corrective action plans? Does this unit have authority to insist that the sponsor take certain steps toward corrective action? What is the RETA's role in regard to accepting or rejecting corrective action plans?

4. How much discretion does an individual regional administrator see himself having to modify the structure and function of different components of the regional office to take into account regional variation? Does the RETA see himself as an advocate of his region at headquarters, even if this might mean controversy with his superiors? What kind of political role does the RETA see himself as having in the region?

5. What kind of input do field representatives and prime sponsors have in the development and modification of regulations and guidelines? Are their comments solicited and if so, are they transmitted directly or through the regional staff to headquarters?

6. What are the official sanctions DOL maintains over prime sponsors? If a prime sponsor insists upon going its own way against the regional office on a specific regulation or in a more discretionary area of program that does not directly violate a regula-

tion but goes contrary to regional advice, what steps would the
DOL regional office take? Has the regional office ever defunded
a prime sponsor in whole or in part, named a substitute sponsor, or assumed sponsorship itself? What sanctions besides
these does the regional office use? Who would make such a
decision?

7. What does the RETA see as the major differences between the
categorical programs and the block grant in relation to program
substance, administration and intergovernmental relations?
How are various federal programs being coordinated at the
local level with the coming of the block grant?

With members of the RETA's regional office staff, interviews
would generally focus more intensively on a particular aspect of field
activities, such as the provision of technical assistance. For a staff unit
in the regional office, we probed in depth about procedures and techniques used, specific field relationships with the area office and with
prime sponsors, and relationships with headquarters. A critical group
of interviews were with the field representatives located in the area office. Each prime sponsor had a field representative who was the primary contact on administrative and programmatic issues between the
federal government and the major administrative and operating elements of the prime sponsors (political contacts generally were handled
in the regional office). We tried to get the field representatives to tell us
in detail specific activities they pursued in administering grants. How
did they get information (e.g., what kind of monitoring efforts did they
undertake); how much time did they spend in the field with prime sponsors and project operators; and what did they do when a prime sponsor
had a major problem? We were also concerned with the field representatives' perceptions of what they thought headquarters and the regional
offices demanded of prime sponsors and how much authority the field
representatives had over prime sponsors.

In interviews with prime sponsors and project operators, we focused on (a) the kinds of services actually provided by federal field
staffs and by the prime sponsors to project operators; and (b) how the
recipients of these services assessed their quality, their usefulness, and
their limitations, including the absence of needed services. With prime
sponsors, we were also concerned about their perceptions of what they
thought the legislation required of them, what the roles of headquarters
and the federal field staffs were, and what specific activities they
thought they should be executing as the primary administrators of manpower projects in the field.

The Washington, D.C. interviews ranged from extremely broad

questions about how the New Federalism was perceived, to details about the nature of contacts between the lower level headquarters staff with regional staffs. In summer 1974, prior to beginning the initial regional office interviews, our interview staff spent 10 weeks in Washington working not only on this study but on a number of policy analysis issues. The latter dominated during that period, but the interview staff did interview agency staff and others about the role of regional offices and about general perceptions of headquarters–field staff–local relationships. Once extensive regional office interviews had been conducted, our Washington interviews usually focused on a particular issue or person in an effort to trace questions first raised in the field. But on occasion, we concentrated on a broad issue, such as how government officials in the agency and elsewhere (e.g., the Office of Management and Budget) perceived the New Federalism or spoke with persons who could provide an overview of CETA.

What has been described for CETA holds for CDBG in that the same rationale guided both sets of interviews. If we had presented questions for a HUD regional director, they would have been similar to those for the RETA.

INTERVIEWS IN REGION IX

HUD
   Regional Office:
      Regional Administrator of HUD
      Assistant Regional Administrator for Community Planning and Development
      Assistant Regional Administrator for Planning and Evaluation and various staff members
   Area Office:
      Director of Area Office
      Head of Community Planning and Development, Area Office
      Area Office Representative for Los Angeles
      Area Office Representative for San Francisco and Santa Clara Counties and staff
   Local Government:
      CDBG Administrator, City of Los Angeles and staff
      CDBG Administrator, County of Los Angeles
      CDBG Administrator, City of Richmond and staff
      CDBG Administrator, City of Oakland and staff
      CDBG Administrator, City of San Francisco

DOL–ETA
  Regional Office:
    Regional Employment and Training Administrator (RETA)
    Deputy Regional Employment and Training Administrator
    CETA Director in Office of Program and Technical Services
    Federal Representative for Los Angeles
    Federal Representative for San Mateo and Santa Cruz Counties
    Federal Representative for Oakland
    Director of Area Office
  Prime Sponsors:
    CETA Administrator for Oakland
    CETA Administrator for San Francisco
    Assistant Administrator for San Francisco
    CETA Administrator for Richmond
    CETA Administrator for Los Angeles
    CETA Administrator for County of Los Angeles
  Local Manpower Project Operators:
    Young Israel Center in Los Angeles
    Careers Planning Center for Women in Los Angeles
    Bay Area Urban League in San Francisco
    Director of Services, Employment, Redevelopment (SER) in Los Angeles

INDEX

QUANTITATIVE STUDIES IN SOCIAL RELATIONS

Consulting Editor: Peter H. Rossi

UNIVERSITY OF MASSACHUSETTS
AMHERST, MASSACHUSETTS